THE WORLD'S CLASSICS

The Oxford Sherlock Holmes

HIS LAST BOW

SIR ARTHUR CONAN DOYLE was born in Edinburgh in 1859 to Irish Catholic parents. A Jesuit pupil at Stonyhurst, he graduated in medicine from Edinburgh (1881), and won his doctorate (1885). He practised medicine at Southsea in the 1880s as well as in a Greenland whaler, a West African trader and (after 20 years' retirement) a Boer War hospital. His literary career began in *Chambers's Edinburgh Journal* before he was 20, and he invented Sherlock Holmes when 26. After moving to London he transferred Holmes and Watson to short stories in the newly launched *Strand* magazine (1891) where he remained the lead author. A master of the short story, Conan Doyle's other great series revolved around Brigadier Gerard and Napoleon, while of his longer stories the same mix of comedy with adventure characterized his historical and scientific fiction, with unforgettable heroes such as the minute bellicose Sir Nigel, the Puritan crook Decimus Saxon, and the Shavian egomaniac Professor Challenger. His influence on the detective story was omnipresent, but his own literary stature as a classic is only now receiving its scholarly due. He died in 1930.

OWEN DUDLEY EDWARDS, the general editor of the Oxford Sherlock Holmes, is Reader in History at the University of Edinburgh and author of *The Quest for Sherlock Holmes: A Biographical Study of Sir Arthur Conan Doyle*.

THE OXFORD SHERLOCK HOLMES

GENERAL EDITOR: OWEN DUDLEY EDWARDS

'Here it is at last, the definitive edition.'
Julian Symons, *Sunday Times*

'This outstanding edition of the five collections of stories and the four novels does Conan Doyle's great creation full justice . . . maintaining the right mixture of scholarly precision and infectious enthusiasm. These volumes, a delight to handle, are a bargain.'   Sean French, *Observer*

'The riches of the textual apparatus . . . will be a source of endless joy to veteran Sherlockians . . .'
John Bayley, *Times Literary Supplement*

'The hawk-faced maestro of Baker Street has been well served.'   Brian Fallon, *Irish Times*

'The definitive and most desirable edition of these milestones in crime fiction.'   F. E. Pardoe, *Brimingham Post*

'The Oxford is the edition to curl up with on a winter's night.'   John McAleer, *Chicago Tribune*

THE WORLD'S CLASSICS

ARTHUR CONAN DOYLE

His Last Bow

Some Reminiscences of Sherlock Holmes

Edited with an Introduction by
OWEN DUDLEY EDWARDS

Oxford   New York

OXFORD UNIVERSITY PRESS

1994

Oxford University Press, Walton Street, Oxford OX2 6DP

Oxford New York
Athens Auckland Bangkok Bombay
Calcutta Cape Town Dar es Salaam Delhi
Florence Hong Kong Istanbul Karachi
Kuala Lumpur Madras Madrid Melbourne
Mexico City Nairobi Paris Singapore
Taipei Tokyo Toronto

and associated companies in
Berlin Ibadan

Oxford is a trade mark of Oxford University Press

First published in the Oxford Sherlock Holmes 1993
First published as a World's Classics paperback 1994

British Library Cataloguing in Publication Data
Data available

Library of Congress Cataloging in Publication Data
Doyle, Arthur Conan, Sir, 1859-1930.
His last bow : some reminiscences of Sherlock Holmes / Arthur Conan
Doyle ; edited with an introduction by Owen Dudley Edwards.
p. cm.—(The World's classics)
Includes bibliographical references (p.).
1. Holmes, Sherlock (Fictitious character)—Fiction. 2. Detective
and mystery stories, English. 3. Private investigators—England—
Fiction. I. Edwards, Owen Dudley. II. Title. III. Series.
PR4622.H5 1994 823'.8—dc20 94-5817
ISBN 0-19-282381-7

1 3 5 7 9 10 8 6 4 2

Printed in Great Britain by
BPC Paperbacks Ltd
Aylesbury, Bucks

CONTENTS

ACKNOWLEDGEMENTS

GRATEFUL thanks are due to A. P. Watt and the Trustees of the Wodehouse Estate for permission to reprint, for the first time, the three unsigned pieces by P. G. Wodehouse. We would also like to express the warmest thanks to John Simpson (Department of Scottish History, Edinburgh University), R. Cairns Craig and Murray Pittock (English Literature, Edinburgh), Neil MacCormick (Law, Edinburgh), Donald Rutherford (Economics, Edinburgh), Jeffrey Richards and Michael Heale (Department of History, University of Lancaster), Ian Walker (Department of American Studies, University of Manchester), Paul Dukes (Aberdeen University), as well as to Nicolas Barker, Leslie Macfarlane, Peter and Liselotte Marshall, Anthony Burgess, John Sutherland, Gerald Roberts, George Richardson, Graham Richardson, Philip French, Julian Symons, the Arthur Conan Doyle Society in general, Morag Kyle and the staff of the Reference Division of Edinburgh Central Library, as well as the staff of the Edinburgh Room, Scottish, Fiction, and Circulation Divisions, the Society of Jesus and present and former members of staff at Stonyhurst College, Allan Boyd and the staff of James Thin of Edinburgh, Christopher Harvie, John Hargreaves, Andrew Rutherford, Malcolm Pittock, Andrew Hook, Fred Urquhart, Colin Affleck, Adam Naylor, Christopher McGimpsey, Paul Schoolman, Justin Avery, John Kerr, Neville Garden, Allen Wright, Allan Massie, David Daiches, George Davie, Tom Nairn, Tom Flanagan, the National Library of Ireland, the Library of Trinity College, Dublin, the British Library, the Library of Trinity College, Cambridge.

We have not troubled Dame Jean Conan Doyle during the preparation of this edition, but her encouragement of Conan Doyle studies has been of the greatest support to us.

GENERAL EDITOR'S PREFACE
TO THE SERIES

ARTHUR CONAN DOYLE told his *Strand* editor, Herbert Greenhough Smith (1855–1935), that 'A story always comes to me as an organic thing and I never can recast it without the Life going out of it.'[1]

On the whole, this certainly seems to describe Conan Doyle's method with the Sherlock Holmes stories, long and short. Such manuscript evidence as survives (approximately half the stories) generally bears this out: there is remarkably little revision. Sketches or scenarios are another matter. Conan Doyle was no more bound by these at the end of his literary life than at the beginning, whence scraps of paper survive to tell us of 221B Upper Baker Street where lived Ormond Sacker and J. Sherrinford Holmes. But very little such evidence is currently available for analysis.

Conan Doyle's relationship with his most famous creation was far from the silly label 'The Man Who Hated Sherlock Holmes': equally, there was no indulgence in it. Though the somewhat too liberal Puritan Micah Clarke was perhaps dearer to him than Holmes, Micah proved unable to sustain a sequel to the eponymous novel of 1889. By contrast, 'Sherlock' (as his creator irreverently alluded to him when not creating him) proved his capacity for renewal 59 times (which Conan Doyle called 'a striking example of the patience and loyalty of the British public'). He dropped Holmes in 1893, apparently into the Reichenbach Falls, as a matter of literary integrity: he did not intend to be written off as 'the Holmes man'. But public clamour turned Holmes into an economic asset that could not be ignored. Even so, Conan Doyle could not have continued to write about

---

[1] Undated letter, quoted by Cameron Hollyer, 'Author to Editor', *ACD— The Journal of the Arthur Conan Doyle Society*, 3 (1992), 19–20. Conan Doyle's remark was probably *à propos* 'The Red Circle' (*His Last Bow*).

Holmes without taking some pleasure in the activity, or indeed without becoming quietly proud of him.

Such Sherlock Holmes manuscripts as survive are frequently in private keeping, and very few have remained in Britain. In this series we have made the most of two recent facsimiles, of 'The Dying Detective' and 'The Lion's Mane'. In general, manuscript evidence shows Conan Doyle consistently underpunctuating, and to show the implications of this 'The Dying Detective' (*His Last Bow*) has been printed from the manuscript. 'The Lion's Mane', however, offers the one case known to us of drastic alterations in the surviving manuscript, from which it is clear from deletions that the story was entirely altered, and Holmes's role transformed, in the process of its creation.

Given Conan Doyle's general lack of close supervision of the Holmes texts, it is not always easy to determine his final wishes. In one case, it is clear that 'His Last Bow', as a deliberate contribution to war propaganda, underwent a ruthless revision at proof stage—although (as we note for the first time) this was carried out on the magazine text and lost when published in book form. But nothing comparable exists elsewhere.

In general, American texts of the stories are closer to the magazine texts than British book texts. Textual discrepancies, in many instances, may simply result from the conflicts of sub-editors. Undoubtedly, Conan Doyle did some re-reading, especially when returning to Holmes after an absence; but on the whole he showed little interest in the constitution of his texts. In his correspondence with editors he seldom alluded to proofs, discouraged ideas for revision, and raised few—if any—objections to editorial changes. For instance, we know that the *Strand*'s preference for 'Halloa' was not Conan Doyle's original usage, and in this case we have restored the original orthography. On the other hand, we also know that the *Strand* texts consistently eliminated anything (mostly expletives) of an apparently blasphemous character, but in the absence of manuscript confirmation we have normally been unable to restore what were probably stronger original versions. (In any case, it is perfectly possible that Conan Doyle, the consummate professional, may have come to exercise self-censorship in the certain knowledge that editorial changes would be imposed.)

Throughout the series we have corrected any obvious errors, though these are comparatively few: the instances are at all times noted. (For a medical man, Conan Doyle's handwriting was commendably legible, though his 'o' could look like an 'a'.) Regarding the order of individual stories, internal evidence makes it clear that 'A Case of Identity' (*Adventures*) was written before 'The Red-Headed League' and was intended to be so printed; but the 'League' was the stronger story and the *Strand*, in its own infancy, may have wanted the Holmes stories established as quickly as possible (at this point the future of both Holmes series and the magazine was uncertain). Surviving letters show that the composition of 'The Solitary Cyclist' (*Return*) preceded that of 'The Dancing Men' (with the exception of the former's first paragraph, which was rewritten later); consequently, the order of these stories has been reversed. Similarly, the stories in *His Last Bow* and *The Case-Book of Sherlock Holmes* have been rearranged in their original order of publication, which—as far as is known—reflects the order of composition. The intention has been to allow readers to follow the fictional evolution of Sherlock Holmes over the forty years of his existence.

The one exception to this principle will be found in *His Last Bow*, where the final and eponymous story was actually written and published after *The Valley of Fear*, which takes its place in the Holmes canon directly after the magazine publication of the other stories in *His Last Bow*; but the removal of the title story to the beginning of the *Case-Book* would have been too radically pedantic and would have made *His Last Bow* ludicrously short. Readers will note that we have already reduced the extent of *His Last Bow* by returning 'The Cardboard Box' to its original location in the *Memoirs of Sherlock Holmes* (after 'Silver Blaze' and before 'The Yellow Face'). The removal of 'The Cardboard Box' from the original sequence led to the inclusion of its introductory passage in 'The Resident Patient': this, too, has been returned to its original position and the proper opening of 'The Resident Patient' restored. Generally, texts have been derived from first book publication collated with magazine texts and, where possible, manuscripts; in the case of 'The Cardboard Box' and 'The Resident Patient', however, we have employed the *Strand* texts, partly because of the restoration of the latter's opening, partly to give readers a flavour of the magazine in which the Holmes stories made their first, vital conquests.

In all textual decisions the overriding desire has been to meet the author's wishes, so far as these can be legitimately ascertained from documentary evidence or application of the rule of reason.

One final plea. If you come to these stories for the first time, proceed now to the texts themselves, putting the introductions and explanatory notes temporarily aside. Our introductions are not meant to introduce: Dr Watson will perform that duty, and no one could do it better. Then, when you have mastered the stories, and they have mastered you, come back to us.

OWEN DUDLEY EDWARDS

University of Edinburgh

INTRODUCTION

THE stories published in this volume provide windows on a much greater span of Arthur Conan Doyle's life and times than any of the six predecessor volumes, none of which seems to have taken more than eighteen months to compose. Up to now it had been a matter of long stories written at high speed, or of series in which episode followed episode with remarkably little delay in creation. The title of *His Last Bow*, both book and story, had intentional ironies. Sherlock Holmes had taken his last bow on several previous occasions—most famously in the apparent death-plunge into the Reichenbach Falls with Professor Moriarty, but most recently (in December 1904) with a firm statement of his retirement in the opening of the last story of *The Return of Sherlock Holmes*, 'The Adventure of the Second Stain'.

But the stories in *His Last Bow*, whose advent Conan Doyle announced to the editor of the *Strand Magazine*, Herbert Greenhough Smith, on 4 March 1908 under the working title 'Reminiscences of Sherlock Holmes', were divergences from the old form. These post-retirement, retrospective glimpses of Holmes were occasional pieces, written at their creator's pleasure rather than under the kind of pressure he had formerly feared might cause him to force into a Holmesian mould what was really not Holmesian matter. The result was Holmes revisited, at intervals ranging from two months to two years.

The first two tales were longer than any of the previous short stories about Holmes except 'The Naval Treaty' (*Memoirs*) and 'The Priory School' (*Return*), while the last of the pre-war group, 'The Dying Detective', was the shortest in length and internal time-span to date. An interval of nearly four years separated it from the 'Epilogue' written during the war, 'His Last Bow' (the last Holmes novel, *The Valley of Fear*, partly filled the gap), which, a little longer than 'The Dying Detective' and even shorter in internal time-span,

was the first story published entirely in third-person narration (as had been initially attempted in *The Valley of Fear*).
Conan Doyle was using his new freedom to experiment.

His experimentation went far beyond form and style. *The
Adventures* and *The Memoirs* had been landmarks in the evolution
of the detective short story, especially in the concentration
on the scientific basis of Holmes's methods, whilst *The
Return*, conscious of the many imitators who had arisen
during the years of Holmes's supposed demise, made less of
exposition and more of revelation. The 'Reminiscences'
continued the movement towards literature for its own sake.
Holmes now has more work to do than detection, and he is
called upon to reflect a wider and increasingly less contained
and ordered world. His creator worked better than he
perhaps fully realized: he observed—though he did not, as
Holmes would say, 'deduce'—phenomena betokening the
advent of world cataclysm in 1914. These stories are milestones for a world on its way to war.

George Dangerfield, in *The Strange Death of Liberal England*
(1936), saw a Britain in 1914 on the verge of social revolution, rescued only by the outbreak of world war. Conan
Doyle, trained as a doctor to observe symptoms, recorded
signs of revolution even in his own changes of conception.
London was never the secure, circumscribed arena of Holmes's
guardianship claimed by Colin Watson in *Snobbery with
Violence* (1971)—'a city whose every crime is soluble and whose
vices are sealed within narrow and defined areas. It is a cosy
place. It is, for as long as a hawk-eyed man broods in Baker
Street, a safe place. It does not exist. It never did. But Doyle
managed to build it in the minds of his readers.' On the
contrary, a tally of the case-backgrounds to the Holmes
stories exhibits a horrifying cascade of social evils, in the
face of which Holmes can do little more than make an
occasional difference, or a solitary improvement. But the
popular notion of Holmes was as the omniscient, omni-
potent figure of Colin (though not of Dr John) Watson's
picture. The stories in *His Last Bow* are an open break with
that myth. In case after case, Holmes is fallible, faulted, or

marginalized. True, Conan Doyle had joyfully proclaimed Holmes's defeat by a woman in the very first short story, 'A Scandal in Bohemia' (*Adventures*), had recounted how Holmes let a client go from his door to death in 'The Five Orange Pips' (*Adventures*), and had revealed limitations of his hero's capabilities in 'The Yellow Face' (*Memoirs*); but these were forgotten in the litany of monthly triumphs. Now, in 1908–13, a disintegrating world is partly symbolized by a Holmes suffering intermittent medical ailments and at times foiled, fooled, or frustrated more by himself than by his adversaries.

Conan Doyle's awareness of increasing loss of British national confidence may have been sporadic, and its artistic expression sometimes unconscious; but the result was to have a palpable effect on the Holmes prescription. He wanted these stories to speak for him on questions of fresh urgency, as well as coming to terms with old problems encountered anew. To do this he now demanded more of Holmes than priestcraft, science, and wit. Private ruminations on brilliant doctors left marooned in the provinces were mingled with the author's new pride in his own rural residence (established from early 1908 at Windlesham, Crowborough, Sussex), so that Holmes, in 'Wisteria Lodge', finds himself confronted by the only police detective who comes close to proving his match—Inspector Baynes of Esher. Baynes's pleasantly bitter 'We stagnate in the provinces', in response to Holmes's 'Your powers, if I may say so without offence, seem superior to your opportunities', signal Conan Doyle's own warning that metropolitan complacency can lead to intellectual bankruptcy—a frequent charge levelled at London by other Scots and Irish writers. Here the logic of the theme works itself out in the two closely matched detectives eyeing each other's progress so narrowly that the miscreant breaks free, and disaster is averted only by the actions of a discharged gardener seeking revenge on his vicious employer. The earlier Holmes stories often show a hard-edged bourgeois revelation of aristocratic depravity or inadequacy: now the honours go to John Warner, a workman in revolt and a suitable emblem of the years ahead.

The Holmes of 'The Bruce-Partington Plans' impedes himself by obsession, not with a rival, but with a superior: his brother Mycroft. There is a resonance here with Conan Doyle's experience of officialdom in his crusade to clear the name of the wrongfully convicted George Edalji (1876–1953), into which he had thrown himself in 1906–7.[1] In that case, which involved a Home Office whitewash of a savagely partisan chief constable, race and class seemed to be factors inhibiting both the vindication of Edalji and the discovery of the true culprits. Mycroft Holmes, representing the government, specifically circumscribes his brother's investigation by declaring at the outset that Sir James Walter, 'whose decorations and sub-titles fill two lines of a book of reference . . . has grown grey in the Service'—that is the Civil Service in which Mycroft is also employed. Sir James is, moreover, 'a gentleman, a favoured guest in the most exalted houses, and above all a man whose patriotism is beyond suspicion'. The effect is to throw a cloak of protection around the person and household of Sir James, who is ultimately shown to have known that his own brother is the traitor but to have chosen to die in silence rather than exculpate his subordinate at the expense of the Walter family. Holmes drives his investigations at a fine pace, but is cold to pleas to vindicate the suspected Cadogan West, and then swings his own suspicions against another innocent subordinate. When his trap catches its gentlemanly rat he confesses: 'You can write me down an ass this time, Watson . . . This was not the bird that I was looking for.'

The sporadic appearance of the adventures was now giving Conan Doyle's audience more time to draw its conclusions and assert itself. In February 1909, while recuperating in Cornwall after a minor operation, Conan Doyle experienced the response that seems to have rankled longest among criticisms of the Holmes stories, for he quoted variants of it for the rest of his life. A Cornish

---

[1] See Richard and Molly Whittington-Egan (eds.), Arthur Conan Doyle, *The Story of Mr George Edalji* (1985).

boatman, clearly referring to the last two published stories, proclaimed (with the author at his mercy): 'When Mr Holmes had that fall he may not have been killed, but he was certainly injured, for he was never the same man afterwards.'[2] So Conan Doyle now had to vindicate Holmes by having him triumph in a Cornish case, and there flashed into his memory one of his own first triumphs, 'The Captain of the *Pole-Star*' (1883), the last words of which describe how the haunted captain had been engaged 'to a young lady of singular beauty residing upon the Cornish coast. During his absence at sea his betrothed died under circumstances of peculiar horror.' The recollection was translated into Holmes's telegram to Watson which launches 'The Devil's Foot'. Well might Holmes remember the case, for he shone in its unravelling; but well also might Watson remember it, for without him Holmes would have ended dead or insane, having in either outcome gone through indescribable mental torture. Yet another of Holmes's mythological qualities crumbled: his invulnerability. Simultaneously, the cycle's progress in affection between Holmes and Watson continued, to reach an epiphany in Holmes's expression of gratitude for the part played by his friend.

Holmes's deductive powers, as well as his capacity for ironic comment, are in good working order in 'The Red Circle'. But the story ultimately sidelines him. Conan Doyle insisted on this, despite Greenhough Smith's objections. As he told his editor, the *Strand*'s publication of the episode in two instalments heightened this effect.[3]

'The Disappearance of Lady Frances Carfax' presents an ageing Holmes apparently showing premature symptoms of the rheumatism Watson mentions in his preface to the collection. He begins by indulging in a rather childish display of exhibitionism, squanders a client's money in sending

---

[2] ACD, 'Some Personalia about Mr Sherlock Holmes', *Strand Magazine* (Dec. 1917); repr. in Richard Lancelyn Green, *The Uncollected Sherlock Holmes*, 276–93.

[3] ACD to Greenhough Smith, n.d. [?Jan. 1911], University of Virginia Library MS.

on a journey whose fruits could have been gathered by the local police, is absurdly abusive—and even more absurdly in disguise—when he finds Watson (and is consequently absent from London when the criminals return there with their victim). Lady Frances almost loses her life as a result of Holmes's failures, which he acknowledges in an exceptionally self-serving admission ('an example of that temporary eclipse to which even the best-balanced mind may be exposed'). It is consistent with the principle of Nemesis already established in 'The Solitary Cyclist' (*Return*) that whenever Holmes is particularly rude to Watson he will have to do penance for it. (Conan Doyle's disciple P. G. Wodehouse works the same rule for Bertie Wooster and Jeeves, although in most other respects Jeeves is his Holmes and Wooster his Watson.) But this case is a much more disquieting revelation of weakness than the comedy of the earlier story.

Holmes at his most vulnerable is present in 'The Dying Detective', which presents a picture of the apparent ruin of his mind in delirium and of his body in disease. But here Conan Doyle suddenly twists this theme of Holmes as Man rather than Superman: his audience, having by now been conditioned by Holmes's intimations of mortality, is caught in its turn. Yet Holmes's triumph at the close is very much a human success, and the words 'Thank you, Watson, you must help me on with my coat' bring him closer to us than ever before. Superman is displaced by the Son of Man (to borrow G. K. Chesterton's image from his *George Bernard Shaw*). Was Conan Doyle—like James Joyce, a child of the Jesuits—conscious of the Christlike aspects of Holmes's character? Deliberate or not, there was redemption by sacrifice in 'The Final Problem' (*Memoirs*) and resurrection in 'The Empty House' (*Return*); and in 'The Dying Detective' there is a version of the fasting in the wilderness, of the illusions created at its close by the devil, and the devil's own visit. Here, though, the temptation is reversed; or, rather, the devil—most ably represented by Culverton Smith—himself succumbs to temptation in gloating over Holmes's condition, whilst Watson (assisted by Simpsonian nutrition) appropriately sustains the role of ministering angel.

The finale of 'His Last Bow' is a kind of ascension, preceded by a walk to Emmaus in which the story's readers talk, as it were, with the risen Christ but do not recognize him. The delusion of Von Bork is an inversion of the doubting Thomas theme. Thomas's 'My Lord and my God' becomes Von Bork's 'There is only one man' when, recovering his senses, he discovers the true identity of Altamont. Holmes's purpose in this story, unlike the pre-war six, is to build up reader morale and reinforce confidence and security—above all, encourage a sense of the moral righteousness of the British cause. Yet the story's departure from Watsonian narration reasserts the unexpected. Hitherto in the series there had been many breaks in the formula: the abrupt opening was sometimes used (as it is in his novels from this period, *The Lost World* and *The Valley of Fear*), demonstrating Conan Doyle's enthusiasm for establishing new conventions. He wrote a charming letter to Ronald Knox when Knox's eleven-point structural analysis of the Holmes stories appeared in 1912; but Conan Doyle the writer took up the challenge much more vigorously and the method of the very next episode, 'The Dying Detective', tore the Knoxian anatomization to rags in what seems a happy defiance of the author's existing guide-lines—and hence an interdiction of the reader's accustomed path.

The most disconcerting feature of the entire volume is surely the *American* Holmes in 'His Last Bow'. The initial inspiration for this seems to have come from the 22-year-old P. G. Wodehouse, who, in ecstasies at Holmes's return, had contributed two Holmesian pastiches and a poem to *Punch* in 1903 (see Appendix). Of these, 'The Prodigal' drew on rumours that, in response to financial inducements, an American location would be supplied for some of Holmes's cases. Watson was made by Wodehouse to encounter a horribly stage-American Holmes in the Strand (of course). (Wodehouse was to live most of his long life in the USA, but did not make his first visit there until 1904: Conan Doyle had travelled there twice before he wrote 'His Last Bow'.) The end of 'The Prodigal' almost seems an anticipation of a passage written fourteen years later in 'His Last Bow':

Just then a look of anxiety passed over my friend's face. I asked the reason.

'It's like this,' he said; 'I've been in the U-nited States so long now, tracking down the toughs there, that I reckon I've ac-quired the Amurrican accent some. Say, do you think the public will object?' (*Punch*, 23 Sept. 1903).

'I shall no doubt reappear at Claridge's to-morrow as I was before this American stunt—I beg your pardon, Watson; my well of English seems to be permanently defiled' ('His Last Bow').

But in 'His Last Bow' Holmes as Altamont has an American reality. Altamont's is the underworld of ethnic conspiracy, not of crookery, although in the Chicago whence he officially hails the 'Triangle' wing of the Clan-na-Gael (successors to the Fenians) had ably mixed the categories in the 1880s. One of the few breaks from realism is Altamont's name. The Clan had been successfuly penetrated in the 1870s and 1880s by an Englishman named Thomas Billis Beach (1841–94) masquerading under the protectively French name of Henri Le Caron, by which he had enlisted in the Union Army in the American Civil War. 'Altamont' would have smacked far too ostentatiously of the English upper classes for Irish-American nationalist stomachs: the device is a little joke—an artist's signature, as might have been used by Conan Doyle's father, Charles Altamont Doyle. We are to understand that Holmes has called himself Doyle—as Irish a name as could be asked for, and one whose acceptability in Clan circles was evidenced by Michael Francis Doyle (1876–1960), the American lawyer sent by the organization to assist in the defence of Conan Doyle's old friend Sir Roger Casement (1864–1916) in his trial for high treason. Sir Arthur Conan Doyle signed the petition for Casement's pardon, believing him insane in his support for Germany in the war; but the episode had alerted him to Clan links with Germany. He also seems to have been familiar with Le

Caron's *Twenty-five Years in the Secret Service* (1892), and Le Caron's chief at the Home Office, Sir Robert Anderson, had written a critical but complimentary appreciation of the Holmes stories in *TP's Weekly* (2 October 1903), in addition to memoirs of his own on the Le Caron case.

For Conan Doyle, writing in 1917 in the aftermath of the German-backed Irish insurrection of Easter Week 1916, the Irish theme in 'His Last Bow' mingled authenticity with propaganda. He wanted to tell Irish supporters of Germany that they were being cynically exploited—as indeed Casement had discovered and was returning to tell the insurgents before his capture. Conan Doyle would not have wanted to make too much publicly of the inspiration provided by Le Caron, even though he was a natural source for himself as the young Liberal Unionist organizer in Southsea when the spy stepped into the witness-box before the 'Parnellism and Crime' Special Commission on 5 February 1889. However gratifying to Unionist supporters Le Caron's evidence was, its effects were obliterated when the main case of *The Times*, for which Anderson had unveiled Le Caron, proved to be based on forged letters. And while Conan Doyle had stood as a Liberal Unionist candidate in two Scottish elections, he had since been converted to Irish Home Rule by Casement. His sympathies in early 1917 were firmly with the Home Ruler MP Major Willie Redmond (1861–1917), libelled by Le Caron's chief as a Fenian supporter and soon to be killed fighting in the Allied cause. He included a letter from Redmond (dated 18 December 1916) in *Memories and Adventures*:

It was very good of you to write to me and I value very much the expression of your opinion. There are a great many Irishmen today who feel that out of this War we should try and build up a new Ireland. The trouble is men are so timid about meeting each other half-way. It would be a fine memorial to the men who have died so splendidly, if we could over their graves build up a bridge between North and South.

In 'His Last Bow', set before the outbreak of war, Von Herling speaks of 'Irish civil war' being stirred up by the Germans. This is an allusion to Ulster Unionist gun-running from Germany in 1914, as well as to the Clan links. The story was intended to tell Ireland, north and south, that the Allied cause was their cause and that their pre-war quarrel had been inflamed by Germany.

Von Herling also takes credit for 'window-breaking furies'—that is the militant suffragettes led by the Pankhursts. The women's revolution was placed by Dangerfield alongside the Irish crisis and the labour unrest in the making of the pre-war death of liberal England. In its violent phases, just before the war, Conan Doyle attacked it, expressed public fear that its votaries would be lynched, and advised against forcible feeding of prisoners (presumably, and if so quite correctly, on medical grounds). But the suffragettes (whose majority, once war broke out, became as vehemently militaristic in the Allied cause as anyone) were but a small proportion of the New Woman movement sweeping across the North Atlantic over the previous twenty years, and Dr A. Conan Doyle had been an early zealot for equality of the sexes in the medical profession, as may be seen from his 'The Doctors of Hoyland' (*Round the Red Lamp*), probably the best and strongest short story written in that cause. And 'His Last Bow' is intended to point the irony that Von Bork and Von Herling, for all their claims of suffragette-inflammation, are themselves victims of the 'New Woman'—old Martha, whom they so comfortably despise, and who has penetrated to the heart of their organization. She has lived without a moment's ease from a permanent threat of discovery and inevitable death where Holmes, operating for the most part in the outside world, would have had solitary breaks of tension. In literature she is the ancestor of Dorothy Sayers's Miss Climpson, Agatha Christie's Miss Marple, and Patricia Wentworth's Miss Silver.

But how do the pre-war stories here reveal the New Woman? Feminist criticism has argued that women in the Sherlock Holmes stories open up a remarkable subtext. Holmes's self-confessed inability to understand women (except, we should remind ourselves, when his creator wants him to) makes for what Catherine Belsey calls 'another narrative' sketched 'on the fringes of the text' (*Critical Practice*, 1980). Shadowy women, silent women, in the stories raise questions that open up new dimensions—questions that many male critics have themselves left in silence and shadow. Some women in the Holmes cycle before 1900 do find voices to considerable purpose: Hattie Doran explains before a fashionable London audience why she committed bigamy and is warmly, though not unanimously, cheered for it ('The Noble Bachelor', *Adventures*); and Effie Grant Munro's ringing affirmation of interracial love in absolute defiance of the times makes 'The Yellow Face' one of the noblest documents in English literature. But many others remain in ambiguity and possibility: the reader is left unsure of whether Rachel Howells murdered the butler who betrayed her ('The Musgrave Ritual', *Memoirs*), or what Elsie Cubitt's real feelings are towards Abe Slaney ('The Dancing Men', *Return*), or indeed of Conan Doyle's view of admirable husbands who break their engagements, marriages, or hearts at the discovery of premarital (though innocent) indiscretion ('Charles Augustus Milverton' and 'The Second Stain', *Return*). Even Irene Adler in 'A Scandal in Bohemia' (*Adventures*) is largely silent, although she says enough to make Holmes refuse the royal hand, if not the royal snuff-box.

Two of the six pre-war cases here have very silent women: Brenda Tregennis (literally terrorized out of her life in 'The Devil's Foot') and Lady Frances Carfax (unseen and then unconscious until the last moment of her eponymous story). But these silences are far less ambiguous than in the earlier narratives. Conan Doyle married Jean Leckie on 18 September 1907, his first wife Louisa having died on 4 July 1906. The new bride and groom had loved one another without consummation for ten years. The agonies of Leon Sterndale and Philip Green reflect ACD's gratitude that Jean Leckie did not die during that long wait, and that she did not flee his society. It does not mean that either woman was based on the second Lady Conan Doyle. There is less of Brenda Tregennis known to us than her original in the *Pole-Star* Captain's ghostly visitant, created fifteen years before Conan Doyle met Jean

Leckie: we are to understand from Sterndale's 'For years Brenda waited. For years I waited' that this love was also unconsummated, although his 'I have got into the way of being a law to myself' hardly suggests the restraint was on his side. Irrespective of her unspeakable brother and murderer, it might be argued that Brenda thereby trapped herself, since it is not implied that the faithless Mrs Sterndale, unlike Louisa Conan Doyle, was terminally ill. But nothing in the author's intentions obtrudes to say so. As president of the Divorce Law Reform Union he gives a case demanding redress, but Brenda Tregennis belongs to a world of Cornish bourgeois respectability which Sterndale, connected to her family, could not ask her to flout. Then the family itself in its feud destroys her. A social milieu that could not countenance adultery becomes the breeding-ground of murder. The New Woman was attacked for seeking independence from her family: 'The Devil's Foot' points out that her survival might depend on it.

It may also be the ugliest sibling murder in English literature. And as a bourgeois murder it constitutes an ominous development. 'Reading Conan Doyle', writes Franco Moretti, 'one discovers that the criminals are *never* members of the bourgeoisie'.[4] A mine-ownership dispute seems bourgeois enough; but the error is instructive. Up to now the Holmes criminal might be upper-class, or an élite figure (such as Professor Moriarty), or working-class. The change is another sign of a darkening world.

Lady Frances Carfax never utters a word to us, but she symbolizes a vanishing aristocracy, and one marked for extinction by its own preoccupations and illusions (as Chekhov exhibits in *The Cherry Orchard*). The crisis here is one of form. The author of *Micah Clarke* knew his history of Puritanism, and the means by which outward signs of piety could impose on an audience unduly convinced by superficialities. Had Lady Frances's piety been much more than a convention, more than a means of creating an artificial barrier between herself and the Hon. Philip Green, she

[4] 'Clues', in his *Signs Taken for Wonders* (1983, 1988), 139.

would have been able to see through the patently false biblical scholarship of the *soi-disant* Dr Shlessinger. She becomes an easy victim, and like that other doomed aristocrat, Sir Charles Baskerville, she turns her back on the security of servants she knows, and flees for help in the direction where help is least likely to be. Conan Doyle was not the only medical writer to comment on the dangers of aristocratic women of the time having nothing to do, but this case is exceptional in its class analysis. Lady Frances in her turn is based on a model long antedating Jean Leckie; her origin lies in the Burke and Hare murders of 1828 in which elderly vagrants in Edinburgh were smothered to supply anatomical specimens for the world-leading medical school. Conan Doyle was old enough to have overlapped at Edinburgh medical school with one of the case's investigators, Professor Sir Robert Christison (1797–1882), whose attempts during the inquiry to determine whether bruises could be produced after death were later ascribed to Sherlock Holmes (*A Study in Scarlet*) and whose near-fatal auto-experiment on the calabar bean is an evident origin of the killer drug in 'The Devil's Foot'. William Burke (1792–1829), with his charm, his interest in Scripture, and the assurance he showed in his relations with the authorities, supplied the lineaments for Shlessinger alias Holy Peters, whose wife's greeting to Holmes on her husband's ability to face the world comes from the words of Burke's mistress to the police before his arrest. But the point was that, whereas in the Edinburgh of 1828 it was the working-class 'drifting and friendless woman' who was in mortal danger if abandoned by her migrant labourer kin and protectors, by 1911 such victims and outcasts are most likely to come from the upper classes. Lady Frances's relatives will spend money for her recovery once an ex-servant starts publicly worrying about her, but nothing is suggested as to family affection for her. Her day is done; her class is done, too; even her ethics are artificial and become the means of her death. We do not see the moment when she realizes the true nature of her missionary protectors: another form of silence, it deliberately makes for ugly imaginings. And the silence becomes sibylline, meaning so much, saying so little, and so easily consumed, with Lady Frances's salvation depending on Holmes's recollection of the words of the wife of the undertaker.

The role of Violet Westbury in 'The Bruce-Partington Plans' obliquely raises another facet of the silent woman—unwilling silence, imposed by want of male trust. Dakin makes the case:

We are supposed to admire the conduct of Cadogan West 'leaving all his private concerns, like the good citizen that he was' in order to pursue the thief, although it meant leaving his unhappy fiancée alone in a dark street on a foggy night, helpless and a prey to the most distressing fears. One wonders if this cult of the noble patriot putting the national interest above the most sacred personal ties . . . cannot perhaps be overdone. Is it not a trifle coldblooded? Even allowing for the problematic disadvantage to the British navy in a problematic war of having the enemy share the knowledge of a problematic submarine, could it properly weigh more with him than the certain distress and probable danger to the woman it was his first duty to protect? Could he not have managed a brief parting word with her to say where he was going? Incidentally, Holmes indirectly supported this view in his pronouncement, 'To treason you added the more terrible crime of murder'—that is, that the crime against the person is more terrible than the crime against the state.

How far did Arthur Conan Doyle intend such a reading? He certainly drew Arthur Cadogan West as a cruelly traduced martyr to duty; yet apart from his unchivalrous zeal West gravely weakens his own cause by his failure to confide in his fiancée. It was an improvident refusal to insure against disaster. Had he done so, she would have put Holmes on the right track from the first instead of giving him information so vague that it simply 'made it blacker' against her dead love, in Holmes's conclusion. A moral of trust in place of male chauvinist secrecy seems clearly asserted. As Dakin says, taken in conjunction with 'The Second Stain' (*Return*) it shows what evil consequences flowed from the automatic presumption that men in public life should not trust their wives, or their betrothed.

But the secondary implication is a different matter. As Dakin sees it, the notion that a man's first duty is to the state and not to his female partner is morally wrong. Sir Arthur Conan Doyle would have indignantly repudiated this thesis, at least when the 1914 war had begun; but Conan Doyle the writer opens up other possibilities. The brave but rash Cadogan West, hurtling to his lonely and silent sacrifice without a word to his loved one, was a symptom of the male chauvinist preserve of official patriotism whose nature drove Europe inexorably to war. It was the ability of all European governments to rely on instinctive male prioritization of this kind which ensured the ruthlessness and recklessness of the spiralling power struggle. The insurrection of Easter 1916 in Dublin set family obligations aside in exactly the same way.

'The Dying Detective' breaks the silence of another woman symbolically enough for the saga, less so for the times. Mrs Hudson, silent in almost all stories, inaugurates the action here, although, as we discover, her rebellion against Holmes was an essential development on which he had counted (a case when he shows himself capable of forecasting female conduct, admittedly with the woman he knew best). But if women are to speak in the stories, it is from governesses and landladies that we may expect the most skilled deployment of potentialities, since Conan Doyle's sisters were among the former and his mother among the latter.

And it is in fact a governess who makes the great break with previous tradition when Miss Burnet, otherwise Señora Victor Durando, tells the true story of 'Wisteria Lodge'. Signora Emilia Lucca performs the same role in 'The Red Circle'. In both cases their ability to do so was far from predictable. Both are distinguished by their thirst for the murder of a man, Miss Burnet having conspired for it without success, Signora Lucca having obtained it at the moment of despair. Age alone separates their expression of it:

[Miss Burnet's] thin hands clenched, and her worn face blanched with the passion of hatred.

[Emilia Lucca] sprang into the air with a cry of joy. Round and round the room she danced, her hands clapping, her dark eyes gleaming with delighted wonder, and a thousand pretty Italian exclamations pouring from her lips. It was terrible and amazing to see such a woman so convulsed with joy at such a sight.

This is the New Woman. It is also the old one, inspired in part by Rob Roy's wife disposing of her family enemy in Scott's novel. (For all of Conan Doyle's warm praise of Poe's pioneer work, it is Scott who seems the most profound fictional influence on his work.) But the shock of both these female partisans expressing naked homicidal hatred against a male oppressor is Conan Doyle's diagnosis of changing sexual leadership: his heart might be with Miss Burnet and Signora Lucca, and subsequently against the militant suffragettes; but his head records their place in the future. His knowledge of secret conspiracies of the kind portrayed in 'Wisteria Lodge', and of secret societies as in 'The Red Circle', would derive above all from his knowledge of Irish history and society, to which his ancestry gave him entry. He would have known something of the part played by the Ladies' Land League in 1881, and would have seen the new prominence of women in Irish politics, nationalism, socialism, and scholarship. He was particularly familiar with one Irishwoman, his mother, very much her own woman.

The Red Circle as described owes much to the circles into which the Irish Republican Brotherhood, or Fenian Brotherhood, was organized in Ireland and the United States in the 1860s, but it has its own lessons for us. In its way this story is the clearest milestone of all on the road to world war, for it was just such an ethnically based group (Bosnian) which was to assassinate the Archduke Franz Ferdinand on 28 June 1914 at Sarajevo and precipitate the war. Such conspiracies had become commonplace since 1848, but 'The Red Circle' is outstanding in its awareness of the social, national, and spiritual tensions inherent in ethnic networks. The Irish prototype is firmly asserted by the great Yugoslav historian Vladimir Dedijer in the very last words of his *Road to Sarajevo* (1968); it is an ominous thought that Gavrilo Princip, who fired the fatal shots inaugurating the world holocaust, was more reminiscent of the sympathetic Gennaro and Emilia Lucca than of Black Gorgiano, although Irish, Italian, and Yugoslav conspiracies had many Gorgiano equivalents.

Conan Doyle's knowledge of Celtic homicidal instincts was self-knowledge, just as Father Brown in G. K. Chesterton's *The Secret of Father Brown* explains that he did all the murders he had solved himself, by imagining them. To take the most obvious example, Conan Doyle had deliberately chosen a name as blazingly Irish as his own for Holmes's destroyer in 'The Final Problem': one can easily transmute the Moriarty–Holmes confrontation into the author confronting his creation. The dates on which Moriarty noted Holmes's impact might be those when Holmes deadlines prevented other work being written by Conan Doyle, or vetoed simple personal pleasures. The same private release of irritation with the demanding Holmes is present in 'The Dying Detective' when Smith (the sixth most popular Irish surname) snarls: 'Who asked you to cross my path? If you had left me alone I would not have hurt you.' Culverton Smith certainly represented a newer style in malignity, the twisted horror of his mind liberating itself in the jeering malice of his speech, and as such at a much greater remove from Conan Doyle than Moriarty, whose courtesy and dignity are very characteristic of the author himself. There is an element of the stage villain in Smith, which is not present in Moriarty, and this derives partly from Conan Doyle's stage success with *The Speckled Band*, first performed on 4 June 1910: 'The Dying Detective' certainly seems written with the thought of theatre performance in mind. But the mock-autobiographical thought of Irish-Edinburgh homicide comes out again in Smith's residence in Burke Street, as it would in giving the German spies in 'His Last Bow' the names 'Von Bork' and 'Von Herling' (pronounced 'Hareling').

The really serious use of Celtic homicide is of course in 'The Devil's Foot'. Conan Doyle in his Cornish convalescence enjoyed himself by playing with phenomena of the Celtic twilight, linguistic quests, linkage with other ancient traditions, comparative data of note in Devonshire, Wales, Scotland, and Ireland. He got up the extinct Cornish language and peppered his text with it. He seems to have wrapped Holmes's singular theory about Chaldean roots around a famous Scottish literary joke in which 'Chaldean' meant 'Caledonian', while at the time of composing 'The Devil's Foot' he was writing stories in which Roman enmity to the Phoenicians ('The Last Galley') and the Celts ('The Last of the Legions') are linked. But 'The Devil's Foot' also seems to imply that he saw a terror in invoking ancient ethnic roots of identity. Celtic legend has its stories of feud and vengeance within families, and some of the physical results are very nasty, if not equal to the mental horror of Conan Doyle's story. Conan Doyle implies the dangers in what Wagnerian cults of ancient heroic roots can induce among the moderns—and in this his story is even more relevant to the Second World War than to the First (and a Wagner night concludes the next case); in an Irish context, as Yeats was then making famous, the cult of the Hound of Ulster, Cuchulain, could become a powerful impetus in the development of modern national self-consciousness, and that was to have its outcome in World War I, with Patrick Pearse leading into insurrection some of the school pupils trained in that spirit. 'The Devil's Foot' comes from Conan Doyle's own ancestral knowledge, and while, like a wise man of medicine, he was much more alive to its inherent psychological danger than most of his fellow-Celts, it gives him an unquestionable place in the Celtic Renaissance. It is certainly the most Celtic story he ever wrote, even awarding Holmes an honorary Celticism by preoccupation; ironically, its main literary beneficiary would seem to have been Angus Wilson's *Anglo-Saxon Attitudes* (1955), arguably one of the greatest English novels of the twentieth century.

The conflict of imperialisms, and their consequent psychological, economic, and strategic interests, played a great part in the coming of World War I, and there might seem enough kinship between Conan Doyle and, say, Rudyard

Kipling, to identify him easily with support for the imperial idea. But any such interpretation breaks down on close analysis. The imperial theme in Conan Doyle's fiction usually amounts to little more than adventure arising from an incident in imperial history, and sometimes he divides his sympathies sharply to preponderate against the agents of empire: it is difficult to read *The Sign of the Four* without greater dislike for Major Sholto than for the Four, while the merchant Achmed is surely the most pitiable figure of all. The idea of empire as a Pandora's Box is symbolically asserted from time to time, less in rejection of the countries colonized as of the uses which British persons might make of their products. Thus Mortimer Tregennis steals *Radix pedis diaboli* from Sterndale's museum of Africana to further his vengeance and greed, and Culverton Smith uses his own Sumatran discoveries and researches for similar ends, both turning weapons of peculiar horror on their own kin. The implication is of empire as exceedingly dangerous in its encouragement of the morally unfit in the vilest forms of avarice. In some ways the principle is similar to that asserted by Holmes at the end of 'The Creeping Man' (*Case-Book*), where he denounces artificial rejuvenation and longevity as a means for 'the material, the sensual, the worldly' to 'prolong their worthless lives', calling it the 'survival of the least fit'.

None of this prevented Conan Doyle from calling himself an imperialist, especially when preaching Home Rule for Ireland. But the man who was to convert him to that only to defect himself into separatism by violence, Sir Roger Casement, first came to his attention when, as British Consul in the Congo, he indicted the Belgian King Leopold II's hideous regime of profiteering by slave labour. Conan Doyle watched further revelations with mounting horror. Britain, a signatory to the treaty establishing Leopold's Congo in 1885, pressed for full transfer of the Congo to Belgium, Foreign Secretary Sir Edward Grey (1862–1933) stating on 26 February 1908 that the regime had 'morally forfeited every right to international recognition': a parliamentary paper providing documentary proof of the ghastly charges was issued the same day. On 5 March Leopold (1835–1909, reigning from 1865) agreed to end his private empire by its cession to Belgium, but received enormous personal compensation such as land in Laeken, property in the Riviera, a villa in Ostend, a 155-square-mile estate in Africa, and £2 million nominally expendable on objects 'connected with and beneficial to the Congo'. Within the next few days Conan Doyle began work on 'Wisteria Lodge', whose main plot turned on a profiteering regime of comparable cruelty and enforcement by ruthless espionage, ending in the chief profiteer's departure from control in similar plutocratic splendour. Personally, he could not give public expression to his views on the Congo while the regime was being transferred; his own government was exerting forceful but delicate leverage, and a blundering intervention could make matters much worse for the sufferers. It was not until 1909, when Belgian rule had been shown after a year to have brought no noticeable improvement, that Conan Doyle burst into visible flame with his searing pamphlet *The Crime of the Congo*; but, as he then revealed, his fires had been banked for many long months before. 'What is progress?' (he would ask there): 'Is it to run a little faster in a motor-car, to listen to gabble in a gramophone—these are the toys of life. But if progress is a spiritual thing, then we do *not* progress. Such a horror as this of Belgium and the Congo would not have been possible fifty years ago. No European nation would have done it, and if they had, no other one would have failed to raise its voice in protest. There was more decorum and principle in those slower days. We live in a time of rush, but do not call it progress. The story of the Congo has made the idea a little absurd' (pp. 86–7).

As Miss Burnet's Philippic at the close of 'Wisteria Lodge' declares, the greatest insurance Injustice has is the simple inability of ordinary people in other countries to see why they should bestir themselves in its cause. Structure, as usual, is the key to Conan Doyle's purpose: we begin with the sybarite Englishman John Scott Eccles, the pattern of respectability whose potential for exploitation the Scots author ironically assesses, but whose selfishness is as clear to us as was his status to the police; we end with the dedicated Englishwoman Miss Burnet, consecrated in the cause which may cost her life. It is

'This is very painful—very painful and terrible,' said Mr Scott Eccles, in a querulous voice; 'but it is really uncommonly hard upon me. I had nothing to do with my host going off upon a nocturnal expedition and meeting so sad an end. How do I come to be mixed up with the case?'

versus

'How can an English lady join in such a murderous affair?'

'I join in it because there is no other way in the world by which justice can be gained. What does the law of England care for the rivers of blood shed years ago in San Pedro, or for the ship-load of treasure which this man has stolen? To you they are like crimes committed in some other planet. But *we* know . . . To us there is no fiend in hell like Juan Murillo, and no peace in life while his victims still cry for vengeance.'

Conan Doyle had real-life precedent for the blood-bathed tyrant as Home Counties resident, but 'Wisteria Lodge' brings an English milieu cosily around the Latin American despot. It was appropriate for Leopold—whom the *Strand*'s artist Arthur Twidle (1865–1936) seems to have used as model for the Tiger of San Pedro: he was Queen Victoria's first cousin, eldest son of her favourite uncle, and as profligate in sexual life as her own eldest son ('whatever his whims may be', notes Holmes of Don Juan Murillo with grim ambiguity, 'he can very easily satisfy them'). A recent scholar, Anthea Trood, builds on Holmes's description of the Tiger's Surrey home ('his house is full of butlers, footmen, maid-servants, and the usual overfed, under-worked staff of a large English country-house') to assert:

If 'The Musgrave Ritual' demonstrates the employer's nightmare of a household taken over by servants, another Holmes story, 'Wisteria Lodge', offers something like the ideal, though one to which many employers might refuse to own:

'. . . It's a double winged house, and the servants live on one side, the family on the other. There's no link between the two save for Henderson's own servant, who serves the family's meals. Everything is carried to a certain door, which forms the one connection'.[5]

So that to an accomplished student of criminal motifs in pre-war fiction, the Tiger of San Pedro had so Englished himself as to become the *beau ideal* of great-house domesticity in his security arrangements. Trood so far accepts his orthodoxy as to state that it is the employee Miss Burnet who brings 'crime into the house'. However questionable this analysis, its importance lies in Trood's instinctive impression that the story is one of social orthodoxy, with the Tiger as its ultimate beneficiary. As against his status in Surrey, his enemies are a badly run household composed of adventurers of dubious origins, racially mixed, gastronomically disappointing, supported by a widow of some foreign envoy masquerading as a spinster governess. Truth is disreputable.

The coalition against the Tiger is in fact impressive in its multiracial and multinational span, and this symbolizes the range of cultures despoiled by Leopold. And the voodoo-worship is essential to bring imperial curses home to roost. To go in and violate the sanctities of remote pagan theologies is to draw them into the heart of whiteness. The sacrifice in the kitchen of Wisteria Lodge reverses Joseph Conrad's story of the Congo, *Heart of Darkness* (1902), and the climax of Kurtz's dying words 'The horror! The horror!' is counterpointed by Holmes's conclusion on the theme of the grotesque (which has made this story, in addition to all else, a dissertation on a word): 'there is but one step from the grotesque to the horrible'.

The bleak and melancholy atmosphere of 'Wisteria Lodge' supplies its tone for the idea of conflicting and dishonoured imperial ambitions. 'The Bruce-Partington Plans' asserts the more obvious theme of resultant inter-power rivalry in the arms race and search for state security. Conan Doyle was

---

[5] *Domestic Crime in the Victorian Novel* (1989), 159.

extraordinarily perceptive in recognizing the future significance of the submarine, whose potential in starving an island such as Britain which is dependent on food imports he would set out five years later in his parable 'Danger!', published in the *Strand* for July 1914. Up to this point the First Lord of the Admiralty, Winston Churchill (1874–1965), could make no headway with his scheme of state insurance against wartime shipping losses, but shipowners pressed the issue in July and a Bill to that effect was introduced on 3 August. Churchill probably privately gave credit to Conan Doyle (he was generous in his respect for authors whose work he liked, other things being equal), but others were less ready to acknowledge how unready Conan Doyle had shown them to be. When on 1 May 1917 Admiral Capelle, Secretary of the German navy, saluted him as the 'real and only prophet' he became something of a target of a widely prevalent wartime vindictiveness, for all of his unrestrained and incessant evangelization for the British war effort from the beginning. Although abominating Casement's treason, he had called for his reprieve from the gallows, in July 1916, and, most unusually, had dismissed the widely circulated 'Black Diaries', with their content of homosexual obsessions and orgies recorded in what looked like Casement's handwriting: Conan Doyle simply said that no sexual offence could be as bad as the treasonable offences Casement had committed and his own signature for clemency would stand. He had breakfast with the Prime Minister David Lloyd George (1863–1945) in April 1917, was complimented on his *Strand* series collected in annual volumes, *The British Campaign in France and Flanders*, and was officially informed by War Intelligence that he was not to publish his account of the campaigns of 1916 until further notice. It hurt him greatly, and seemed to call into question his loyalty, a particularly sensitive point for persons of Irish parentage after the Easter Rising. And he desperately wanted to contribute further to raise public morale, which was slipping in the apparently endless deadlock on the Western Front.

This introduction has implied a divisive tension between Conan Doyle the man and Conan Doyle the writer. As he wrote to Herbert Greenhough Smith concerning 'The Red Circle', he found that his stories came into being as organic entities (Metropolitan Toronto Library MS: (January 1911)), all the more so with the Holmes cycle, for which he needed little research; so Conan Doyle the writer scanned and took pulse, charted symptoms and diagnosed phenomena of contemporary history, where Conan Doyle the man responded in partisan terms. As he rose in society he diverged a little more from his essentially democratic writer's perspective. It might seem that Holmes, so much of a popular joke, was at the remotest pole from the rising, newly installed squire of Windlesham, Crowborough, and perhaps 'Wisteria Lodge' asks whether Windlesham is so much more virtuous than Henderson's (or Murillo's) High Gable. But that won't do. Both Conan Doyles rebelled against new social pressures and class dictates, and High Gable may be more of a product of accord than tension. Certainly 'Wisteria Lodge' testified that social advancement would not silence Conan Doyle and where his pen led, in crusade, his voice would follow. Holmes himself was less of an incubus when he did not bring with him the pressure of a deadline. And war made for strange bedfellows, none stranger than when, muzzled by censorship, Conan Doyle turned for the voice being denied him to the notoriously disreputable one among his literary offspring. Sherlock Holmes leaped lightly to the rescue from a Ford car. In using his aid Conan Doyle offered a suitably propagandist version of the origins of the Great War such as might inspire his increasingly disillusioned readers to recover the first, fine, careless rapture in the chivalric tradition so wholeheartedly invoked here by Holmes and Watson. Skilfully, the case for the United Kingdom as champion and as victim is mixed, using the old intermingling of hero and martyr so dear to Irish national myth. And the Holmesian ironies are in finest shape: if all else fails, the audience is invited to laugh its way to victory.

It is propaganda, and hence great care is taken to make the British cause that of the little man, symbolized in the small car contrasting with the Benz, the old lady as against the grand embassy retinue, the *Handbook of Bee Culture* as sole answer to the magnificently efficient range of German filing-systems and combination codes, Watson at the wheel versus the mobilized Reich. Yet the story is document no less than design. So are Holmes and Watson. Holmes proclaims their death, and Watson their survival, in the last lines. They constitute a quintessential Britishness, and, given their creator, Irishness, drawing on the roots of cultural identity in the Allied cause. But their car is American, Holmes's voice for half the story is American, and they appear in an episode of 1914 written in 1917 when the cause had also become American.

His Last Bow, whether it knew it or not, bowed in the American century.

OWEN DUDLEY EDWARDS

NOTE ON THE TEXT

The text has been taken from the John Murray collection *His Last Bow*, first published on 22 October 1917, collated against initial publication of the individual items in the *Strand* magazine at dates given in the Explanatory Notes, as well as with the American edition of the collection, published by George H. Doran of New York in October 1917, and with subsequent UK and US editions. But in this series 'The Cardboard Box' is now in the *Memoirs*. In this series 'The Dying Detective' has been based on the MS, other than occasional punctuation and hyphenization from the *Strand*, whilst 'His Last Bow' is based on the *Strand* text, for reasons indicated in the Explanatory Notes together with all significant variations.

SELECT BIBLIOGRAPHY

I. A. CONAN DOYLE. PRINCIPAL WORKS

(a) *Fiction*

A Study in Scarlet (Ward, Lock, & Co., 1888)
The Mystery of Cloomber (Ward & Downey, 1888)
Micah Clarke (Longmans, Green, & Co., 1889)
The Captain of the Pole-Star and Other Tales (Longmans, Green, & Co., 1890)
The Sign of the Four (Spencer Blackett, 1890)
The Firm of Girdlestone (Chatto & Windus, 1890)
The White Company (Smith, Elder, & Co., 1891)
The Adventures of Sherlock Holmes (George Newnes, 1892)
The Great Shadow (Arrowsmith, 1892)
The Refugees (Longmans, Green, & Co., 1893)
The Memoirs of Sherlock Holmes (George Newnes, 1893)
Round the Red Lamp (Methuen & Co., 1894)
The Stark Munro Letters (Longmans, Green, & Co., 1895)
The Exploits of Brigadier Gerard (George Newnes, 1896)
Rodney Stone (Smith, Elder, & Co., 1896)
Uncle Bernac (Smith, Elder, & Co., 1897)
The Tragedy of the Korosko (Smith, Elder, & Co., 1898)
A Duet With an Occasional Chorus (Grant Richards, 1899)
The Green Flag and Other Stories of War and Sport (Smith, Elder, & Co., 1900)
The Hound of the Baskervilles (George Newnes, 1902)
Adventures of Gerard (George Newnes, 1903)
The Return of Sherlock Holmes (George Newnes, 1905)
Sir Nigel (Smith, Elder, & Co., 1906)
Round the Fire Stories (Smith, Elder, & Co., 1908)
The Last Galley (Smith, Elder, & Co., 1911)
The Lost World (Hodder & Stoughton, 1912)
The Poison Belt (Hodder & Stoughton, 1913)
The Valley of Fear (Smith, Elder, & Co., 1915)
His Last Bow (John Murray, 1917)
Danger! and Other Stories (John Murray, 1918)
The Land of Mist (Hutchinson & Co., 1926)
The Case-Book of Sherlock Holmes (John Murray, 1927)
The Maracot Deep and Other Stories (John Murray, 1929)

The Complete Sherlock Holmes Short Stories (John Murray, 1928)
The Conan Doyle Stories (John Murray, 1929)
The Complete Sherlock Holmes Long Stories (John Murray, 1929)

(b) *Non-fiction*

The Great Boer War (Smith, Elder, & Co., 1900)
The Story of Mr George Edalji (T. Harrison Roberts, 1907)
Through the Magic Door (Smith, Elder, & Co., 1907)
The Crime of the Congo (Hutchinson & Co., 1909)
The Case of Oscar Slater (Hodder & Stoughton, 1912)
The German War (Hodder & Stoughton, 1914)
The British Campaign in France and Flanders (Hodder & Stoughton, 6 vols., 1916–20)
The Poems of Arthur Conan Doyle (John Murray, 1922)
Memories and Adventures (Hodder & Stoughton, 1924; revised edn., 1930)
The History of Spiritualism (Cassell & Co., 1926)

2. MISCELLANEOUS

A Bibliography of A. Conan Doyle (Soho Bibliographies 23: Oxford, 1983) by Richard Lancelyn Green and John Michael Gibson, with a foreword by Graham Greene, is the standard—and indispensable—source of bibliographical information, and of much else besides. Green and Gibson have also assembled and introduced *The Unknown Conan Doyle*, comprising *Uncollected Stories* (those never previously published in book form); *Essays on Photography* (documenting a little-known enthusiasm of Conan Doyle's during his time as a student and young doctor), both published in 1982; and *Letters to the Press* (1986). Alone, Richard Lancelyn Green has compiled (1) *The Uncollected Sherlock Holmes* (1983), an impressive assemblage of Holmesiana, containing almost all Conan Doyle's writing about his creation (other than the stories themselves) together with related material by Joseph Bell, J. M. Barrie, and Beverley Nichols; (2) *The Further Adventures of Sherlock Holmes* (1985), a selection of eleven apocryphal Holmes adventures by various authors, all diplomatically introduced; (3) *The Sherlock Holmes Letters* (1986), a collection of noteworthy public correspondence on Holmes and Holmesiana and far more valuable than its title suggests; and (4) *Letters to Sherlock Holmes* (1984), a powerful testimony to the power of the Holmes stories.

Though much of Conan Doyle's work is now readily available there are still gaps. Some of his very earliest fiction now only survives in rare piracies (apart, that is, from the magazines in which they were first published), including items of intrinsic genre interest such as 'The Gully of Bluemansdyke' (1881) and its sequel 'My Friend the Murderer' (1882), which both turn on the theme of the murderer-informer (handled very differently—and far better in the Holmes story of 'The Resident Patient' (*Memoirs*)): both of these were used as book-titles for the same pirate collection first issued as *Mysteries and Adventures* (1889). Other stories achieved book publication only after severe pruning—for example, 'The Surgeon of Gaster Fell', reprinted in *Danger!* many years after magazine publication (1890). Some items given initial book publication were not included in the collected edition of *The Conan Doyle Stories*. Particularly deplorable losses were 'John Barrington Cowles' (1884: included subsequently in *Edinburgh Stories of Arthur Conan Doyle* (1981)), 'A Foreign Office Romance' (1894), 'The Club-Footed Grocer' (1898), 'A Shadow Before' (1898), and 'Danger!' (1914). Three of these may have been post-war casualties, as seeming to deal too lightheartedly with the outbreak of other wars; 'John Barrington Cowles' may have been dismissed as juvenile work; but why Conan Doyle discarded a story as good as 'The Club-Footed Grocer' would baffle even Holmes.

At the other end of his life, Conan Doyle's tidying impaired the survival of his most recent work, some of which well merited lasting recognition. *The Maracot Deep and Other Stories* appeared in 1929, a little over a month after *The Conan Doyle Stories*; 'Maracot' itself found a separate paperback life as a short novel; the two Professor Challenger stories, 'The Disintegration Machine' and 'When the World Screamed', were naturally included in John Murray's *The Professor Challenger Stories* (1952); but the fourth item, 'The Story of Spedegue's Dropper', passed beyond the ken of most of Conan Doyle's readers. These three stories show the author, in his seventieth year, still at the height of his powers.

In 1980 Gaslight Publications, of Bloomington, Ind., reprinted *The Mystery of Cloomber, The Firm of Girdlestone, The Doings of Raffles Haw* (1892), *Beyond the City* (1893), *The Parasite* (1894; also reprinted in *Edinburgh Stories of Arthur Conan Doyle*), *The Stark Munro Letters, The Tragedy of the Korosko*, and *A Duet*. *Memories and Adventures*, Conan Doyle's enthralling but impressionistic recollections, are best read in the revised (1930) edition. *Through the Magic Door* remains the best introduction to the literary mind of Conan Doyle, whilst some of his volumes on Spiritualism have autobiographical material of literary significance.

ACD: The Journal of the Arthur Conan Doyle Society (ed. Christopher Roden, David Stuart Davies [to 1991], and Barbara Roden [from 1992]), together with its newsletter, *The Parish Magazine*, is a useful source of critical and biographical material on Conan Doyle. The enormous body of 'Sherlockiana' is best pursued in *The Baker Street Journal*, published by Fordham University Press, or in the *Sherlock Holmes Journal* (Sherlock Holmes Society of London), itemized up to 1974 in the colossal *World Bibliography of Sherlock Holmes and Doctor Watson* (1974) by Ronald Burt De Waal (see also De Waal, *The International Sherlock Holmes* (1980)) and digested in *The Annotated Sherlock Holmes* (2 vols., 1968) by William S. Baring-Gould, whose industry has been invaluable for the Oxford Sherlock Holmes editors. Jack Tracy, *The Encyclopaedia Sherlockiana* (1979) is a very helpful compilation of relevant data. Those who can nerve themselves to consult it despite its title will benefit greatly from Christopher Redmond, *In Bed With Sherlock Holmes* (1984). The classic 'Sherlockian' work is Ronald A. Knox, 'Studies in the Literature of Sherlock Holmes', first published in *The Blue Book* (July 1912) and reprinted in his *Essays in Satire* (1928).

The serious student of Conan Doyle may perhaps deplore the vast extent of 'Sherlockian' literature, even though the size of this output is testimony in itself to the scale and nature of Conan Doyle's achievement. But there is undoubtedly some wheat amongst the chaff. At the head stands Dorothy L. Sayers, *Unpopular Opinions* (1946); also of some interest are T. S. Blakeney, *Sherlock Holmes: Fact or Fiction* (1932), H. W. Bell, *Sherlock Holmes and Dr Watson* (1932), Vincent Starrett, *The Private Life of Sherlock Holmes* (1934), Gavin Brend, *My Dear Holmes* (1951), S. C. Roberts, *Holmes and Watson* (1953) and Roberts's introduction to *Sherlock Holmes: Selected Stories* (Oxford: The World's Classics, 1951), James E. Holroyd, *Baker Street Byways* (1959), Ian McQueen, *Sherlock Holmes Detected* (1974), and Trevor H. Hall, *Sherlock Holmes and his Creator* (1978). One Sherlockian item certainly falls into the category of the genuinely essential: D. Martin Dakin, *A Sherlock Holmes Commentary* (1972), to which all the editors of the present series are indebted.

Michael Pointer, *The Public Life of Sherlock Holmes* (1975) contains invaluable information concerning dramatizations of the Sherlock Holmes stories for radio, stage, and the cinema; of complementary interest are Chris Steinbrunner and Norman Michaels, *The Films of Sherlock Holmes* (1978) and David Stuart Davies, *Holmes of the Movies* (1976), whilst Philip Weller with Christopher Roden, *The Life and Times of Sherlock Holmes* (1992) summarizes a great deal of useful information concerning Conan Doyle's life and Holmes's cases, and in addition is delightfully illustrated. The more concrete products of the Holmes industry are dealt with in Charles Hall, *The Sherlock Holmes Collection* (1987). For a useful retrospective view, Allen Eyles, *Sherlock Holmes: A Centenary Celebration* (1986) rises to the occasion. Both useful and ongoing are Peter Haining, *The Sherlock Holmes Scrapbook* (1973) and Charles Viney, *Sherlock Holmes in London* (1989).

Of the many anthologies of Holmesiana, P. A. Shreffler (ed.), *The Baker Street Reader* (1984) is exceptionally useful. D. A. Redmond, *Sherlock Holmes: A Study in Sources* (1982) is similarly indispensable. Michael Hardwick, *The Complete Guide to Sherlock Holmes* (1986) is both reliable and entertaining; Michael Harrison, *In the Footsteps of Sherlock Holmes* (1958) is occasionally helpful.

For more general studies of the detective story, the standard history is Julian Symons, *Bloody Murder* (1972, 1985, 1992). Necessary but a great deal less satisfactory is Howard Haycraft, *Murder for Pleasure* (1942); of more value is Haycraft's critical anthology *The Art of the Mystery Story* (1946), which contains many choice period items. Both R. F. Stewart, *... And Always a Detective* (1980) and Colin Watson, *Snobbery with Violence* (1971) are occasionally useful. Dorothy Sayers's pioneering introduction to *Great Short Stories of Detection, Mystery and Horror* (First Series, 1928), despite some inspired howlers, is essential reading; Raymond Chandler's riposte, 'The Simple Art of Murder' (1944), is reprinted in Haycraft, *The Art of the Mystery Story* (see above). Less well known than Sayers's essay but with an equal claim to poineer status is E. M. Wrong's introduction to *Crime and Detection*, First Series (Oxford: The World's Classics, 1926). See also Michael Cox (ed.), *Victorian Tales of Mystery and Detection: An Oxford Anthology* (1992).

Amongst biographical studies of Conan Doyle one of the most distinguished is Jon L. Lellenberg's survey, *The Quest for Sir Arthur Conan Doyle* (1987), with a Foreword by Dame Jean Conan Doyle (much the best piece of writing on ACD by any member of his family). The four earliest biographers—the Revd John Lamond (1931), Hesketh Pearson (1943), John Dickson Carr (1949), and Pierre Nordon (1964)—all had access to the family archives, subsequently closed to researchers following a lawsuit; hence all four biographies contain valuable documentary material, though Nordon handles the evidence best (the French text is fuller than the English version, published in 1966). Of the others, Lamond seems only to have made little use of the material available to him;

Pearson is irreverent and wildly careless with dates; Dickson Carr has a strong fictionalizing element. Both he and Nordon paid a price for their access to the Conan Doyle papers by deferring to the far from impartial editorial demands of Adrian Conan Doyle; Nordon nevertheless remains the best available biography. The best short sketch is Julian Symons, *Conan Doyle* (1979) (and for the late Victorian milieu of the Holmes cycle some of Symons's own fiction, such as *The Blackheath Poisonings* and *The Detling Secret*, can be thoroughly recommended). Harold Orel (ed.), *Critical Essays on Sir Arthur Conan Doyle* (1992) is a good and varied collection, whilst Robin Winks, *The Historian as Detective* (1969) contains many insights and examples applicable to the Holmes corpus; Winks's *Detective Fiction: A Collection of Critical Essays* (1980) is an admirable working handbook, with a useful critical bibliography. Edmund Wilson's famous essay 'Mr Holmes, they were the footprints of a gigantic hound' (1944) may be found in his *Classics and Commercials: A Literary Chronicle of the Forties* (1950).

Specialized biographical areas are covered in Owen Dudley Edwards, *The Quest for Sherlock Holmes: A Biographical Study of Arthur Conan Doyle* (1983) and in Geoffrey Stavert, *A Study in Southsea: The Unrevealed Life of Dr Arthur Conan Doyle* (1987), which respectively assess the significance of the years up to 1882, and from 1882 to 1890. Alvin E. Rodin and Jack D. Key provide a thorough study of Conan Doyle's medical career and its literary implications in *Medical Casebook of Dr Arthur Conan Doyle* (1984). Peter Costello, in *The Real World of Sherlock Holmes: The True Crimes Investigated by Arthur Conan Doyle* (1991) claims too much, but it is useful to be reminded of events that came within Conan Doyle's orbit, even if they are sometimes tangential or even irrelevant. Christopher Redmond, *Welcome to America, Mr Sherlock Holmes* (1987) is a thorough account of Conan Doyle's tour of North America in 1894.

Other than Baring-Gould (see above), the only serious attempt to annotate the nine volumes of the Holmes cycle has been in the Longman Heritage of Literature series (1979–80), to which the present editors are also indebted. Of introductions to individual texts, H. R. F. Keating's to the *Adventures* and *The Hound of the Baskervilles* (published in one volume under the dubious title *The Best of Sherlock Holmes* (1992)) is worthy of particular mention.

A CHRONOLOGY OF ARTHUR CONAN DOYLE

1855   Charles Altamont Doyle, youngest son of the political cartoonist John Doyle ('HB'), and Mary Foley, his Irish landlady's daughter, marry in Edinburgh on 31 July.

1859   Arthur Ignatius Conan Doyle, third child and elder son of ten siblings, born at 11 Picardy Place, Edinburgh, on 22 May and baptized into the Roman Catholic religion of his parents.

1868–75 ACD commences two years' education under the Jesuits at Hodder, followed by five years at its senior sister college, Stonyhurst, both in the Ribble Valley, Lancashire; becomes a popular storyteller amongst his fellow pupils, writes verses, edits a school paper, and makes one close friend, James Ryan of Glasgow and Ceylon. Doyle family resides at 3 Sciennes Hill Place, Edinburgh.

1875–6 ACD passes London Matriculation Examination at Stonyhurst and studies for a year in the Jesuit college at Feldkirch, Austria.

1876–7 ACD becomes a student of medicine at Edinburgh University on the advice of Bryan Charles Waller, now lodging with the Doyle family at 2 Argyle Park Terrace.

1877–80 Waller leases 23 George Square, Edinburgh as a 'consulting pathologist', with all the Doyles as residents. ACD continues medical studies, becoming surgeon's clerk to Joseph Bell at Edinburgh; also takes temporary medical assistantships at Sheffield, Ruyton (Salop), and Birmingham, the last leading to a close friendship with his employer's family, the Hoares. First story published, 'The Mystery of Sasassa Valley', in *Chambers's Journal* (6 Sept. 1879); fiirst non-fiction published—'Gelseminum as a Poison', *British Medical Journal* (20 Sept. 1879). Some time previously ACD sends 'The Haunted Grange of Goresthorpe' to *Blackwood's Edinburgh Magazine*, but it is filed and forgotten.

1880   (Feb.–Sept.) ACD serves as surgeon on the Greenland whaler *Hope* of Peterhead.

1881   ACD graduates MB, CM (Edin.); Waller and the Doyles living at 15 Lonsdale Terrace, Edinburgh.

1881–2   (Oct.–Jan.) ACD serves as surgeon on the steamer *Mayumba* to West Africa, spending three days with US Minister to Liberia, Henry Highland Garnet, black abolitionist leader, then dying. (July–Aug.) Visits Foley relatives in Lismore, Co. Waterford.

1882   Ill-fated partnership with George Turnavine Budd in Plymouth. ACD moves to Southsea, Portsmouth, in June. ACD published in *London Society*, *All the Year Round*, *Lancet*, and *British Journal of Photography*. Over the next eight years ACD becomes an increasingly successful general practitioner at Southsea.

1882–3   Breakup of the Doyle family in Edinburgh. Charles Altamont Doyle henceforth confined because of alcoholism and epilepsy. Mary Foley Doyle resident in Masongill Cottage on the Waller estate at Masongill, Yorkshire. Innes Doyle (b. 1873) resident with ACD as schoolboy and surgery page from Sept. 1882.

1883   'The Captain of the *Pole-Star*' published (*Temple Bar*, Jan.), as well as a steady stream of minor pieces. Works on *The Mystery of Cloomber*.

1884   ACD publishes 'J. Habakuk Jephson's Statement' (*Cornhill Magazine*, Jan.), 'The Heiress of Glenmahowley' (*Temple Bar*, Jan.), 'The Cabman's Story' (*Cassell's Saturday Journal*, May); working on *The Firm of Girdlestone*.

1885   Publishes 'The Man from Archangel' (*London Society*, Jan.). John Hawkins, briefly a resident patient with ACD, dies of cerebral meningitis. Louisa Hawkins, his sister, marries ACD. (Aug.) Travels in Ireland for honeymoon. Awarded Edinburgh MD.

1886   Writing *A Study in Scarlet*.

1887   *A Study in Scarlet* published in *Beeton's Christmas Annual*.

1888   (July) First book edition of *A Study in Scarlet* published by Ward, Lock; (Dec.) *The Mystery of Cloomber* published.

1889   (Feb.) *Micah Clarke* (ACD's novel of the Monmouth Rebellion of 1685) published. Mary Louise Conan Doyle, ACD's eldest child, born. Unauthorized publication of *Mysteries and Adventures* (published later as *The*

Gully of Bluemansdyke and *My Friend the Murderer*). *The Sign of the Four* and Oscar Wilde's *The Picture of Dorian Gray* commissioned by Lippincott's.

1890   (Jan.) 'Mr [R. L.] Stevenson's Methods in Fiction' published in the *National Review*. (Feb.) *The Sign of the Four* published in *Lippincott's Monthly Magazine*; (Mar.) First authorized short-story collection, *The Captain of the Pole-Star and Other Tales*, published; (Apr.) *The Firm of Girdle-stone* published; (Oct.) First book edition of the *Sign* published by Spencer Blackett.

1891   ACD sets up as an eye specialist in 2 Upper Wimpole Street, off Harley Street, while living at Montague Place. Moves to South Norwood. (July–Dec.) The first six 'Adventures of Sherlock Holmes' published in George Newnes's *Strand Magazine*. (Oct.) *The White Company* published; *Beyond the City* first published in *Good Cheer*, the special Christmas number of *Good Words*.

1892   (Jan.–June) Six more Holmes stories published in the *Strand*, with another in Dec. (Mar.) *The Doings of Raffles Haw* published (first serialized in Alfred Harmsworth's penny paper *Answers*, Dec. 1891–Feb. 1892). (14 Oct.) *The Adventures of Sherlock Holmes* published by Newnes. (31 Oct.) Waterloo story *The Great Shadow* published. Alleyne Kingsley Conan Doyle born. Newnes republishes the *Sign*.

1893   'Adventures of Sherlock Holmes' (second series) continues in the *Strand*, to be published by Newnes as *The Memoirs of Sherlock Holmes* (Dec.), minus 'The Cardboard Box'. Holmes apparently killed in 'The Final Problem' (Dec.) to free ACD for 'more serious literary work'. (May) *The Refugees* published. *Jane Annie: or, the Good Conduct Prize* (musical comedy co-written with J. M. Barrie) fails at the Savoy Theatre. (10 Oct.) Charles Altamont Doyle dies.

1894   (Oct.) *Round the Red Lamp*, a collection of medical short stories, published, several for the first time. *The Stark Munro Letters*, a fictionalized autobiography, begun, to be concluded the following year. ACD on US lecture tour with Innes Doyle. (Dec.) *The Parasite* published; 'The Medal of Brigadier Gerard' published in the *Strand*.

1895   'The Exploits of Brigadier Gerard' published in the *Strand*.

1896   (Feb.) *The Exploits of Brigadier Gerard* published by Newnes. ACD settles at Hindhead, Surrey, to minimize effects of his wife's tuberculosis. (Nov.) *Rodney Stone*, a pre-Regency mystery, published. Self-pastiche, 'The Field Bazaar', appears in the Edinburgh University *Student* (20 Nov.).

1897   (May) Napoleonic novel *Uncle Bernac* published; three 'Captain Sharkey' pirate stories published in *Pearson's Magazine* (Jan., Mar., May). Home at Undershaw, Hindhead.

1898   (Feb.) *The Tragedy of the Korosko* published. (June) Publishes *Songs of Action*, a verse collection. (June–Dec.) Begins to publish 'Round the Fire Stories' in the *Strand*—'The Beetle Hunter', 'The Man with the Watches', 'The Lost Special', 'The Sealed Room', 'The Black Doctor', 'The Club-Footed Grocer', and 'The Brazilian Cat'. Ernest William Hornung (ACD's brother-in-law) creates A. J. Raffles and in 1899 dedicates the first stories to ACD.

1899   (Jan.–May) Concludes 'Round the Fire' series in the *Strand* with 'The Japanned Box', 'The Jew's Breast-Plate', 'B. 24', 'The Latin Tutor', and 'The Brown Hand'. (Mar.) Publishes *A Duet with an Occasional Chorus*, a version of his own romance. (Oct.–Dec.) 'The Croxley Master', a boxing story, published in the *Strand*. William Gillette begins 33 years starring in *Sherlock Holmes*, a play by Gillette and ACD.

1900   Accompanies volunteer-staffed Langman hospital as unofficial supervisor to support British forces in the Boer War. (Mar.) Publishes short-story collection, *The Green Flag and Other Stories of War and Sport*. (Oct.) *The Great Boer War* published. Unsuccessful Liberal Unionist parliamentary candidate for Edinburgh Central.

1901   (Aug.) 'The Hound of the Baskervilles' begins serialization in the *Strand*, subtitled 'Another Adventure of Sherlock Holmes'.

1902   (Jan.) *The War in South Africa: Its Cause and Conduct* published. 'Sherlockian' higher criticism begun by Frank Sidgwick in the *Cambridge Review* (23 Jan.). (Mar.) *The Hound of the Baskervilles* published by Newnes. ACD accepts knighthood with reluctance.

1903   (Sept.) *Adventures of Gerard* published by Newnes (previously serialized in the *Strand*). (Oct.) 'The Return of

Sherlock Holmes' begins in the *Strand*. Author's Edition of ACD's major works published in twelve volumes by Smith, Elder and thirteen by D. Appleton & Co. of New York, with prefaces by ACD; many titles omitted.

1904   'Return of Sherlock Holmes' continues in the *Strand*, series designed to conclude with 'The Abbey Grange' (Sept.), but ACD develops earlier allusions and produces 'The Second Stain' (Dec.).

1905   (Mar.) *The Return of Sherlock Holmes* published by Newnes. (Dec.) Serialization of 'Sir Nigel' begun in the *Strand* (concluded Dec. 1906).

1906   (Nov.) Book publication of *Sir Nigel*. ACD defeated as Unionist candidate for Hawick District in general election. (4 July) Death of Louisa ('Touie'), Lady Conan Doyle. ACD deeply affected.

1907   ACD clears the name of George Edalji (convicted in 1903 of cattle-maiming). (18 Sept.) Marries Jean Leckie. (Nov.) Publishes *Through the Magic Door*, a celebration of his literary mentors (earlier version serialized in *Great Thoughts*, 1894).

1908   Moves to Windlesham, Crowborough, Sussex. (Jan.) Death of Sidney Paget. (Sept.) *Round the Fire Stories* published, including some not in earlier *Strand* series. (Sept.–Oct.) 'The Singular Experience of Mr John Scott Eccles' (later retitled as 'The Adventure of Wisteria Lodge') begins occasional series of Holmes stories in the *Strand*.

1909   ACD becomes President of the Divorce Law Reform Union (until 1919). Denis Percy Stewart Conan Doyle born. Takes up agitation against Belgian oppression in the Congo.

1910   (Sept.) 'The Marriage of the Brigadier', the last Gerard story, published in the *Strand*, and (Dec.) the Holmes story of 'The Devil's Foot'. ACD takes six-month lease on Adelphi Theatre; the play *The Speckled Band* opens there, eventually running to 346 performances. Adrian Malcolm Conan Doyle born.

1911   (Apr.) *The Last Galley* (short stories, mostly historical) published. Two more Holmes stories appear in the *Strand*: 'The Red Circle' (Mar., Apr.) and 'The Disappearance of Lady Frances Carfax' (Dec.). ACD declares for Irish Home Rule, under the influence of Sir Roger Casement.

1912   (Apr.–Nov.) The first Professor Challenger story, *The Lost World*, published in the *Strand*, book publication in Oct. Jean Lena Annette Conan Doyle (afterwards Air Commandant Dame Jean Conan Doyle, Lady Bromet) born.

1913   (Feb.) Writes 'Great Britain and the Next War' (*Fortnightly Review*). (Aug.) Second Challenger story, *The Poison Belt*, published. (Dec.) 'The Dying Detective' published in the *Strand*. ACD campaigns for a channel tunnel.

1914   (July) 'Danger!', warning of the dangers of a war-time blockade of Britain, published in the *Strand*. (4 Aug.) Britain declares war on Germany; ACD forms local volunteer force.

1914–15   (Sept.) *The Valley of Fear* begins serialization in the *Strand* (concluding May 1915).

1915   (27 Feb.) *The Valley of Fear* published by George H. Doran in New York. (June) *The Valley of Fear* published in London by Smith, Elder (transferred with rest of ACD stock to John Murray when the firm is sold on the death of Reginald Smith). Five Holmes films released in Germany (ten more during the war).

1916   (Apr., May) First instalments of *The British Campaign in France and Flanders 1914* appear in the *Strand*. (Aug.) *A Visit to Three Fronts* published. Sir Roger Casement convicted of high treason after Dublin Easter Week Rising and executed despite appeals for clemency by ACD and others.

1917   War censor interdicts ACD's history of the 1916 campaigns in the *Strand*. (Sept.) 'His Last Bow' published in the *Strand*. (Oct.) *His Last Bow* published by John Murray (includes 'The Cardboard Box').

1918   (Apr.) ACD publishes *The New Revelation*, proclaiming himself a Spiritualist. (Dec.) *Danger! and Other Stories* published. Permitted to resume accounts of 1916 and 1917 campaigns in the *Strand*, but that for 1918 never serialized. Death of eldest son, Captain Kingsley Conan Doyle, from influenza aggravated by war wounds.

1919   Death of Brigadier-General Innes Doyle, from post-war pneumonia.

1920–30 ACD engaged in world-wide crusade for Spiritualism.

1921–2 ACD's one-act play, *The Crown Diamond*, tours with Dennis Neilson-Terry as Holmes.

1921 (Oct.) 'The Mazarin Stone' (apparently based on *The Crown Diamond*) published in the *Strand*. Death of mother, Mary Foley Doyle.

1922 (Feb.–Mar.) 'The Problem of Thor Bridge' in the *Strand*. (July) John Murray publishes a collected edition of the non-Holmes short stories in six volumes: *Tales of the Ring and the Camp*, *Tales of Pirates and Blue Water*, *Tales of Terror and Mystery*, *Tales of Twilight and the Unseen*, *Tales of Adventure and Medical Life*, and (Nov.) *Tales of Long Ago*. (Sept.) Collected edition of ACD's *Poems* published by Murray.

1923 (Mar.) 'The Creeping Man' published in the *Strand*.

1924 (Jan.) 'The Sussex Vampire' appears in the *Strand*. (June) 'How Watson Learned the Trick', ACD's own Holmes pastiche, appears in *The Book of the Queen's Dolls' House Library*. (Sept.) *Memories and Adventures* published (reprinted with additions and deletions 1930).

1925 (Jan.) 'The Three Garridebs' and (Feb.–Mar.) 'The Illustrious Client' published in the *Strand*. (July) *The Land of Mist*, a Spiritualist novel featuring Challenger, begins serialization in the *Strand*.

1926 (Mar.) *The Land of Mist* published. *Strand* publishes 'The Three Gables' (Oct.), 'The Blanched Soldier' (Nov.), and 'The Lion's Mane' (Dec.).

1927 *Strand* publishes 'The Retired Colourman' (Jan.), 'The Veiled Lodger' (Feb.), and 'Shoscombe Old Place' (Apr.). (June) Murray publishes *The Case-Book of Sherlock Holmes*.

1928 (Oct.) *The Complete Sherlock Holmes Short Stories* published by Murray.

1929 (June) *The Conan Doyle Stories* (containing the six separate volumes issued by Murray in 1922) published. (July) *The Maracot Deep and Other Stories*, ACD's last collection of his fictional work.

1930 (7 July, 8.30 a.m.) Death of Arthur Conan Doyle. 'Education never ends, Watson. It is a series of lessons with the greatest for the last' ('The Red Circle').

His Last Bow

PREFACE*

T HE friends of Mr Sherlock Holmes will be glad to learn that he is still alive and well, though somewhat crippled by occasional attacks of rheumatism. He has, for many years, lived in a small farm upon the Downs five miles from Eastbourne, where his time is divided between philosophy and agriculture.* During this period of rest he has refused the most princely offers to take up various cases, having determined that his retirement was a permanent one. The approach of the German war caused him, however, to lay his remarkable combination of intellectual and practical activity at the disposal of the Government, with historical results which are recounted in 'His Last Bow'. Several previous experiences which have lain long in my portfolio, have been added to 'His Last Bow' so as to complete the volume.*

JOHN H. WATSON, MD

Wisteria Lodge*

1 THE SINGULAR EXPERIENCE OF MR JOHN SCOTT ECCLES

I FIND it recorded in my notebook that it was a bleak and windy day towards the end of March in the year 1895.* Holmes had received a telegram whilst we sat at our lunch, and he had scribbled a reply. He made no remark, but the matter remained in his thoughts, for he stood in front of the fire afterwards with a thoughtful face, smoking his pipe, and casting an occasional glance at the message. Suddenly he turned upon me with a mischievous twinkle in his eyes.

'I suppose, Watson, we must look upon you as a man of letters,' said he. 'How do you define the word "grotesque"?'

'Strange—remarkable,' I suggested.

He shook his head at my definition.

'There is surely something more than that,' said he; 'some underlying suggestion of the tragic and the terrible. If you cast your mind back to some of those narratives with which you have afflicted a long-suffering public, you will recognize how often the grotesque has deepened into the criminal. Think of that little affair of the red-headed men. That was grotesque enough in the outset, and yet it ended in a desperate attempt at robbery. Or, again, there was that most grotesque affair of the five orange pips,* which led straight to a murderous conspiracy. The word puts me on the alert.'

'Have you it there?' I asked.

He read the telegram aloud.

' "Have just had most incredible and grotesque experience. May I consult you?—Scott Eccles, Post Office, Charing Cross." '*

'Man or woman?' I asked.

'Oh, man, of course. No woman would ever send a reply-paid telegram.* She would have come.'

'Will you see him?'

5

'My dear Watson, you know how bored I have been since we locked up Colonel Carruthers.* My mind is like a racing engine, tearing itself to pieces because it is not connected up with the work for which it was built. Life is commonplace, the papers are sterile; audacity and romance seem to have passed for ever from the criminal world. Can you ask me, then, whether I am ready to look into any new problem, however trivial it may prove? But here, unless I am mistaken, is our client.'

A measured step was heard upon the stairs, and a moment later a stout, tall, grey-whiskered and solemnly respectable person was ushered into the room. His life history was written in his heavy features and pompous manner. From his spats* to his gold-rimmed spectacles he was a Conservative, a Churchman, a good citizen, orthodox and conventional to the last degree. But some amazing experience had disturbed his native composure and left its traces in his bristling hair, his flushed, angry cheeks, and his flurried, excited manner. He plunged instantly into his business.

'I have had a most singular and unpleasant experience, Mr Holmes,' said he. 'Never in my life have I been placed in such a situation. It is most improper—most outrageous. I must insist upon some explanation.' He swelled and puffed in his anger.

'Pray sit down, Mr Scott Eccles,' said Holmes, in a soothing voice. 'May I ask, in the first place, why you came to me at all?'

'Well, sir, it did not appear to be a matter which concerned the police, and yet, when you have heard the facts, you must admit that I could not leave it where it was. Private detectives are a class with whom I have absolutely no sympathy, but none the less, having heard your name—'

'Quite so. But, in the second place, why did you not come at once?'

'What do you mean?'

Holmes glanced at his watch.

'It is a quarter past two,' he said. 'Your telegram was dispatched about one. But no one can glance at your toilet* and attire without seeing that your disturbance dates from the moment of your waking.'

Our client smoothed down his unbrushed hair and felt his unshaven chin.

'You are right, Mr Holmes. I never gave a thought to my toilet. I was only too glad to get out of such a house. But I have been running round making inquiries before I came to you. I went to the house agents, you know, and they said Mr Garcia's* rent was paid up all right, and that everything was in order at Wisteria Lodge.'*

'Come, come, sir,' said Holmes, laughing. 'You are like my friend Dr Watson, who has a bad habit of telling his stories wrong end foremost.* Please arrange your thoughts and let me know, in their due sequence, exactly what those events are which have sent you out unbrushed and unkempt, with dress boots and waistcoat buttoned awry, in search of advice and assistance.'

Our client looked down with a rueful face at his own unconventional appearance.

'I'm sure it must look very bad, Mr Holmes, and I am not aware that in my whole life such a thing has ever happened before. But I will tell you the whole queer business, and when I have done so you will admit, I am sure, that there has been enough to excuse me.'

But his narrative was nipped in the bud. There was a bustle outside, and Mrs Hudson opened the door to usher in two robust and official-looking individuals, one of whom was well known to us as Inspector Gregson* of Scotland Yard, an energetic, gallant, and, within his limitations, a capable officer. He shook hands with Holmes, and introduced his comrade as Inspector Baynes of the Surrey Constabulary.

'We are hunting together, Mr Holmes, and our trail lay in this direction.' He turned his bulldog eyes upon our visitor. 'Are you Mr John Scott Eccles, of Popham House, Lee?'*

'I am.'

'We have been following you about all the morning.'

'You traced him through the telegram,* no doubt,' said Holmes.

'Exactly, Mr Holmes. We picked up the scent at Charing Cross Post Office and came on here.'

'But why do you follow me? What do you want?'

'We wish a statement, Mr Scott Eccles, as to the events which led up to the death last night of Mr Aloysius Garcia, of Wisteria Lodge, near Esher.'

Our client had sat up with staring eyes and every tinge of colour struck from his astonished face.

'Dead? Did you say he was dead?'

'Yes, sir, he is dead.'

'But how? An accident?'

'Murder, if ever there was one upon earth.'

'Good God! This is awful! You don't mean—you don't mean that I am suspected?'

'A letter of yours was found in the dead man's pocket, and we know by it that you had planned to pass last night at his house.'

'So I did.'

'Oh, you did, did you?'

Out came the official notebook.

'Wait a bit, Gregson,' said Sherlock Holmes. 'All you desire is a plain statement, is it not?'

'And it is my duty to warn Mr Scott Eccles that it may be used against him.'

'Mr Eccles was going to tell us about it when you entered the room. I think, Watson, a brandy and soda would do him no harm. Now, sir, I suggest that you take no notice of this addition to your audience, and that you proceed with your narrative exactly as you would have done had you never been interrupted.'

Our visitor had gulped off the brandy and the colour had returned to his face. With a dubious glance at the inspector's notebook, he plunged at once into his extraordinary statement.

'I am a bachelor,' said he, 'and, being of a sociable turn, I cultivate a large number of friends. Among these are the family of a retired brewer called Melville, living at Albemarle Mansion, Kensington. It was at his table that I met some weeks ago a young fellow named Garcia. He was, I understood, of Spanish descent and connected in some way with the Embassy. He spoke perfect English, was pleasing in his manners, and as good-looking a man as ever I saw in my life.

'In some way we struck up quite a friendship, this young fellow and I. He seemed to take a fancy to me from the first, and within two days of our meeting he came to see me at Lee. One thing led to another, and it ended in his inviting me out to spend a few days at his house, Wisteria Lodge, between Esher and Oxshott. Yesterday evening I went to Esher to fulfil this engagement.

'He had described his household to me before I went there. He lived with a faithful servant, a countryman of his own, who looked after all his needs. This fellow could speak English and did his housekeeping for him. Then there was a wonderful cook, he said, a half-breed whom he had picked up in his travels, who could serve an excellent dinner. I remember that he remarked what a queer household it was to find in the heart of Surrey, and that I agreed with him, though it has proved a good deal queerer than I thought.

'I drove to the place—about two miles on the south side of Esher. The house was a fair-sized one, standing back from the road, with a curving drive which was banked with high evergreen shrubs. It was an old, tumbledown building in a crazy state of disrepair. When the trap pulled up on the grass-grown drive in front of the blotched and weather-stained door, I had doubts as to my wisdom in visiting a man whom I knew so slightly. He opened the door himself, however, and greeted me with a great show of cordiality. I was handed over to the man-servant, a melancholy, swarthy individual, who led the way, my bag in his hand, to my bedroom. The whole place was depressing. Our dinner was *tête-à-tête*,* and though my host did his best to be entertaining, his thoughts seemed to continually wander, and he talked so vaguely and wildly that I could hardly understand him. He continually drummed his fingers on the table, gnawed his nails, and gave other signs of nervous impatience. The dinner itself was neither well served nor well cooked, and the gloomy presence of the taciturn servant did not help to enliven us. I can assure you that many times in the course of the evening I wished that I could invent some excuse which would take me back to Lee.

'One thing comes back to my memory which may have a bearing upon the business that you two gentlemen are investigating. I thought nothing of it at the time. Near the end of dinner a note was handed in by the servant. I noticed that after my host had read it he seemed even more distrait and strange than before. He gave up all pretence at conversation and sat, smoking endless cigarettes, lost in his own thoughts, but he made no remark as to the contents. About eleven I was glad to go to bed. Some time later Garcia looked in at my door—the room was dark at the time—and asked me if I had rung. I said that I had not. He apologized for having disturbed me so late, saying that it was nearly one o'clock. I dropped off after this and slept soundly all night.

'And now I come to the amazing part of my tale. When I woke it was broad daylight. I glanced at my watch, and the time was nearly nine. I had particularly asked to be called at eight, so I was very much astonished at this forgetfulness. I sprang up and rang for the servant. There was no response. I rang again and again, with the same result. Then I came to the conclusion that the bell was out of order. I huddled on my clothes and hurried downstairs in an exceedingly bad temper to order some hot water. You can imagine my surprise when I found that there was no one there. I shouted in the hall. There was no answer. Then I ran from room to room. All were deserted. My host had shown me which was his bedroom the night before, so I knocked at the door. No reply. I turned the handle and walked in. The room was empty, and the bed had never been slept in. He had gone with the rest. The foreign host, the foreign footman, the foreign cook, all had vanished in the night! That was the end of my visit to Wisteria Lodge.'

Sherlock Holmes was rubbing his hands and chuckling as he added this bizarre incident to his collection of strange episodes.

'Your experience is, so far as I know, perfectly unique,' said he. 'May I ask, sir, what you did then?'

'I was furious. My first idea was that I had been the victim of some absurd practical joke. I packed my things, banged the hall door behind me, and set off for Esher, with my bag in my hand. I called at Allan Brothers', the chief land agents in the village, and found that it was from this firm that the villa had been rented. It struck me that the whole proceeding could hardly be for the purpose of making a fool of me, and that the main object must be to get out of the rent. It is late in March, so quarter-day is at hand.* But this theory would not work. The agent was obliged to me for my warning, but told me that the rent had been paid in advance. Then I made my way to town and called at the Spanish Embassy. The man was unknown there. After this I went to see Melville, at whose house I had first met Garcia, but I found that he really knew rather less about him than I did. Finally, when I got your reply to my wire I came out to you, since I understand that you are a person who gives advice in difficult cases. But now, Mr Inspector, I gather, from what you said when you entered the room, that you can carry the story on, and that some tragedy has occurred. I can assure you that every word I have said is the truth, and that, outside of what I have told you, I know absolutely nothing about the fate of this man. My only desire is to help the law in every possible way.'

'I am sure of it, Mr Scott Eccles—I am sure of it,' said Inspector Gregson, in a very amiable tone. 'I am bound to say that everything which you have said agrees very closely with the facts as they have come to our notice. For example, there was that note which arrived during dinner. Did you chance to observe what became of it?'

'Yes, I did. Garcia rolled it up and threw it into the fire.'

'What do you say to that, Mr Baynes?'

The country detective was a stout, puffy, red man, whose face was only redeemed from grossness by two extraordinarily bright eyes, almost hidden behind the heavy creases of cheek and brow. With a slow smile he drew a folded and discoloured scrap of paper from his pocket.

'It was a dog-grate,* Mr Holmes, and he overpitched it. I picked this out unburned from the back of it.'

Holmes smiled his appreciation.

'You must have examined the house very carefully, to find a single pellet of paper.'

'I did, Mr Holmes. It's my way. Shall I read it, Mr Gregson?'

The Londoner nodded.

'The note is written upon ordinary cream-laid paper without watermark. It is a quarter-sheet. The paper is cut off in two snips with a short-bladed scissors. It has been folded over three times and sealed with purple wax,* put on hurriedly and pressed down with some flat, oval object. It is addressed to Mr Garcia, Wisteria Lodge. It says: "Our own colours, green and white. Green open, white shut. Main stair, first corridor, seventh right, green baize. God speed. D." It is a woman's writing, done with a sharp-pointed pen, but the address is either done with another pen or by someone else. It is thicker and bolder, as you see.'

'A very remarkable note,' said Holmes, glancing it over. 'I must compliment you, Mr Baynes, upon your attention to detail in your examination of it. A few trifling points might perhaps* be added. The oval seal is undoubtedly a plain sleeve-link*—what else is of such a shape? The scissors were bent nail-scissors. Short as the two snips are, you can distinctly see the same slight curve in each.'

The country detective chuckled.

'I thought I had squeezed all the juice out of it, but I see there was a little over,' he said. 'I'm bound to say that I make nothing of the note except that there was something on hand, and that a woman, as usual, was at the bottom of it.'

Mr Scott Eccles had fidgeted in his seat during this conversation.

'I am glad you found the note, since it corroborates my story,' said he. 'But I beg to point out that I have not yet heard what has happened to Mr Garcia, nor what has become of his household.'

'As to Garcia,' said Gregson, 'that is easily answered. He was found dead this morning upon Oxshott Common, nearly a mile from his home. His head had been smashed to pulp by heavy blows of a sand-bag or some such instrument, which had crushed rather than wounded. It is a lonely corner, and there is no house within a quarter of a mile of the spot. He had apparently been struck down first from behind, but his assailant had gone on beating him long after he was dead. It was a most furious assault. There are no footsteps nor any clue to the criminals.'

'Robbed?'

'No, there was no attempt at robbery.'

'This is very painful—very painful and terrible,' said Mr Scott Eccles, in a querulous voice; 'but it is really uncommonly hard upon me. I had nothing to do with my host going off upon a nocturnal excursion and meeting so sad an end. How do I come to be mixed up with the case?'

'Very simply, sir,' Inspector Baynes answered. 'The only document found in the pocket of the deceased was a letter from you saying that you would be with him on the night of his death. It was the envelope of this letter which gave us the dead man's name and address. It was after nine this morning when we reached his house and found neither you nor anyone else inside it. I wired to Mr Gregson to run you down in London while I examined Wisteria Lodge. Then I came into town, joined Mr Gregson, and here we are.'

'I think now,' said Gregson, rising, 'we had best put this matter into an official shape. You will come round with us to the station, Mr Scott Eccles, and let us have your statement in writing.'

'Certainly, I will come at once. But I retain your services, Mr Holmes. I desire you to spare no expense and no pains to get at the truth.'

My friend turned to the country inspector.

'I suppose that you have no objection to my collaborating with you, Mr Baynes?'

'Highly honoured, sir, I am sure.'

'You appear to have been very prompt and businesslike in all that you have done. Was there any clue, may I ask, as to the exact hour that the man met his death?'

'He had been there since one o'clock. There was rain about that time, and his death had certainly been before the rain.'

'But that is perfectly impossible, Mr Baynes,' cried our client. 'His voice is unmistakable. I could swear to it that it was he who addressed me in my bedroom at that very hour.'

'Remarkable, but by no means impossible,' said Holmes, smiling.

'You have a clue?' asked Gregson.

'On the face of it the case is not a very complex one, though it certainly presents some novel and interesting features. A further knowledge of facts is necessary before I would venture to give a final and definite opinion. By the way, Mr Baynes, did you find anything remarkable besides this note in your examination of the house?'

The detective looked at my friend in a singular way.

'There were,' said he, 'one or two *very* remarkable things. Perhaps when I have finished at the police-station you would care to come out and give me your opinion of them.'

'I am entirely at your service,' said Sherlock Holmes, ringing the bell. 'You will show these gentlemen out, Mrs Hudson, and kindly send the boy with this telegram. He is to pay a five-shilling reply.'*

We sat for some time in silence after our visitors had left. Holmes smoked hard, with his brows drawn down over his keen eyes, and his head thrust forward in the eager way characteristic of the man.

'Well, Watson,' he asked, turning suddenly upon me, 'what do you make of it?'

'I can make nothing of this mystification of Scott Eccles.'

'But the crime?'

'Well, taken with the disappearance of the man's companions, I should say that they were in some way concerned in the murder and had fled from justice.'

'That is certainly a possible point of view. On the face of it you must admit, however, that it is very strange that his two servants should have been in a conspiracy against him and should have attacked him on the one night when he had a guest. They had him alone at their mercy every other night in the week.'

'Then why did they fly?'

'Quite so. Why did they fly? There is a big fact. Another big fact is the remarkable experience of our client, Scott Eccles. Now, my dear Watson, is it beyond the limits of human ingenuity to furnish an explanation which would cover both these big facts? If it were one which would also admit of the mysterious note with its very curious phraseology, why, then it would be worth accepting as a temporary hypothesis. If the fresh facts which come to our knowledge all fit themselves into the scheme, then our hypothesis may gradually become a solution.'

'But what is our hypothesis?'

Holmes leaned back in his chair with half-closed eyes.

'You must admit, my dear Watson, that the idea of a joke is impossible. There were grave events afoot, as the sequel showed, and the coaxing of Scott Eccles to Wisteria Lodge had some connection with them.'

'But what possible connection?'

'Let us take it link by link. There is, on the face of it, something unnatural about this strange and sudden friendship between the young Spaniard and Scott Eccles. It was the former who forced the pace. He called upon Eccles at the other end of London on the very day after he first met him, and he kept in close touch with him until he got him down to Esher. Now, what did he want with Eccles? What could Eccles supply? I see no charm in the man.* He is not particularly intelligent—not a man likely to be congenial to a quick-witted Latin. Why, then, was he picked out from all the other people whom Garcia met as particularly suited to his purpose? Has he any one outstanding quality? I say that he has. He is the very type of conventional British respectability, and the very man as a witness to impress another Briton. You saw yourself how neither of the inspectors dreamed of questioning his statement, extraordinary as it was.'

'But what was he to witness?'

'Nothing, as things turned out, but everything had they gone another way. That is how I read the matter.'

'I see, he might have proved an alibi.'

'Exactly, my dear Watson; he might have proved an alibi. We will suppose, for argument's sake, that the household of Wisteria Lodge are confederates in some design. The attempt, whatever it may be, is to come off, we will say, before one o'clock. By some juggling of the clocks it is quite possible that they may have got Scott Eccles to bed earlier than he thought, but in any case it is likely that when Garcia went out of his way to tell him that it was one it was really not more than twelve. If Garcia could do whatever he had to do and be back by the hour mentioned he had evidently a powerful reply to any accusation. Here was this irreproachable Englishman ready to swear in any court of law that the accused was in his house all the time. It was an insurance against the worst.'

'Yes, yes, I see that. But how about the disappearance of the others?'

'I have not all my facts yet, but I do not think there are any insuperable difficulties. Still, it is an error to argue in front of your data. You find yourself insensibly twisting them round to fit your theories.'

'And the message?'

'How did it run? "Our own colours, green and white." Sounds like racing. "Green open, white shut." That is clearly a signal. "Main stair, first corridor, seventh right, green baize." This is an assignation. We may find a jealous husband at the bottom of it all. It was clearly a dangerous quest. She could not have said "God speed" had it not been so. "D"—that should be a guide.'

'The man was a Spaniard. I suggest that "D" stands for Dolores, a common female name in Spain.'

'Good, Watson, very good—but quite inadmissible. A Spaniard would write to a Spaniard in Spanish. The writer of this note is certainly English. Well, we can only possess our souls in patience,* until this excellent inspector comes back for us. Meanwhile we can thank our lucky fate which has rescued us for a few short hours from the insufferable fatigues of idleness.'

An answer had arrived to Holmes's telegram before our Surrey officer had returned. Holmes read it, and was about to place it in his note-book when he caught a glimpse of my expectant face. He tossed it across with a laugh.

'We are moving in exalted circles,' said he.

The telegram was a list of names and addresses: 'Lord Harringby, The Dingle; Sir George Ffolliott, Oxshott Towers; Mr Hynes Hynes, JP,* Purdey Place; Mr James Baker Williams, Forton Old Hall; Mr Henderson, High Gable;* Rev. Joshua Stone, Nether Walsling.'

'This is a very obvious way of limiting our field of operations,' said Holmes. 'No doubt Baynes, with his methodical mind, has already adopted some similar plan.'

'I don't quite understand.'

'Well, my dear fellow, we have already arrived at the conclusion that the message received by Garcia at dinner was an appointment or an assignation. Now, if the obvious reading of it is correct, and in order to keep this tryst one has to ascend a main stair and seek the seventh door in a corridor, it is perfectly clear that the house is a very large one. It is equally certain that this house cannot be more than a mile or two from Oxshott, since Garcia was walking in that direction, and hoped, according to my reading of the facts, to be back again in Wisteria Lodge in time to avail himself of an alibi, which would only be valid up to one o'clock. As the number of large houses close to Oxshott must be limited, I adopted the obvious method of sending to the agents mentioned by Scott Eccles and obtaining a list of them. Here they are in this telegram, and the other end of our tangled skein* must lie among them.'

It was nearly six o'clock before we found ourselves in the pretty Surrey village of Esher, with Inspector Baynes as our companion.

Holmes and I had taken things for the night, and found comfortable quarters at the Bull.* Finally we set out in the company of the detective on our visit to Wisteria Lodge. It was a cold, dark March evening, with a sharp wind and a fine rain beating upon our faces, a fit setting for the wild common over which our road passed and the tragic goal to which it led us.

2   THE TIGER OF SAN PEDRO*

A cold and melancholy walk of a couple of miles brought us to a high wooden gate, which opened into a gloomy avenue of chestnuts. The curved and shadowed drive led us to a low, dark house, pitch-black against a slate-coloured sky. From the front window upon the left of the door there peeped a glimmer of a feeble light.

'There's a constable in possession,' said Baynes. 'I'll knock at the window.' He stepped across the grass plot and tapped with his hand on the pane. Through the fogged glass I dimly saw a man spring up from a chair beside the fire, and heard a sharp cry from within the room. An instant later a white-faced, hard-breathing policeman had opened the door, the candle wavering in his trembling hand.

'What's the matter, Walters?' asked Baynes, sharply.

The man mopped his forehead with his handkerchief and gave a long sigh of relief.

'I am glad you have come, sir. It has been a long evening and I don't think my nerve is as good as it was.'

'Your nerve, Walters? I should not have thought you had a nerve in your body.'

'Well, sir, it's this lonely, silent house and the queer thing in the kitchen. Then when you tapped at the window I thought it had come again.'

'That what had come again?'

'The devil, sir, for all I know. It was at the window.'

'What was at the window, and when?'

'It was just about two hours ago. The light was just fading. I was sitting reading in the chair. I don't know what made me look up, but there was a face looking in at me through the lower pane. Lord, sir, what a face it was! I'll see it in my dreams.'

'Tut, tut, Walters! This is not talk for a police-constable.'

'I know, sir, I know; but it shook me, sir, and there's no use to deny it. It wasn't black, sir, nor was it white, nor any colour that I know, but a kind of queer shade like clay with a splash of milk in it. Then there was the size of it—it was twice yours, sir. And the look of it—the great staring goggle eyes, and the line of white teeth like a hungry beast. I tell you, sir, I couldn't move a finger, nor get my breath, till it whisked away and was gone. Out I ran and through the shrubbery, but thank God there was no one there.'

'If I didn't know you were a good man, Walters, I should put a black mark against you for this. If it were the devil himself, a constable on duty should never thank God that he could not lay his hands upon him. I suppose the whole thing is not a vision and a touch of nerves?'

'That, at least, is very easily settled,' said Holmes, lighting his little pocket lantern. 'Yes,' he reported, after a short examination of the grass bed, 'a number twelve shoe, I should say. If he was all on the same scale as his foot he must certainly have been a giant.'

'What became of him?'

'He seems to have broken through the shrubbery and made for the road.'

'Well,' said the inspector, with a grave and thoughtful face, 'whoever he may have been, and whatever he may have wanted, he's gone for the present, and we have more immediate things to attend to. Now, Mr Holmes, with your permission, I will show you round the house.'

The various bedrooms and sitting-rooms had yielded nothing to a careful search. Apparently the tenants had brought little or nothing with them, and all the furniture down to the smallest details had been taken over with the house. A good deal of clothing with the stamp of Marx and Co., High Holborn, had been left behind. Telegraphic inquiries had been already made which showed that Marx knew nothing of his customer save that he was a good payer. Odds and ends, some pipes, a few novels, two of them in Spanish, an old-fashioned pinfire revolver, and a guitar were amongst the personal property.

'Nothing in all this,' said Baynes, stalking, candle in hand, from room to room. 'But now, Mr Holmes, I invite your attention to the kitchen.'

It was a gloomy, high-ceilinged room at the back of the house, with a straw litter in one corner, which served apparently as a bed for the cook. The table was piled with half-eaten dishes and dirty plates, the débris of last night's dinner.

'Look at this,' said Baynes. 'What do you make of it?'

He held up his candle before an extraordinary object which stood at the back of the dresser. It was so wrinkled and shrunken and withered that it was difficult to say what it might have been. One could but say that it was black and leathery and that it bore some resemblance to a dwarfish human figure. At first, as I examined it, I thought that it was a mummified negro baby, and then it seemed a very twisted and ancient monkey. Finally I was left in doubt as to whether it was animal or human. A double band of white shells was strung round the centre of it.

'Very interesting—very interesting, indeed!' said Holmes, peering at this sinister relic.* 'Anything more?'

In silence Baynes led the way to the sink and held forward his candle. The limbs and body of some large, white bird, torn savagely to pieces with the feathers still on, were littered all over it. Holmes pointed to the wattles on the severed head.

'A white cock,' said he; 'most interesting! It is really a very curious case.'

But Mr Baynes had kept his most sinister exhibit to the last. From under the sink he drew a zinc pail which contained a quantity of blood. Then from the table he took a platter heaped with small pieces of charred bone.

'Something has been killed and something has been burned. We raked all these out of the fire. We had a doctor in this morning. He says that they are not human.'

Holmes smiled and rubbed his hands.

'I must congratulate you, inspector, on handling so distinctive and instructive a case. Your powers, if I may say so without offence, seem superior to your opportunities.'

Inspector Baynes's small eyes twinkled with pleasure.

'You're right, Mr Holmes. We stagnate in the provinces. A case of this sort gives a man a chance, and I hope that I shall take it. What do you make of these bones?'

'A lamb, I should say, or a kid.'

'And the white cock?'

'Curious, Mr Baynes, very curious. I should say almost unique.'

'Yes, sir, there must have been some very strange people with some very strange ways in this house. One of them is dead. Did his companions follow him and kill him? If they did we should have them, for every port is watched. But my own views are different. Yes, sir, my own views are very different.'

'You have a theory, then?'

'And I'll work it myself, Mr Holmes. It's only due to my own credit to do so. Your name is made, but I have still to make mine. I should be glad to be able to say afterwards that I had solved it without your help.'

Holmes laughed good-humouredly.

'Well, well, inspector,' said he. 'Do you follow your path and I will follow mine. My results are always very much at your service if you care to apply to me for them. I think that I have seen all that I wish in this house, and that my time may be more profitably employed elsewhere. *Au revoir** and good luck!'

I could tell by numerous subtle signs, which might have been lost upon anyone but myself, that Holmes was on a hot scent. As impassive as ever to the casual observer, there

were none the less a subdued eagerness and suggestion
of tension in his brightened eyes and brisker manner
which assured me that the game was afoot.* After his habit
he said nothing, and after mine I asked no questions.
Sufficient for me to share the sport and lend my humble
help to the capture without distracting that intent brain with
needless interruption. All would come round to me in due
time.

I waited, therefore—but, to my ever-deepening disappointment, I waited in vain. Day succeeded day, and my
friend took no step forward. One morning he spent in town,
and I learned from a casual reference that he had visited the
British Museum.* Save for this one excursion, he spent his
days in long and often solitary walks, or in chatting with
a number of village gossips whose acquaintance he had
cultivated.

'I'm sure, Watson, a week in the country will be invaluable to you,' he remarked. 'It is very pleasant to see the first
green shoots upon the hedges and the catkins on the hazels
once again. With a spud,* a tin box, and an elementary
book on botany, there are instructive days to be spent.' He
prowled about with this equipment himself, but it was a
poor show of plants which he would bring back of an
evening.

Occasionally in our rambles we came across Inspector
Baynes. His fat, red face wreathed itself in smiles and his
small eyes glittered as he greeted my companion. He said
little about the case, but from that little we gathered that he
also was not dissatisfied at the course of events. I must
admit, however, that I was somewhat surprised when, some
five days after the crime, I opened my morning paper to find
in large letters:

THE OXSHOTT MYSTERY

A SOLUTION

ARREST OF SUPPOSED ASSASSIN

Holmes sprang in his chair as if he had been stung when I
read the head-lines.

'By Jove!' he cried. 'You don't mean that Baynes has got him?'

'Apparently,' said I, as I read the following report:

Great excitement was caused in Esher and the neighbouring district when it was learned late last night that an arrest had been effected in connection with the Oxshott murder. It will be remembered that Mr Garcia, of Wisteria Lodge, was found dead on Oxshott Common, his body showing signs of extreme violence, and that on the same night his servant and his cook fled, which appeared to show their participation in the crime. It was suggested, but never proved, that the deceased gentleman may have had valuables in the house, and that their abstraction was the motive of the crime. Every effort was made by Inspector Baynes, who has the case in hand, to ascertain the hiding place of the fugitives, and he had good reason to believe that they had not gone far, but were lurking in some retreat which had been already prepared. It was certain from the first, however, that they would eventually be detected, as the cook, from the evidence of one or two trades-people who have caught a glimpse of him through the window, was a man of most remarkable appearance—being a huge and hideous mulatto,* with yellowish features of a pronounced negroid type. This man has been seen since the crime, for he was detected and pursued by Constable Walters on the same evening, when he had the audacity to revisit Wisteria Lodge. Inspector Baynes, considering that such a visit must have some purpose in view, and was likely, therefore, to be repeated, abandoned the house, but left an ambuscade in the shrubbery. The man walked into the trap, and was captured last night after a struggle, in which Constable Downing was badly bitten by the savage. We understand that when the prisoner is brought before the magistrates a remand will be applied for by the police, and that great developments are hoped from his capture.

'Really we must see Baynes at once,' cried Holmes, picking up his hat. 'We will just catch him before he starts.' We hurried down the village street and found, as we had expected, that the inspector was just leaving his lodgings.

'You've seen the paper, Mr Holmes?' he asked, holding one out to us.

'Yes, Baynes, I've seen it. Pray don't think it a liberty if I give you a word of friendly warning.'

'Of warning, Mr Holmes?'

'I have looked into this case with some care, and I am not convinced that you are on the right lines. I don't want you to commit yourself too far, unless you are sure.'

'You're very kind, Mr Holmes.'

'I assure you I speak for your good.'

It seemed to me that something like a wink quivered for an instant over one of Mr Baynes's tiny eyes.

'We agreed to work on our own lines, Mr Holmes. That's what I am doing.'

'Oh, very good,' said Holmes. 'Don't blame me.'

'No, sir; I believe you mean well by me. But we all have our own systems, Mr Holmes. You have yours, and maybe I have mine.'

'Let us say no more about it.'

'You're welcome always to my news. This fellow is a perfect savage, as strong as a carthorse and as fierce as the devil. He chewed Downing's thumb nearly off before they could master him. He hardly speaks a word of English, and we can get nothing out of him but grunts.'

'And you think you have evidence that he murdered his late master?'

'I didn't say so, Mr Holmes; I didn't say so. We all have our little ways. You try yours and I will try mine. That's the agreement.'

Holmes shrugged his shoulders as we walked away together. 'I can't make the man out. He seems to be riding for a fall. Well, as he says, we must each try our own way and see what comes of it. But there's something in Inspector Baynes which I can't quite understand.'*

'Just sit down in that chair, Watson,' said Sherlock Holmes, when we had returned to our apartment at the Bull. 'I want to put you in touch with the situation, as I may need your help to-night. Let me show you the evolution of this case, so far as I have been able to follow it. Simple as it has been in its leading features, it has none the less presented surprising difficulties in the way of an arrest. There are gaps in that direction which we have still to fill.

'We will go back to the note which was handed in to Garcia upon the evening of his death. We may put aside this idea of Baynes's that Garcia's servants were concerned in the matter. The proof of this lies in the fact that it was *he* who had arranged for the presence of Scott Eccles, which could only have been done for the purpose of an alibi. It was Garcia, then, who had an enterprise, and apparently a criminal enterprise, in hand that night, in the course of which he met his death. I say criminal because only a man with a criminal enterprise desires to establish an alibi. Who, then, is most likely to have taken his life? Surely the person against whom the criminal enterprise was directed. So far it seems to me that we are on safe ground.

'We can now see a reason for the disappearance of Garcia's household. They were *all* confederates in the same unknown crime. If it came off then Garcia returned, any possible suspicion would be warded off by the Englishman's evidence, and all would be well. But the attempt was a dangerous one, and if Garcia did *not* return by a certain hour it was probable that his own life had been sacrificed. It had been arranged, therefore, that in such a case his two subordinates were to make for some prearranged spot, where they could escape investigation and be in a position afterwards to renew their attempt. That would fully explain the facts, would it not?'

The whole inexplicable tangle seemed to straighten out before me. I wondered, as I always did, how it had not been obvious to me before.

'But why should one servant return?'

'We can imagine that, in the confusion of flight, something precious, something which he could not bear to part with, had been left behind. That would explain his persistence, would it not?'

'Well, what is the next step?'

'The next step is the note received by Garcia at the dinner. It indicates a confederate at the other end. Now, where was the other end? I have already shown you that it could only lie in some large house, and that the number of large houses is limited. My first days in this village were devoted to a series of walks, in which in the intervals of my botanical researches I made a reconnaissance of all the large houses and an examination of the family history of the occupants. One house, and only one, riveted my attention. It is the famous old Jacobean grange of High Gable, one mile on the farther side of Oxshott, and less than half a mile from the scene of the tragedy. The other mansions belonged to prosaic and respectable people who live far aloof from romance. But Mr Henderson, of High Gable, was by all accounts a curious man, to whom curious adventures might befall. I concentrated my attention, therefore, upon him and his household.

'A singular set of people, Watson—the man himself the most singular of them all. I managed to see him on a plausible pretext, but I seemed to read in his dark, deep-set, brooding eyes that he was perfectly aware of my true business. He is a man of fifty, strong, active, with iron-grey hair, great bunched black eyebrows, the step of a deer, and the air of an emperor—a fierce, masterful man, with a red-hot spirit behind his parchment face. He is either a foreigner or has lived long in the Tropics, for he is yellow and sapless, but tough as whipcord. His friend and secretary, Mr Lucas, is undoubtedly a foreigner, chocolate brown, wily, suave and cat-like, with a poisonous gentleness of speech. You see, Watson, we have come already upon two sets of foreigners—one at Wisteria Lodge and one at High Gable—so our gaps are beginning to close.

'These two men, close and confidential friends, are the centre of the household; but there is one other person, who for our immediate purpose may be even more important. Henderson has two children—girls of eleven and thirteen. Their governess is a Miss Burnet, an Englishwoman of forty or thereabouts. There is also one confidential man-servant. This little group forms the real family, for they travel about together, and Henderson is a great traveller, always on the move. It is only within the last few weeks that he has returned, after a year's absence, to High Gable. I may add that he is enormously rich, and whatever his whims may be he can very easily satisfy them. For the rest, his house is full of butlers, footmen, maid-servants, and the usual overfed, underworked staff of a large English country-house.*

'So much I learned partly from village gossip and partly from my own observation. There are no better instruments than discharged servants with a grievance, and I was lucky enough to find one. I call it luck, but it would not have come my way had I not been looking out for it. As Baynes remarks, we all have our systems. It was my system which enabled me to find John Warner, late gardener of High Gable, sacked in a moment of temper by his imperious employer. He in turn had friends among the indoor servants, who unite in their fear and dislike of their master. So I had my key to the secrets of the establishment.

'Curious people, Watson! I don't pretend to understand it all yet, but very curious people anyway. It's a double-winged house, and the servants live on one side, the family on the other. There's no link between the two save for Henderson's own servant, who serves the family's meals. Everything is carried to a certain door, which forms the one connection. Governess and children hardly go out at all, except into the garden. Henderson never by any chance walks alone. His dark secretary is like his shadow. The gossip among the servants is that their master is terribly afraid of something. "Sold his soul to the devil in exchange for money," says Warner, "and expects his creditor to come up and claim his own." Where they came from, or who they are, nobody has an idea. They are very violent. Twice Henderson has lashed at folk with his dog-whip, and only his long purse and heavy compensation have kept him out of the courts.

'Well, now, Watson, let us judge the situation by this new information. We may take it that the letter came out of this strange household, and was an invitation to Garcia to carry out some attempt which had already been planned. Who wrote the note? It was someone within the citadel, and it was a woman. Who then, but Miss Burnet, the governess? All our reasoning seems to point that way. At any rate, we may take it as a hypothesis, and see what consequences it would entail. I may add that Miss Burnet's age and character make it certain that my first idea that there might be a love interest in our story is out of the question.

'If she wrote the note she was presumably the friend and confederate of Garcia. What, then, might she be expected to do if she heard of his death? If he met it in some nefarious enterprise her lips might be sealed. Still, in her heart she must retain bitterness and hatred against those who had killed him, and would presumably help so far as she could to have revenge upon them. Could we see her, then, and try to use her? That was my first thought. But now we come to a sinister fact. Miss Burnet has not been seen by any human eye since the night of the murder. From that evening she has utterly vanished. Is she alive? Has she perhaps met her end on the same night as the friend whom she had summoned? Or is she merely a prisoner? There is the point which we still have to decide.

'You will appreciate the difficulty of the situation, Watson. There is nothing upon which we can apply for a warrant. Our whole scheme might seem fantastic if laid before a magistrate. The woman's disappearance counts for nothing, since in that extraordinary household any member of it might be invisible for a week. And yet she may at the present moment be in danger of her life. All I can do is to watch the house and leave my agent, Warner, on guard at the gates. We can't let such a situation continue. If the law can do nothing we must take the risk ourselves.'

'What do you suggest?'

'I know which is her room. It is accessible from the top of an outhouse. My suggestion is that you and I go to-night and see if we can strike at the very heart of the mystery.'

It was not, I must confess, a very alluring prospect. The old house with its atmosphere of murder, the singular and formidable inhabitants, the unknown dangers of the approach, and the fact that we were putting ourselves legally in a false position, all combined to damp my ardour. But there was something in the ice-cold reasoning of Holmes which made it impossible to shrink from any adventure which he might recommend. One knew that thus, and only thus, could a solution be found. I clasped his hand in silence, and the die was cast.

But it was not destined that our investigation should have so adventurous an ending. It was about five o'clock, and the shadows of the March evening were beginning to fall, when an excited rustic rushed into our room.

'They've gone, Mr Holmes. They went by the last train. The lady broke away, and I've got her in a cab downstairs.'

'Excellent, Warner!' cried Holmes, springing to his feet. 'Watson, the gaps are closing rapidly.'

In the cab was a woman, half-collapsed from nervous exhaustion. She bore upon her aquiline and emaciated face the traces of some recent tragedy. Her head hung listlessly upon her breast, but as she raised it and turned her dull eyes upon us, I saw that her pupils were dark dots in the centre of the broad grey iris. She was drugged with opium.

'I watched at the gate, same as you advised, Mr Holmes,' said our emissary, the discharged gardener. 'When the carriage came out I followed it to the station. She was like one walking in her sleep; but when they tried to get her into the train she came to life and struggled. They pushed her into the carriage. She fought her way out again. I took her part, got her into a cab, and here we are. I shan't forget* the face at the carriage window as I led her away. I'd have a short life if he had his way—the black-eyed, scowling, yellow devil.'

We carried her upstairs, laid her on the sofa, and a couple of cups of the strongest coffee soon cleared her brain from the mists of the drug. Baynes had been summoned by Holmes, and the situation rapidly explained to him.

'Why, sir, you've got me the very evidence I want,' said the inspector, warmly, shaking my friend by the hand. 'I was on the same scent as you from the first.'

'What! You were after Henderson?'

'Why, Mr Holmes, when you were crawling in the shrubbery at High Gable I was up one of the trees in the plantation and saw you down below. It was just who would get his evidence first.'

'Then why did you arrest the mulatto?'

Baynes chuckled.

'I was sure Henderson, as he calls himself, felt that he was suspected, and that he would lie low and make no move so long as he thought he was in any danger. I arrested the wrong man to make him believe that our eyes were off him. I knew he would be likely to clear off then and give us a chance of getting at Miss Burnet.'

Holmes laid his hand upon the inspector's shoulder.

'You will rise high in your profession. You have instinct and intuition,' said he.

Baynes flushed with pleasure.

'I've had a plain-clothes man waiting at the station all the week. Wherever the High Gable folk go he will keep them in sight. But he must have been hard put to it when Miss Burnet broke away. However, your man picked her up, and it all ends well. We can't arrest without her evidence, that is clear, so the sooner we get a statement the better.'

'Every minute she gets stronger,' said Holmes, glancing at the governess. 'But tell me, Baynes, who is this man Henderson?'

'Henderson', the inspector answered, 'is Don Murillo,* once called the Tiger of San Pedro.'

The Tiger of San Pedro! The whole history of the man came back to me in a flash. He had made his name as the most lewd and bloodthirsty tyrant that had ever governed any country with a pretence to civilization. Strong, fearless, and energetic, he had sufficient virtue to enable him to impose his odious vices upon a cowering people for ten or twelve years. His name was a terror through all Central America. At the end of that time there was a universal rising against him. But he was as cunning as he was cruel, and at the first whisper of coming trouble he had secretly conveyed his treasures aboard a ship which was manned by devoted adherents. It was an empty palace which was stormed by the insurgents next day. The Dictator, his two children, his secretary, and his wealth had all escaped them. From that moment he had vanished from the world, and his identity had been a frequent subject for comment in the European Press.

'Yes, sir; Don Murillo, the Tiger of San Pedro,' said Baynes. 'If you look it up you will find that the San Pedro colours are green and white, same as in the note, Mr Holmes. Henderson he called himself, but I traced him back, Paris and Rome and Madrid to Barcelona, where his ship came in in '86. They've been looking for him all the time for their revenge, but it is only now that they have begun to find him out.'

'They discovered him a year ago,' said Miss Burnet, who had sat up and was now intently following the conversation. 'Once already his life has been attempted; but some evil spirit shielded him. Now, again, it is the noble, chivalrous Garcia who has fallen, while the monster goes safe. But another will come, and yet another, until some day justice will be done; that is as certain as the rise of to-morrow's sun.' Her thin hands clenched, and her worn face blanched with the passion of her hatred.

'But how come you into this matter, Miss Burnet?' asked Holmes. 'How can an English lady join in such a murderous affair?'

'I join in it because there is no other way in the world by which justice can be gained. What does the law of England care for the rivers of blood shed years ago in San Pedro, or for the ship-load of treasure which this man has stolen?* To you they are like crimes committed in some other planet. But *we* know. We have learned the truth in sorrow and in suffering. To us there is no fiend in hell like Juan Murillo, and no peace in life while his victims still cry for vengeance.'

'No doubt,' said Holmes, 'he was as you say. I have heard that he was atrocious. But how are you affected?'

'I will tell you it all. This villain's policy was to murder, on one pretext or another, every man who showed such promise that he might in time come to be a dangerous rival.

My husband—yes, my real name is Señora Victor Durando*—was the San Pedro Minister in London. He met me and married me there. A nobler man never lived upon earth. Unhappily, Murillo heard of his excellence, recalled him on some pretext, and had him shot. With a premonition of his fate he had refused to take me with him. His estates were confiscated, and I was left with a pittance and a broken heart.

'Then came the downfall of the tyrant. He escaped as you have just described. But the many whose lives he had ruined, whose nearest and dearest had suffered torture and death at his hands, would not let the matter rest.* They banded themselves into a society which should never be dissolved until the work was done. It was my part after we had discovered in the transformed Henderson the fallen despot, to attach myself to his household and keep the others in touch with his movements. This I was able to do by securing the position of governess in his family. He little knew that the woman who faced him at every meal was the woman whose husband he had hurried at an hour's notice into eternity. I smiled on him, did my duty to his children, and bided my time. An attempt was made in Paris, and failed. We zigzagged swiftly here and there over Europe, to throw off the pursuers, and finally returned to this house, which he had taken upon his first arrival in England.

'But here also the ministers of justice were waiting. Knowing that he would return there, Garcia, who is the son of the former highest dignitary in San Pedro, was waiting with two trusty companions of humble station, all three fired with the same reasons for revenge. He could do little during the day, for Murillo took every precaution, and never went out save with his satellite Lucas, or Lopez as he was known in the days of his greatness. At night, however, he slept alone, and the avenger might find him. On a certain evening, which had been prearranged, I sent my friend final instructions, for the man was for ever on the alert, and continually changed his room. I was to see that the doors were open and the signal of a green or white light in a window which faced the drive was to give notice if all was safe, or if the attempt had better be postponed.

'But everything went wrong with us. In some way I had excited the suspicion of Lopez, the secretary. He crept up behind me, and sprang upon me just as I had finished the note. He and his master dragged me to my room, and held judgement upon me as a convicted traitress. Then and there they would have plunged their knives into me, could they have seen how to escape the consequence of the deed. Finally, after much debate, they concluded that my murder was too dangerous. But they determined to get rid for ever of Garcia. They had gagged me, and Murillo twisted my arm round until I gave him the address. I swear that he might have twisted it off had I understood what it would mean to Garcia. Lopez addressed the note which I had written, sealed it with his sleeve-link, and sent it by the hand of the servant, José. How they murdered him I do not know, save that it was Murillo's hand who struck him down, for Lopez had remained to guard me. I believe he must have waited among the gorse bushes through which the path winds and struck him down as he passed. At first they were of a mind to let him enter the house and to kill him as a detected burglar; but they argued that if they were mixed up in an inquiry their own identity would at once be publicly disclosed and they would be open to further attacks. With the death of Garcia the pursuit might cease, since such a death might frighten others from the task.

'All would now have been well for them had it not been for my knowledge of what they had done. I have no doubt that there were times when my life hung in the balance. I was confined to my room, terrorized by the most horrible threats, cruelly ill-used to break my spirit—see this stab on my shoulder and the bruises from end to end of my arms—and a gag was thrust into my mouth on the one occasion when I tried to call from the window. For five days this cruel imprisonment continued, with hardly enough food to hold body and soul together. This afternoon a good lunch was brought me, but the moment after I took it I knew that

I had been drugged. In a sort of dream I remember being half-led, half-carried to the carriage; in the same state I was conveyed to the train. Only then, when the wheels were almost moving, did I suddenly realize that my liberty lay in my own hands. I sprang out, they tried to drag me back, and had it not been for the help of this good man, who led me to the cab, I should never have broken away. Now, thank God, I am beyond their power for ever.'

We had all listened intently to this remarkable statement. It was Holmes who broke the silence.

'Our difficulties are not over,' he remarked, shaking his head. 'Our police work ends, but our legal work begins.'

'Exactly,' said I. 'A plausible lawyer could make it out as an act of self-defence. There may be a hundred crimes in the background, but it is only on this one that they can be tried.'

'Come, come,' said Baynes, cheerily; 'I think better of the law than that. Self-defence is one thing. To entice a man in cold blood with the object of murdering him is another, whatever danger you may fear from him. No, no; we shall all be justified when we see the tenants of High Gable at the next Guildford Assizes.'*

It is a matter of history, however, that a little time was still to elapse before the Tiger of San Pedro should meet with his deserts. Wily and bold, he and his companion threw their pursuer off their track by entering a lodging-house in Edmonton Street and leaving by the back-gate into Curzon Square. From that day they were seen no more in England. Some six months afterwards the Marquess of Montalva and Signor Rulli, his secretary, were both murdered in their rooms at the Hotel Escurial at Madrid. The crime was ascribed to Nihilism,* and the murderers were never arrested. Inspector Baynes visited us at Baker Street with a printed description of the dark face of the secretary, and of the masterful features, the magnetic black eyes, and the tufted brows of his master. We could not doubt that justice, if belated, had come at last.

'A chaotic case, my dear Watson,' said Holmes, over an evening pipe. 'It will not be possible for you to present it in that compact form which is dear to your heart. It covers two continents, concerns two groups of mysterious persons, and is further complicated by the highly respectable presence of our friend Scott Eccles, whose inclusion shows me that the deceased Garcia had a scheming mind and a well-developed instinct of self-preservation. It is remarkable only for the fact that amid a perfect jungle of possibilities we, with our worthy collaborator the inspector, have kept our close hold on the essentials and so been guided along the crooked and winding path. Is there any point which is not quite clear to you?'

'The object of the mulatto cook's return?'

'I think that the strange creature* in the kitchen may account for it. The man was a primitive savage from the backwoods of San Pedro, and this was his fetish. When his companion and he had fled to some prearranged retreat—already occupied, no doubt by a confederate—the companion had persuaded him to leave so compromising an article of furniture. But the mulatto's heart was with it, and he was driven back to it next day, when, on reconnoitring through the window, he found policeman Walters in possession. He waited three days longer, and then his piety or his superstition drove him to try once more. Inspector Baynes, who, with his usual astuteness, had minimized the incident before me, had really recognized its importance, and had left a trap into which the creature* walked. Any other point, Watson?'

'The torn bird, the pail of blood, the charred bones, all the mystery of that weird kitchen?'

Holmes smiled as he turned up an entry in his note-book.

'I spent a morning in the British Museum reading up that and other points. Here is a quotation from Eckermann's *Voodooism and the Negroid Religions:**

The true Voodoo-worshipper attempts nothing of importance without certain sacrifices which are intended to propitiate his unclean gods. In extreme cases these rites take the form of human sacrifices followed by cannibalism. The more usual victims are a white cock, which is plucked in pieces alive, or a black goat, whose throat is cut and body burned.

'So you see our savage friend was very orthodox in his ritual. It is grotesque, Watson,' Holmes added, as he slowly fastened his notebook; 'but, as I have had occasion to remark, there is but one step from the grotesque to the horrible.'*

The Bruce-Partington Plans

IN the third week of November, in the year 1895, a dense yellow fog settled down upon London. From the Monday to the Thursday I doubt whether it was ever possible from our windows in Baker Street to see the loom of the opposite houses. The first day Holmes had spent in cross-indexing his huge book of references. The second and third had been patiently occupied upon a subject which he had recently made his hobby—the music of the Middle Ages. But when, for the fourth time, after pushing back our chairs from breakfast we saw the greasy, heavy brown swirl still drifting past us and condensing in oily drops upon the window-panes, my comrade's impatient and active nature could endure this drab existence no longer. He paced restlessly about our sitting-room in a fever of suppressed energy, biting his nails, tapping the furniture, and chafing against inaction.

'Nothing of interest in the paper, Watson?' he said.

I was aware that by anything of interest, Holmes meant anything of criminal interest. There was the news of a revolution, of a possible war, and of an impending change of Government;* but these did not come within the horizon of my companion. I could see nothing recorded in the shape of crime which was not commonplace and futile. Holmes groaned and resumed his restless meanderings.

'The London criminal is certainly a dull fellow,' said he, in the querulous voice of the sportsman whose game has failed him. 'Look out of this window, Watson. See how the figures loom up, are dimly seen, and then blend once more into the cloud-bank. The thief or the murderer could roam London on such a day as the tiger does the jungle, unseen until he pounces, and then evident only to his victim.'

'There have,' said I, 'been numerous petty thefts.'

Holmes snorted his contempt.

'This great and sombre stage is set for something more worthy than that,' said he. 'It is fortunate for this community that I am not a criminal.'

'It is, indeed!' said I, heartily.

'Suppose that I were Brooks or Woodhouse, or any of the fifty men who have good reason for taking my life, how long could I survive against my own pursuit? A summons, a bogus appointment, and all would be over. It is well they don't have days of fog in the Latin countries—the countries of assassination. By Jove! here comes something at last to break our dead monotony.'

It was the maid with a telegram. Holmes tore it open and burst out laughing.

'Well, well! What next?' said he. 'Brother Mycroft* is coming round.'

'Why not?' I asked.

'Why not? It is as if you met a tram-car coming down a country lane. Mycroft has his rails and he runs on them. His Pall Mall lodgings, the Diogenes Club,* Whitehall—that is his cycle. Once, and only once, he has been here.* What upheaval can possibly have derailed him?'

'Does he not explain?'

Holmes handed me his brother's telegram.

'Must see you over Cadogan West. Coming at once. MYCROFT.'

'Cadogan West? I have heard the name.'

'It recalls nothing to my mind. But that Mycroft should break out in this erratic fashion! A planet might as well leave its orbit. By the way, do you know what Mycroft is?'

I had some vague recollection of an explanation at the time of the Adventure of the Greek Interpreter.

'You told me that he had some small office under the British Government.'

Holmes chuckled.

'I did not know you quite so well in those days. One has to be discreet when one talks of high matters of State. You are right in thinking that he is under the British Government. You would also be right in a sense if you said that occasionally he *is* the British Government.'

'My dear Holmes!'

'I thought I might surprise you. Mycroft draws four hundred and fifty pounds a year, remains a subordinate, has no ambitions of any kind, will receive neither honour nor title, but remains the most indispensable man in the country.'

'But how?'

'Well, his position is unique. He has made it for himself. There has never been anything like it before, nor will be again. He has the tidiest and most orderly brain, with the greatest capacity for storing facts, of any man living. The same great powers which I have turned to the detection of crime he has used for this particular business. The conclusions of every department are passed to him, and he is the central exchange, the clearing-house, which makes out the balance. All other men are specialists, but his specialism is omniscience.* We will suppose that a Minister needs information as to a point which involves the Navy, India, Canada, and the bi-metallic question;* he could get his separate advices from various departments upon each, but only Mycroft can focus them all, and say off-hand how each factor would affect the other. They began by using him as a short-cut, a convenience; now he has made himself an essential. In that great brain of his everything is pigeon-holed, and can be handed out in an instant. Again and again his word has decided the national policy. He lives in it. He thinks of nothing else save when, as an intellectual exercise, he unbends if I call upon him and ask him to advise me on one of my little problems. But Jupiter is descending to-day.* What on earth can it mean? Who is Cadogan West, and what is he to Mycroft?'*

'I have it!' I cried, and plunged among the litter of papers upon the sofa. 'Yes, yes, here he is, sure enough! Cadogan West was the young man who was found dead on the Underground* on Tuesday morning.'

Holmes sat up at attention, his pipe half-way to his lips.

'This must be serious, Watson. A death which has caused my brother to alter his habits can be no ordinary one. What in the world can he have to do with it? The case was featureless as I remember it. The young man had apparently fallen out of the train and killed himself. He had not been robbed, and there was no particular reason to suspect violence. Is that not so?'

'There has been an inquest,' said I, 'and a good many fresh facts have come out. Looked at more closely, I should certainly say that it was a curious case.'

'Judging by its effect upon my brother, I should think it must be a most extraordinary one.' He snuggled down in his arm-chair. 'Now, Watson, let us have the facts.'

'The man's name was Arthur Cadogan West. He was twenty-seven years of age, unmarried, and a clerk at Woolwich Arsenal.'*

'Government employ. Behold the link with brother Mycroft!'

'He left Woolwich suddenly on Monday night. Was last seen by his *fiancée*, Miss Violet Westbury, whom he left abruptly in the fog about 7.30 that evening. There was no quarrel between them and she can give no motive for his action. The next thing heard of him was when his dead body was discovered by a plate-layer* named Mason, just outside Aldgate Station* on the Underground system in London.'

'When?'

'The body was found at six on the Tuesday morning. It was lying wide of the metals upon the left hand of the track as one goes eastward, at a point close to the station, where the line emerges from the tunnel in which it runs. The head was badly crushed—an injury which might well have been caused by a fall from the train. The body could only have come on the line in that way. Had it been carried down from any neighbouring street, it must have passed the station barriers, where a collector is always standing. This point seems absolutely certain.'

'Very good. The case was definite enough. The man, dead or alive, either fell or was precipitated from a train. So much is clear to me. Continue.'

'The trains which traverse the lines of rail beside which the body was found are those which run from west to east, some being purely Metropolitan, and some from Willesden* and out-lying junctions. It can be stated for certain that this young man, when he met his death, was travelling in this direction at some late hour of the night, but at what point he entered the train it is impossible to state.'

'His ticket, of course, would show that.'

'There was no ticket in his pockets.'

'No ticket! Dear me, Watson, this is really very singular. According to my experience it is not possible to reach the platform of a Metropolitan train without exhibiting one's ticket. Presumably, then, the young man had one. Was it taken from him in order to conceal the station from which he came? It is possible. Or did he drop it in the carriage? That also is possible. But the point is of curious interest. I understand that there was no sign of robbery?'

'Apparently not. There is a list here of his possessions. His purse contained two pounds fifteen. He had also a cheque-book on the Woolwich branch of the Capital and Counties Bank.* Through this his identity was established. There were also two dress-circle* tickets for the Woolwich Theatre, dated for that very evening. Also a small packet of technical papers.'

Holmes gave an exclamation of satisfaction.

'There we have it at last, Watson! British Government—Woolwich Arsenal—Technical papers—Brother Mycroft, the chain is complete. But here he comes, if I am not mistaken, to speak for himself.'

A moment later the tall and portly form of Mycroft Holmes was ushered into the room. Heavily built and massive, there was a suggestion of uncouth physical inertia in the figure, but above this unwieldy frame there was perched a head so masterful in its brow, so alert in its steel-grey, deep-set eyes, so firm in its lips, and so subtle in its play of expression, that after the first glance one forgot the gross body and remembered only the dominant mind.

At his heels came our old friend Lestrade, of Scotland Yard—thin and austere. The gravity of both their faces foretold some weighty quest. The detective shook hands without a word. Mycroft Holmes struggled out of his overcoat and subsided into an arm-chair.

'A most annoying business, Sherlock,' said he. 'I extremely dislike altering my habits, but the powers that be would take no denial. In the present state of Siam* it is most awkward that I should be away from the office. But it is a real crisis. I have never seen the Prime Minister* so upset. As to the Admiralty—it is buzzing like an overturned bee-hive. Have you read up the case?'

'We have just done so. What were the technical papers?'

'Ah, there's the point! Fortunately, it has not come out. The Press would be furious if it did. The papers which this wretched youth had in his pocket were the plans of the Bruce-Partington submarine.'

Mycroft Holmes spoke with a solemnity which showed his sense of the importance of the subject. His brother and I sat expectant.

'Surely you have heard of it? I thought everyone had heard of it.'

'Only as a name.'

'Its importance can hardly be exaggerated. It has been the most jealously guarded of all Government secrets. You may take it from me that naval warfare becomes impossible within the radius of a Bruce-Partington's operation. Two years ago a very large sum was smuggled through the Estimates and was expended in acquiring a monopoly of the invention. Every effort has been made to keep the secret.* The plans, which are exceedingly intricate, comprising some thirty separate patents, each essential to the working of the whole, are kept in an elaborate safe in a confidential office adjoining the Arsenal, with burglar-proof doors and windows. Under no conceivable circumstances were the plans to be taken from the office. If the Chief Constructor of the Navy desired to consult them, even he was forced to go to the Woolwich office for the purpose. And yet here we find them in the pockets of a dead junior clerk in the heart of London. From an official point of view it's simply awful.'

'But you have recovered them?'

'No, Sherlock, no! That's the pinch. We have not. Ten papers were taken from Woolwich. There were seven in the pockets of Cadogan West. The three most essential are gone—stolen, vanished. You must drop everything, Sherlock. Never mind your usual petty puzzles of the police-court. It's a vital international problem that you have to solve. Why did Cadogan West take the papers, where are the missing ones, how did he die, how came his body where it was found, how can the evil be set right? Find an answer to all these questions, and you will have done good service for your country.'

'Why do you not solve it yourself, Mycroft? You can see as far as I.'

'Possibly, Sherlock. But it is a question of getting details. Give me your details, and from an arm-chair I will return you an excellent expert opinion. But to run here and run there, to cross-question railway guards, and lie on my face with a lens to my eye—it is not my *métier*. No, you are the one man who can clear the matter up. If you have a fancy to see your name in the next honours list—'*

My friend smiled and shook his head.

'I play the game for the game's own sake,' said he. 'But the problem certainly presents some points of interest, and I shall be very pleased to look into it. Some more facts, please.'

'I have jotted down the more essential ones upon this sheet of paper, together with a few addresses which you will find of service. The actual official guardian of the papers is the famous Government expert, Sir James Walter, whose decorations and sub-titles fill two lines of a book of reference. He has grown grey in the service, is a gentleman,* a favoured guest in the most exalted houses, and above all a man whose patriotism is beyond suspicion. He is one of two who have a key of the safe. I may add that the papers were undoubtedly in the office during working hours on Monday, and that Sir James left for London about three o'clock taking his key with him. He was at the house of Admiral

Sinclair at Barclay Square during the whole of the evening when this incident occurred.'

'Has the fact been verified?'

'Yes; his brother, Colonel Valentine Walter, has testified to his departure from Woolwich, and Admiral Sinclair to his arrival in London; so Sir James is no longer a direct factor in the problem.'

'Who was the other man with a key?'

'The senior clerk and draughtsman,* Mr Sidney Johnson. He is a man of forty, married, with five children. He is a silent, morose man, but he has, on the whole, an excellent record in the public service. He is unpopular with his colleagues, but a hard worker. According to his own account, corroborated only by the word of his wife, he was at home the whole of Monday evening after office hours, and his key has never left the watch-chain upon which it hangs.'

'Tell us about Cadogan West.'

'He has been ten years in the Service, and has done good work. He has the reputation of being hot-headed and impetuous, but a straight, honest man. We have nothing against him. He was next Sidney Johnson in the office. His duties brought him into daily, personal contact with the plans. No one else had the handling of them.'

'Who locked the plans up that night?'

'Mr Sidney Johnson, the senior clerk.'

'Well, it is surely perfectly clear who took them away. They are actually found upon the person of this junior clerk, Cadogan West. That seems final, does it not?'

'It does, Sherlock, and yet it leaves so much unexplained. In the first place, why did he take them?'

'I presume they were of value?'

'He could have got several thousands for them very easily.'

'Can you suggest any possible motive for taking the papers to London except to sell them?'

'No, I cannot.'

'Then we must take that as our working hypothesis. Young West took the papers. Now this could only be done by having a false key—'

'Several false keys. He had to open the building and the room.'

'He had, then, several false keys. He took the papers to London to sell the secret, intending, no doubt, to have the plans themselves back in the safe next morning before they were missed. While in London on this treasonable mission he met his end.'

'How?'

'We will suppose that he was travelling back to Woolwich when he was killed and thrown out of the compartment.'

'Aldgate, where the body was found, is considerably past the station for London Bridge,* which would be his route to Woolwich.'

'Many circumstances could be imagined under which he would pass London Bridge. There was someone in the carriage, for example, with whom he was having an absorbing interview. This interview led to a violent scene, in which he lost his life. Possibly he tried to leave the carriage,* fell out on the line, and so met his end. The other closed the door. There was a thick fog, and nothing could be seen.'

'No better explanation can be given with our present knowledge; and yet consider, Sherlock, how much you leave untouched. We will suppose, for argument's sake, that young Cadogan West *had* determined to convey these papers to London. He would naturally have made an appointment with the foreign agent and kept his evening clear. Instead of that, he took two tickets for the theatre, escorted his *fiancée* half-way there, and then suddenly disappeared.

'A blind,' said Lestrade, who had sat listening with some impatience to the conversation.

'A very singular one. That is objection No. 1. Objection No. 2: We will suppose that he reaches London and sees the foreign agent. He must bring back the papers before morning or the loss will be discovered. He took away ten. Only seven were in his pocket. What had become of the other three? He certainly would not leave them of his own free will. Then, again, where is the price of his treason? One would have expected to find a large sum of money in his pocket.'

'It seems to me perfectly clear,' said Lestrade. 'I have no doubt at all as to what occurred. He took the papers to sell them. He saw the agent. They could not agree as to price. He started home again, but the agent went with him. In the train the agent murdered him, took the more essential papers, and threw his body from the carriage. That would account for everything, would it not?'

'Why had he no ticket?'

'The ticket would have shown which station was nearest the agent's house. Therefore he took it from the murdered man's pocket.'

'Good, Lestrade, very good,' said Holmes. 'Your theory holds together. But if this is true, then the case is at an end. On the one hand the traitor is dead. On the other the plans of the Bruce-Partington submarine are presumably already on the Continent. What is there for us to do?'

'To act, Sherlock—to act!' cried Mycroft, springing to his feet. 'All my instincts are against this explanation. Use your powers! Go to the scene of the crime! See the people concerned! Leave no stone unturned! In all your career you have never had so great a chance of serving your country.'

'Well, well!' said Holmes, shrugging his shoulders. 'Come, Watson! And you, Lestrade, could you favour us with your company for an hour or two? We will begin our investigation by a visit to Aldgate Station. Good-bye, Mycroft. I shall let you have a report before evening, but I warn you in advance that you have little to expect.'

An hour later, Holmes, Lestrade, and I, stood upon the Underground railroad at the point where it emerges from the tunnel immediately before Aldgate Station. A courteous, red-faced old gentleman represented the railway company.

'This is where the young man's body lay,' said he, indicating a spot about three feet from the metals. 'It could not have fallen from above, for these, as you see, are all blank walls. Therefore, it could only have come from a train, and that train, so far as we can trace it, must have passed about midnight on Monday.'

46

'Have the carriages been examined for any sign of violence?'

'There are no such signs, and no ticket has been found.'

'No record of a door being found open?'

'None.'

'We have had some fresh evidence this morning,' said Lestrade. 'A passenger who passed Aldgate in an ordinary Metropolitan train about 11.40 on Monday night declares that he heard a heavy thud, as of a body striking the line, just before the train reached the station. There was dense fog, however, and nothing could be seen. He made no report of it at the time. Why, whatever is the matter with Mr Holmes?'

My friend was standing with an expression of strained intensity upon his face, staring at the railway metals where they curved out of the tunnel. Aldgate is a junction,* and there was a network of points. On these his eager, questioning eyes were fixed, and I saw on his keen, alert face that tightening of the lips, that quiver of the nostrils, and concentration of the heavy tufted brows which I knew so well.

'Points,' he muttered; 'the points.'

'What of it? What do you mean?'

'I suppose there are no great number of points on a system such as this?'

'No; there are very few.'

'And a curve, too. Points, and a curve. By Jove! if it were only so.'

'What is it, Mr Holmes? Have you a clue?'

'An idea—an indication, no more. But the case certainly grows in interest. Unique, perfectly unique, and yet why not? I do not see any indications of bleeding on the line.'

'There were hardly any.'

'But I understand that there was a considerable wound.'

'The bone was crushed, but there was no great external injury.'

'And yet one would have expected some bleeding. Would it be possible for me to inspect the train which contained the passenger who heard the thud of a fall in the fog?'

'I fear not, Mr Holmes. The train has been broken up before now, and the carriages redistributed.'

'I can assure you, Mr Holmes,' said Lestrade, 'that every carriage has been carefully examined. I saw to it myself.'

It was one of my friend's most obvious weaknesses that he was impatient with less alert intelligences than his own.

'Very likely,' said he, turning away. 'As it happens, it was not the carriages which I desired to examine. Watson, we have done all we can here. We need not trouble you any further, Mr Lestrade. I think our investigations must now carry us to Woolwich.'

At London Bridge Holmes wrote a telegram to his brother, which he handed to me before dispatching it. It ran thus:

See some light in the darkness, but it may possibly flicker out. Meanwhile, please send by messenger, to await return at Baker Street, a complete list of all foreign spies or international agents known to be in England,* with full address.

SHERLOCK

'That should be helpful, Watson,' he remarked, as we took our seats in the Woolwich train. 'We certainly owe brother Mycroft a debt for having introduced us to what promises to be a really very remarkable case.'

His eager face still wore that expression of intense and high-strung energy, which showed me that some novel and suggestive circumstance had opened up a stimulating line of thought. See the foxhound with hanging ears and drooping tail as it lolls about the kennels, and compare it with the same hound as, with gleaming eyes and straining muscles, it runs upon a breast-high scent—such was the change in Holmes since the morning. He was a different man to the limp and lounging figure in the mouse-coloured* dressing-gown who had prowled so restlessly only a few hours before round the fog-girt room.

'There is material here. There is scope,' said he. 'I am dull indeed not to have understood its possibilities.'

'Even now they are dark to me.'

'The end is dark to me also, but I have hold of one idea which may lead us far. The man met his death elsewhere, and his body was on the *roof* of a carriage.'

'On the roof!'

'Remarkable, is it not? But consider the facts. Is it a coincidence that it is found at the very point where the train pitches and sways as it comes round on the points? Is not that the place where an object upon the roof might be expected to fall off? The points would affect no object inside the train. Either the body fell from the roof, or a very curious coincidence has occurred. But now consider the question of the blood. Of course, there was no bleeding on the line if the body had bled elsewhere. Each fact is suggestive in itself. Together they have a cumulative force.'

'And the ticket, too!' I cried.

'Exactly. We could not explain the absence of a ticket. This would explain it. Everything fits together.'

'But suppose it were so, we are still as far as ever from unravelling the mystery of his death. Indeed, it becomes not simpler, but stranger.'

'Perhaps,' said Holmes, thoughtfully; 'perhaps.' He relapsed into a silent reverie, which lasted until the slow train drew up at last in Woolwich Station. There he called a cab and drew Mycroft's paper from his pocket.

'We have quite a little round of afternoon calls to make,' said he. 'I think that Sir James Walter claims our first attention.'

The house of the famous official was a fine villa with green lawns stretching down to the Thames. As we reached it the fog was lifting, and a thin, watery sunshine was breaking through. A butler answered our ring.

'Sir James, sir!' said he, with solemn face. 'Sir James died this morning.'

'Good heavens!' cried Holmes, in amazement. 'How did he die?'

'Perhaps you would care to step in, sir, and see his brother, Colonel Valentine?'*

'Yes, we had best do so.'

49

We were ushered into a dim-lit drawing-room, where an instant later we were joined by a very tall, handsome, light-bearded man of fifty, the younger brother of the dead scientist. His wild eyes, stained cheeks, and unkempt hair all spoke of the sudden blow which had fallen upon the household. He was hardly articulate as he spoke of it.

'It was this horrible scandal,' said he. 'My brother, Sir James, was a man of very sensitive honour, and he could not survive such an affair. It broke his heart. He was always so proud of the efficiency of his department, and this was a crushing blow.'

'We had hoped that he might have given us some indications which would have helped us to clear the matter up.'

'I assure you that it was all a mystery to him as it is to you and to all of us. He had already put all his knowledge at the disposal of the police. Naturally, he had no doubt that Cadogan West was guilty. But all the rest was inconceivable.'

'You cannot throw any new light upon the affair?'

'I know nothing myself save what I have read or heard. I have no desire to be discourteous, but you can understand, Mr Holmes, that we are much disturbed at present, and I must ask you to hasten this interview to an end.'

'This is indeed an unexpected development,' said my friend when we had regained the cab. 'I wonder if the death was natural, or whether the poor old fellow killed himself! If the latter, may it be taken as some sign of self-reproach for duty neglected? We must leave that question to the future. Now we shall turn to the Cadogan Wests.'

A small but well-kept house in the outskirts of the town sheltered the bereaved mother. The old lady was too dazed with grief to be of any use to us, but at her side was a white-faced young lady, who introduced herself as Miss Violet Westbury, the *fiancée* of the dead man, and the last to see him upon that fatal night.

'I cannot explain it, Mr Holmes,' she said. 'I have not shut an eye since the tragedy, thinking, thinking, thinking, night and day, what the true meaning of it can be. Arthur* was the most single-minded, chivalrous, patriotic man upon earth. He would have cut his right hand off before he would sell a State secret confided to his keeping. It is absurd, impossible, preposterous to anyone who knew him.'

'But the facts, Miss Westbury?'

'Yes, yes; I admit I cannot explain them.'

'Was he in any want of money?'

'No; his needs were very simple and his salary ample. He had saved a few hundreds, and we were to marry at the New Year.'

'No signs of any mental excitement? Come, Miss Westbury, be absolutely frank with us.'

The quick eye of my companion had noted some change in her manner. She coloured and hesitated.

'Yes,' she said, at last. 'I had a feeling that there was something on his mind.'

'For long?'

'Only for the last week or so. He was thoughtful and worried. Once I pressed him about it. He admitted that there was something, and that it was concerned with his official life. "It is too serious for me to speak about, even to you," said he. I could get nothing more.'

Holmes looked grave.

'Go on, Miss Westbury. Even if it seems to tell against him, go on. We cannot say what it may lead to.'

'Indeed, I have nothing more to tell. Once or twice it seemed to me that he was on the point of telling me something. He spoke one evening of the importance of the secret, and I have some recollection that he said that no doubt foreign spies would pay a great deal to have it.'

My friend's face grew graver still.

'Anything else?'

'He said that we were slack about such matters—that it would be easy for a traitor to get the plans.'

'Was it only recently that he made such remarks?'

'Yes, quite recently.'

'Now tell us of that last evening.'

'We were to go to the theatre. The fog was so thick that a cab was useless. We walked, and our way took us close to the office. Suddenly he darted away into the fog.'

'Without a word?'

'He gave an exclamation; that was all. I waited, but he never returned. Then I walked home. Next morning, after the office opened, they came to inquire. About twelve o'clock we heard the terrible news. Oh, Mr Holmes, if you could only, only save his honour! It was so much to him.'

Holmes shook his head sadly.

'Come, Watson,' said he, 'our ways lie elsewhere. Our next station must be the office from which the papers were taken.

'It was black enough before against this young man, but our inquiries make it blacker,' he remarked, as the cab lumbered off. 'His coming marriage gives a motive for the crime. He naturally wanted money. The idea was in his head, since he spoke about it. He nearly made the girl an accomplice in the treason by telling her his plans. It is all very bad.'

'But surely, Holmes, character goes for something? Then, again, why should he leave the girl in the street and dart away to commit a felony?'

'Exactly! There are certainly objections. But it is a formidable case which they have to meet.'

Mr Sidney Johnson, the senior clerk, met us at the office, and received us with that respect which my companion's card always commanded. He was a thin, gruff, bespectacled man of middle age, his cheeks haggard, and his hands twitching from the nervous strain to which he had been subjected.

'It is bad, Mr Holmes, very bad! Have you heard of the death of the chief?'

'We have just come from his house.'

'The place is disorganized. The chief dead, Cadogan West dead, our papers stolen. And yet, when we closed our door on Monday evening we were as efficient an office as any in the Government service. Good God, it's dreadful to think of! That West, of all men, should have done such a thing!'

'You are sure of his guilt, then?'

'I can see no other way out of it. And yet I would have trusted him as I trust myself.'

'At what hour was the office closed on Monday?'

'At five.'

'Did you close it?'

'I am always the last man out.'

'Where were the plans?'

'In that safe. I put them there myself.'

'Is there no watchman to the building?'

'There is, but he has other departments to look after as well. He is an old soldier and a most trustworthy man. He saw nothing that evening. Of course, the fog was very thick.'

'Suppose that Cadogan West wished to make his way into the building after hours; he would need three keys, would he not, before he could reach the papers?'

'Yes, he would. The key of the outer door, the key of the office, and the key of the safe.'

'Only Sir James Walter and you had those keys?'

'I had no keys of the doors—only of the safe.'*

'Was Sir James a man who was orderly in his habits?'

'Yes, I think he was. I know that so far as those three keys are concerned he kept them on the same ring. I have often seen them there.'

'And that ring went with him to London?'

'He said so.'

'And your key never left your possession?'

'Never.'

'Then West, if he is the culprit, must have had a duplicate. And yet none was found upon his body. One other point: if a clerk in this office desired to sell the plans, would it not be simpler to copy the plans for himself than to take the originals, as was actually done?'

'It would take considerable technical knowledge to copy the plans in an effective way.'

'But I suppose either Sir James, or you, or West had that technical knowledge?'

'No doubt we had, but I beg you won't try to drag me into the matter, Mr Holmes. What is the use of our speculating in this way when the original plans were actually found on West?'

'Well, it is certainly singular that he should run the risk of taking originals if he could safely have taken copies, which would have equally served his turn.'

'Singular, no doubt—and yet he did so.'

'Every inquiry in this case reveals something inexplicable. Now there are three papers still missing. They are, as I understand, the vital ones.'

'Yes, that is so.'

'Do you mean to say that anyone holding these three papers, and without the seven others, could construct a Bruce-Partington submarine?'

'I reported to that effect to the Admiralty. But to-day I have been over the drawings again, and I am not so sure of it. The double valves with the automatic self-adjusting slots are drawn in one of the papers which have been returned. Until the foreigners had invented that for themselves they could not make the boat. Of course, they might soon get over the difficulty.'

'But the three missing drawings are the most important?'

'Undoubtedly.'

'I think, with your permission, I will now take a stroll round the premises. I do not recall any other question which I desired to ask.'

He examined the lock of the safe, the door of the room, and finally the iron shutters of the window. It was only when we were on the lawn outside that his interest was strongly excited. There was a laurel bush outside the window, and several of the branches bore signs of having been twisted or snapped. He examined them carefully with his lens, and then some dim and vague marks upon the earth beneath. Finally he asked the chief clerk to close the iron shutters, and he pointed out to me that they hardly met in the centre, and that it would be possible for anyone outside to see what was going on within the room.

'The indications are ruined by the three days' delay. They may mean something or nothing. Well, Watson, I do not think that Woolwich can help us further. It is a small crop which we have gathered. Let us see if we can do better in London.'

Yet we added one more sheaf to our harvest before we left Woolwich Station. The clerk in the ticket office was able to say with confidence that he saw Cadogan West—whom he knew well by sight—upon the Monday night, and that he went to London by the 8.15 to London Bridge. He was alone, and took a single third-class ticket.* The clerk was struck at the time by his excited and nervous manner. So shaky was he that he could hardly pick up his change, and the clerk had helped him with it. A reference to the time-table showed that the 8.15 was the first train which it was possible for West to take after he had left the lady about 7.30.

'Let us reconstruct, Watson,' said Holmes, after half an hour of silence. 'I am not aware that in all our joint researches we have ever had a case which was more difficult to get at. Every fresh advance which we make only reveals a fresh ridge beyond. And yet we have surely made some appreciable progress.

'The effect of our inquiries at Woolwich has in the main been against young Cadogan West; but the indications at the window would lend themselves to a more favourable hypothesis. Let us suppose, for example, that he had been approached by some foreign agent. It might have been done under such pledges as would have prevented him from speaking of it, and yet would have affected his thoughts in the direction indicated by his remarks to his *fiancée*. Very good. We will now suppose that as he went to the theatre with the young lady he suddenly, in the fog, caught a glimpse of this same agent going in the direction of the office. He was an impetuous man, quick in his decisions. Everything gave way to his duty. He followed the man, reached the window, saw the abstraction of the documents, and pursued the thief.* In this way we get over the objection that no one would take originals when he could make copies. This outsider had to take originals. So far it holds together.'

'What is the next step?'

'Then we come into difficulties. One would imagine that under such circumstances the first act of young Cadogan West would be to seize the villain and raise the alarm. Why did he not do so? Could it have been an official superior who took the papers? That would explain West's conduct. Or could the thief have given West the slip in the fog, and West started at once to London to head him off from his own rooms, presuming that he knew where the rooms were? The call must have been very pressing, since he left his girl standing in the fog, and made no effort to communicate with her. Our scent runs cold here, and there is a vast gap between either hypothesis and the laying of West's body, with seven papers in his pocket, on the roof of a Metropolitan train. My instinct now is to work from the other end. If Mycroft has given us the list of addresses we may be able to pick our man, and follow two tracks instead of one.'

Surely enough, a note awaited us at Baker Street. A Government messenger had brought it post-haste. Holmes glanced at it and threw it over to me.

There are numerous small fry, but few who would handle so big an affair. The only men worth considering are Adolph Meyer, of 13, Great George Street, Westminster; Louis La Rothière, of Campden Mansions, Notting Hill; and Hugo Oberstein, 13, Caulfield Gardens, Kensington.* The latter was known to be in town in Monday, and is now reported as having left. Glad to hear you have seen some light. The Cabinet awaits your final report with the utmost anxiety. Urgent representations have arrived from the very highest quarter. The whole force of the State is at your back if you should need it.

MYCROFT

'I'm afraid,' said Holmes, smiling, 'that all the Queen's horses* and all the Queen's men cannot avail in this matter.' He had spread out his big map of London, and leaned eagerly over it. 'Well, well,' said he presently, with an exclamation of satisfaction, 'things are turning a little in our direction at last. Why, Watson, I do honestly believe that we are going to pull it off after all.' He slapped me on the shoulder with a sudden burst of hilarity. 'I am going out now. It is only a reconnaissance. I will do nothing serious without my trusted comrade and biographer at my elbow.

Do you stay here, and the odds are that you will see me again in an hour or two. If time hangs heavy get foolscap and a pen, and begin your narrative of how we saved the State.'

I felt some reflection of his elation in my own mind, for I knew well that he would not depart so far from his usual austerity of demeanour unless there was good cause for exultation. All the long November evening I waited, filled with impatience for his return. At last, shortly after nine o'clock there arrived a messenger with a note:

Am dining at Goldini's* Restaurant, Gloucester Road, Kensington. Please come at once and join me there. Bring with you a jemmy,* a dark lantern,* a chisel, and a revolver.

S.H.

It was a nice equipment for a respectable citizen* to carry through the dim, fog-draped streets. I stowed them all discreetly away in my overcoat, and drove straight to the address given. There sat my friend at a little round table near the door of the garish Italian restaurant.

'Have you had something to eat? Then join me in a coffee and curaçao.* Try one of the proprietor's cigars. They are less poisonous than one would expect. Have you the tools?'

'They are here, in my overcoat.'

'Excellent. Let me give you a short sketch of what I have done, with some indication of what we are about to do. Now it must be evident to you, Watson, that this young man's body was *placed* on the roof of the train. That was clear from the instant that I determined the fact that it was from the roof, and not from a carriage, that he had fallen.'

'Could it not have been dropped from a bridge?'

'I should say it was impossible. If you examine the roofs you will find that they are slightly rounded, and there is no railing round them. Therefore, we can say for certain that young Cadogan West was placed on it.'

'How could he be placed there?'

'That was the question which we had to answer. There is only one possible way. You are aware that the Underground runs clear of tunnels at some points in the West-end. I had a vague memory that as I have travelled by it I have occasionally seen windows just above my head. Now, suppose that a train halted under such a window, would there be any difficulty in laying a body upon the roof?'

'It seems most improbable.'

'We must fall back upon the old axiom that when all other contingencies fail, whatever remains, however improbable, must be the truth. Here all other contingencies *have* failed. When I found that the leading international agent, who had just left London, lived in a row of houses which abutted upon the Underground, I was so pleased that you were a little astonished at my sudden frivolity.'

'Oh, that was it, was it?'

'Yes, that was it. Mr Hugo Oberstein, of 13, Caulfield Gardens, had become my objective. I began my operations at Gloucester Road Station, where a very helpful official walked with me along the track, and allowed me to satisfy myself, not only that the back-stair windows of Caulfield Gardens open on the line, but the even more essential fact that, owing to the intersection of one of the larger railways, the Underground trains are frequently held motionless for some minutes at that very spot.'

'Splendid, Holmes! You have got it!'

'So far—so far, Watson. We advance, but the goal is afar. Well, having seen the back of Caulfield Gardens, I visited the front and satisfied myself that the bird was indeed flown. It is a considerable house, unfurnished, so far as I could judge, in the upper rooms. Oberstein lived there with a single valet, who was probably a confederate entirely in his confidence. We must bear in mind that Oberstein has gone to the Continent to dispose of his booty, but not with any idea of flight; for he had no reason to fear a warrant, and the idea of an amateur domiciliary visit would certainly never occur to him. Yet this is precisely what we are about to make.'

'Could we not get a warrant and legalize it?'

'Hardly on the evidence.'

'What can we hope to do?'

'We cannot tell what correspondence may be there.'

'I don't like it, Holmes.'

'My dear fellow, you shall keep watch in the street. I'll do the criminal part. It's not a time to stick at trifles. Think of Mycroft's note, of the Admiralty, the Cabinet, the exalted person who waits for news. We are bound to go.'

My answer was to rise from the table.*

'You are right, Holmes. We are bound to go.'

He sprang up and shook me by the hand.

'I knew you would not shrink at the last,' said he, and for a moment I saw something in his eyes which was nearer to tenderness than I had ever seen. The next instant he was his masterful, practical self once more.

'It is nearly half a mile, but there is no hurry. Let us walk,' said he. 'Don't drop the instruments, I beg. Your arrest as a suspicious character would be a most unfortunate complication.'

Caulfield Gardens was one of those lines of flat-faced, pillared, and porticoed houses which are so prominent a product of the middle Victorian epoch in the West-end of London. Next door there appeared to be a children's party, for the merry buzz of young voices and the clatter of a piano resounded through the night. The fog still hung about and screened us with its friendly shade. Holmes had lit his lantern and flashed it upon the massive door.

'This is a serious proposition,' said he. 'It is certainly bolted as well as locked. We would do better in the area.* There is an excellent archway down yonder in case a too zealous policeman should intrude. Give me a hand, Watson, and I'll do the same for you.'

A minute later we were both in the area. Hardly had we reached the dark shadows before the step of the policeman was heard in the fog above. As its soft rhythm died away, Holmes set to work upon the lower door. I saw him stoop and strain until with a sharp crash it flew open. We sprang through into the dark passage, closing the area door behind us. Holmes led the way up the curving, uncarpeted stair. His little fan of yellow light shone upon a low window.

'Here we are, Watson—this must be the one.' He threw it open, and as he did so there was a low, harsh murmur, growing steadily into a loud roar as a train dashed past us in the darkness. Holmes swept his light along the window-sill. It was thickly coated with soot from the passing engines, but the black surface was blurred and rubbed in places.

'You can see where they rested the body. Hullo, Watson! what is this? There can be no doubt that it is a blood mark.' He was pointing to faint discolorations along the woodwork of the window. 'Here it is on the stone of the stair also. The demonstration is complete. Let us stay here until a train stops.'

We had not long to wait. The very next train roared from the tunnel as before, but slowed in the open, and then, with a creaking of brakes, pulled up immediately beneath us. It was not four feet from the window-ledge to the roof of the carriages. Holmes softly closed the window.

'So far we are justified,' said he. 'What do you think of it, Watson?'

'A masterpiece. You have never risen to a greater height.'

'I cannot agree with you there. From the moment that I conceived the idea of the body being upon the roof, which surely was not a very abstruse one, all the rest was inevitable. If it were not for the grave interests involved, the affair up to this point would be insignificant. Our difficulties are still before us. But perhaps we may find something here which may help us.'

We had ascended the kitchen stair and entered the suite of rooms upon the first floor. One was a dining-room, severely furnished and containing nothing of interest. A second was a bedroom, which also drew blank. The remaining room appeared more promising, and my companion settled down to a systematic examination. It was littered with books and papers, and was evidently used as a study. Swiftly and methodically Holmes turned over the contents of drawer after drawer and cupboard after cupboard, but no gleam of success came to brighten his austere face. At the end of an hour he was no further than when he started.

'The cunning dog has covered his tracks,' said he. 'He has left nothing to incriminate him. His dangerous correspondence has been destroyed or removed. This is our last chance.'

It was a small tin cash-box which stood upon the writing-desk. Holmes prised it open with his chisel. Several rolls of paper were within, covered with figures and calculations, without any note to show to what they referred. The recurring words, 'Water pressure' and 'Pressure to the square inch' suggested some possible relation to a submarine. Holmes tossed them all impatiently aside. There only remained an envelope with some small newspaper slips inside it. He shook them out on the table, and at once I saw by his eager face that his hopes had been raised.

'What's this, Watson? Eh? What's this? Record of a series of messages in the advertisements of a paper. *Daily Telegraph* agony column* by the print and paper. Right-hand top corner of a page. No date—but messages arrange themselves. This must be the first:

' "Hoped to hear sooner. Terms agreed to. Write fully to address given on card.—Pierrot."

'Next comes: "Too complex for description. Must have full report. Stuff awaits you when goods delivered.—Pierrot."

'Then comes: "Matter presses. Must withdraw offer unless contract completed. Make appointment by letter. Will confirm by advertisement.—Pierrot."

'Finally: "Monday night after nine. Two taps. Only ourselves. Do not be so suspicious. Payment in hard cash when goods delivered.—Pierrot."

'A fairly complete record, Watson! If we could only get at the man at the other end!' He sat lost in thought, tapping his fingers on the table. Finally he sprang to his feet.

'Well, perhaps it won't be so difficult after all. There is nothing more to be done here, Watson. I think we might drive round to the offices of the *Daily Telegraph*, and so bring a good day's work to a conclusion.'

Mycroft Holmes and Lestrade had come round by appointment after breakfast next day, and Sherlock Holmes had recounted to them our proceedings of the day before. The professional shook his head over our confessed burglary.

'We can't do these things in the force, Mr Holmes,' said he. 'No wonder you get results that are beyond us. But some of these days you'll go too far, and you'll find yourself and your friend in trouble.'

'For England, home and beauty*—eh, Watson? Martyrs on the altar of our country. But what do you think of it, Mycroft?'

'Excellent, Sherlock! Admirable! But what use will you make of it?'

Holmes picked up the *Daily Telegraph* which lay upon the table.

'Have you seen Pierrot's advertisement today?'

'What! Another one?'

'Yes, here it is: "Tonight. Same hour. Same place. Two taps. Most vitally important. Your own safety at stake.—Pierrot." '

'By George!' cried Lestrade. 'If he answers that we've got him!'

'That was my idea when I put it in. I think if you could both make it convenient to come with us about eight o'clock to Caulfield Gardens we might possibly get a little nearer to a solution.'

One of the most remarkable characteristics of Sherlock Holmes was his power of throwing his brain out of action and switching all his thoughts on to lighter things whenever he had convinced himself that he could no longer work to advantage. I remember that during the whole of that memorable day he lost himself in a monograph which he had undertaken upon the Polyphonic Motets of Lassus. For my own part I had none of this power of detachment, and the day, in consequence, appeared to be interminable. The great national importance of the issue, the suspense in high quarters, the direct nature of the experiment which we were trying, all combined to work upon my nerves. It was a relief to me when at last, after a light dinner, we set out upon our expedition. Lestrade and Mycroft met us by appointment at the outside of Gloucester Road Station. The area door of Oberstein's house had been left open the night before, and it was necessary for me, as Mycroft Holmes absolutely and indignantly declined to climb the railings, to pass in and open the hall door. By nine o'clock we were all seated in the study, waiting patiently for our man.

An hour passed and yet another. When eleven struck the measured beat of the great church clock* seemed to sound the dirge of our hopes. Lestrade and Mycroft were fidgeting in their seats and looking twice a minute at their watches. Holmes sat silent and composed, his eyelids half shut, but every sense on the alert. He raised his head with a sudden jerk.

'He is coming,' said he.

There had been a furtive step past the door. Now it returned. We heard a shuffling sound outside, and then two sharp taps with the knocker. Holmes rose, motioning to us to remain seated. The gas in the hall was a mere point of light. He opened the outer door, and then as a dark figure slipped past him he closed and fastened it. 'This way!' we heard him say, and a moment later our man stood before us. Holmes had followed him closely, and as the man turned with a cry of surprise and alarm he caught him by the collar and threw him back into the room. Before our prisoner had recovered his balance the door was shut and Holmes standing with his back against it. The man glared round him, staggered, and fell senseless upon the floor. With the shock, his broad-brimmed hat flew from his head, his cravat slipped down from his lips, and there was the long light beard and the soft, handsome, delicate features of Colonel Valentine Walter.

Holmes gave a whistle of surprise.

'You can write me down an ass this time, Watson,' said he. 'This was not the bird that I was looking for.'*

'Who is he?' asked Mycroft, eagerly.

'The younger brother of the late Sir James Walter, the head of the Submarine Department. Yes, yes; I see the fall of the cards. He is coming to. I think that you had best leave his examination to me.'

We had carried the prostrate body to the sofa. Now our prisoner sat up, looked round him with a horror-stricken face, and passed his hand over his forehead, like one who cannot believe his own senses.

'What is this?' he asked. 'I came here to visit Mr Oberstein.'

'Everything is known, Colonel Walter,' said Holmes. 'How an English gentleman could behave in such a manner is beyond my comprehension.* But your whole correspondence and relations with Oberstein are within our knowledge. So also are the circumstances connected with the death of young Cadogan West. Let me advise you to gain at least the small credit for repentance and confession, since there are still some details which we can only learn from your lips.'

The man groaned and sank his face in his hands. We waited, but he was silent.

'I can assure you,' said Holmes, 'that every essential is already known. We know that you were pressed for money; that you took an impress of the keys which your brother held; and that you entered into a correspondence with Oberstein, who answered your letters through the advertisement columns of the *Daily Telegraph*. We are aware that you went down to the office in the fog of Monday night, but that you were seen and followed by young Cadogan West, who had probably some previous reason to suspect you. He saw your theft, but could not give the alarm, as it was just possible that you were taking the papers to your brother in London. Leaving all his private concerns, like the good citizen that he was, he followed you closely in the fog, and kept at your heels until you reached this very house. There he intervened, and then it was, Colonel Walter, that to treason you added the more terrible crime of murder.'*

'I did not! I did not! Before God I swear that I did not!' cried our wretched prisoner.

'Tell us, then, how Cadogan West met his end before you laid him upon the roof of a railway carriage.'

'I will. I swear to you that I will. I did the rest. I confess it. It was just as you say. A Stock Exchange debt had to be paid. I needed the money badly. Oberstein offered me five thousand. It was to save myself from ruin. But as to murder, I am as innocent as you.'

'What happened then?'

'He had his suspicions before, and he followed me as you describe. I never knew it until I was at the very door. It was thick fog, and one could not see three yards. I had given two taps and Oberstein had come to the door. The young man rushed up and demanded to know what we were about to do with the papers. Oberstein had a short life-preserver. He always carried it with him. As West forced his way after us into the house Oberstein struck him on the head. The blow was a fatal one. He was dead within five minutes. There he lay in the hall, and we were at our wits' end what to do. Then Oberstein had this idea about the trains which halted under his back window. But first he examined the papers which I had brought. He said that three of them were essential, and that he must keep them. "You cannot keep them," said I. "There will be a dreadful row at Woolwich if they are not returned." "I must keep them," said he, "for they are so technical that it is impossible in the time to make copies." "Then they must all go back together to-night," said I. He thought for a little, and then he cried out that he had it. "Three I will keep," said he. "The others we will stuff into the pocket of this young man. When he is found the whole business will assuredly be put to his account." I could see no other way out of it, so we did as he suggested. We waited half an hour at the window before a train stopped. It was so thick that nothing could be seen, and we had no difficulty in lowering West's body on to the train. That was the end of the matter so far as I was concerned.'

'And your brother?'

'He said nothing, but he had caught me once with his keys, and I think that he suspected. I read in his eyes that he suspected. As you know, he never held up his head again.'*

65

There was silence in the room. It was broken by Mycroft Holmes.

'Can you not make reparation? It would ease your conscience, and possibly your punishment.'

'What reparation can I make?'

'Where is Oberstein with the papers?'

'I do not know.'

'Did he give you no address?'

'He said that letters to the Hôtel du Louvre, Paris, would eventually reach him.'

'Then reparation is still within your power,' said Sherlock Holmes.

'I will do anything I can. I owe this fellow no particular good-will. He has been my ruin and my downfall.'

'Here are paper and pen. Sit at this desk and write to my dictation. Direct the envelope to the address given. That is right. Now the letter: "Dear Sir,—With regard to our transaction, you will no doubt have observed by now that one essential detail is missing. I have a tracing which will make it complete. This has involved me in extra trouble, however, and I must ask you for a further advance of five hundred pounds. I will not trust it to the post, nor will I take anything but gold or notes. I would come to you abroad, but it would excite remark if I left the country at present. Therefore I shall expect to meet you in the smoking-room of the Charing Cross Hotel at noon on Saturday. Remember that only English notes, or gold, will be taken." That will do very well. I shall be very much surprised if it does not fetch our man.'

And it did! It is a matter of history—that secret history of a nation which is often so much more intimate and interesting than its public chronicles—that Oberstein, eager to complete the coup of his lifetime, came to the lure and was safely engulfed for fifteen years in a British prison.* In his trunk were found the invaluable Bruce-Partington plans, which he had put up for auction in all the naval centres of Europe.*

Colonel Walter died in prison towards the end of the second year of his sentence. As to Holmes, he returned refreshed to his monograph upon the Polyphonic Motets of Lassus, which has since been printed for private circulation, and is said by experts to be the last word upon the subject.* Some weeks afterwards I learned incidentally that my friend spent a day at Windsor, whence he returned with a remarkably fine emerald tie-pin. When I asked him if he had bought it, he answered that it was a present from a certain gracious lady in whose interests he had once been fortunate enough to carry out a small commission. He said no more; but I fancy that I could guess at the lady's august name, and I have little doubt that the emerald pin will for ever recall to my friend's memory the adventure of the Bruce-Partington plans.*

The Devil's Foot

IN recording from time to time some of the curious experiences and interesting recollections which I associate with my long and intimate friendship with Mr Sherlock Holmes, I have continually been faced by difficulties caused by his own aversion to publicity. To his sombre and cynical spirit all popular applause was always abhorrent, and nothing amused him more at the end of a successful case than to hand over the actual exposure to some orthodox official, and to listen with a mocking smile to the general chorus of misplaced congratulation. It was indeed this attitude upon the part of my friend, and certainly not any lack of interesting material, which has caused me of late years to lay very few of my records before the public. My participation in some of his adventures was always a privilege which entailed discretion and reticence upon me.

It was, then, with considerable surprise that I received a telegram from Holmes last Tuesday—he has never been known to write where a telegram would serve—in the following terms: 'Why not tell them of the Cornish horror—strangest case I have handled.' I have no idea what backward sweep of memory had brought the matter fresh to his mind, or what freak had caused him to desire that I should recount it; but I hasten, before another cancelling telegram may arrive, to hunt out the notes which give me the exact details of the case, and to lay the narrative before my readers.

It was, then, in the spring of the year 1897 that Holmes's iron constitution showed some symptoms of giving way in the face of constant hard work of a most exacting kind, aggravated, perhaps, by occasional indiscretions of his own.* In March of that year Dr Moore Agar, of Harley Street,* whose dramatic introduction to Holmes I may some day recount, gave positive injunctions that the famous private agent would* lay aside all his cases and surrender himself to complete rest if he wished to avert an absolute breakdown. The state of his health was not a matter in which he himself took the faintest interest, for his mental detachment was absolute, but he was induced at last, on the threat of being permanently disqualified from work, to give himself a complete change of scene and air. Thus it was that in the early spring of that year we found ourselves together in a small cottage near Poldhu Bay,* at the further extremity of the Cornish peninsula.

It was a singular spot, and one peculiarly well suited to the grim humour of my patient. From the windows of our little whitewashed house, which stood high upon a grassy headland, we looked down upon the whole sinister semi-circle of Mounts Bay,* that old death-trap of sailing vessels, with its fringe of black cliffs and surge-swept reefs on which innumerable seamen have met their end. With a northerly breeze it lies placid and sheltered, inviting the storm-tossed craft to tack into it for rest and protection.

Then comes the sudden swirl round of the wind, the blustering gale from the south-west, the dragging anchor, the lee shore, and the last battle in the creaming breakers. The wise mariner stands far out from that evil place.

On the land side our surroundings were as sombre as on the sea. It was a country of rolling moors, lonely and dun-coloured, with an occasional church tower to mark the site of some old-world village. In every direction upon these moors there were traces of some vanished race which had passed utterly away, and left as its sole record strange monuments of stone, irregular mounds which contained the burned ashes of the dead, and curious earth-works which hinted at prehistoric strife. The glamour and mystery of the place, with its sinister atmosphere of forgotten nations, appealed to the imagination of my friend, and he spent much of his time in long walks and solitary meditations upon the moor. The ancient Cornish language had also arrested his attention, and he had, I remember, conceived the idea that it was akin to the Chaldean,* and had been largely derived from the Phoenician traders in tin. He had received a consignment of books upon philology* and was settling down to develop this thesis, when suddenly, to my sorrow and to his unfeigned delight, we found ourselves, even in that land of dreams, plunged into a problem at our very doors which was more intense, more engrossing, and infinitely more mysterious than any of those which had driven us from London. Our simple life and peaceful, healthy routine were violently interrupted, and we were precipitated into the midst of a series of events which caused the utmost excitement not only in Cornwall, but throughout the whole West of England. Many of my readers may retain some recollection of what was called at the time 'The Cornish Horror', though a most imperfect account of the matter reached the London Press. Now, after thirteen years, I will give the true details of this inconceivable affair to the public.

I have said that scattered towers marked the villages which dotted this part of Cornwall. The nearest of these was the hamlet of Tredannick Wollas,* where the cottages of a couple of hundred inhabitants clustered round an ancient, moss-grown church. The vicar of the parish, Mr Roundhay,* was something of an archaeologist, and as such Holmes had made his acquaintance. He was a middle-aged man, portly and affable, with a considerable fund of local lore. At his invitation we had taken tea at the vicarage, and had come to know, also, Mr Mortimer Tregennis,* an independent gentleman,* who increased the clergyman's scanty resources by taking rooms in his large, straggling house. The vicar, being a bachelor, was glad to come to such an arrangement, though he had little in common with his lodger, who was a thin, dark, spectacled man, with a stoop which gave the impression of actual physical deformity. I remember that during our short visit we found the vicar garrulous, but his lodger strangely reticent, a sad-faced, introspective man, sitting with averted eyes, brooding apparently upon his own affairs.

These were the two men who entered abruptly into our little sitting-room on Tuesday, March the 16th, shortly after our breakfast hour, as we were smoking together, preparatory to our daily excursion upon the moors.

'Mr Holmes,' said the vicar, in an agitated voice, 'the most extraordinary and tragic affair has occurred during the night. It is the most unheard-of business. We can only regard it as a special Providence that you should chance to be here at the time, for in all England you are the one man we need.'

I glared at the intrusive vicar with no very friendly eyes; but Holmes took his pipe from his lips and sat up in his chair like an old hound who hears the view-hallo.* He waved his hand to the sofa, and our palpitating visitor with his agitated companion sat side by side upon it. Mr Mortimer Tregennis was more self-contained than the clergyman, but the twitching of his thin hands and the brightness of his dark eyes showed that they shared a common emotion.

'Shall I speak or you?' he asked of the vicar.

'Well, as you seem to have made the discovery, whatever it may be, and the vicar to have had it second-hand, perhaps you had better do the speaking,' said Holmes.

I glanced at the hastily-clad clergyman, with the formally-dressed lodger seated beside him, and was amused at the surprise which Holmes's simple deduction had brought to their faces.

'Perhaps I had best say a few words first,' said the vicar, 'and then you can judge if you will listen to the details from Mr Tregennis, or whether we should not hasten at once to the scene of this mysterious affair. I may explain, then, that our friend here spent last evening in the company of his two brothers, Owen* and George,* and of his sister Brenda,* at their house of Tredannick Wartha,* which is near the old stone cross upon the moor. He left them shortly after ten o'clock, playing cards round the dining-room table, in excellent health and spirits. This morning, being an early riser, he walked in that direction before breakfast, and was overtaken by the carriage of Dr Richards, who explained that he had just been sent for on a most urgent call to Tredannick Wartha. Mr Mortimer Tregennis naturally went with him. When he arrived at Tredannick Wartha he found an extraordinary state of things. His two brothers and his sister were seated round the table exactly as he had left them, the cards still spread in front of them and the candles burned down to their sockets. The sister lay back stone-dead in her chair, while the two brothers sat on each side of her laughing, shouting, and singing, the senses stricken clean out of them. All three of them, the dead woman and the two demented men, retained upon their faces an expression of the utmost horror—a convulsion of terror which was dreadful to look upon. There was no sign of the presence of anyone in the house, except Mrs Porter, the old cook and housekeeper, who declared that she had slept deeply and heard no sound during the night. Nothing had been stolen or disarranged, and there is absolutely no explanation of what the horror can be which has frightened a woman to death and two strong men out of their senses. There is the situation, Mr Holmes, in a nutshell, and if you can help us to clear it up you will have done a great work.'

I had hoped that in some way I could coax my companion back into the quiet which had been the object of our journey; but one glance at his intense face and contracted eyebrows told me how vain was now the expectation. He sat for some little time in silence, absorbed in the strange drama which had broken in upon our peace.

'I will look into this matter,' he said at last. 'On the face of it, it would appear to be a case of a very exceptional nature. Have you been there yourself, Mr Roundhay?'

'No, Mr Holmes. Mr Tregennis brought back the account to the vicarage, and I at once hurried over with him to consult you.'

'How far is it to the house where this singular tragedy occurred?'

'About a mile inland.'

'Then we shall walk over together. But, before we start, I must ask you a few questions, Mr Mortimer Tregennis.'

The other had been silent all this time, but I had observed that his more controlled excitement was even greater than the obtrusive emotion of the clergyman. He sat with a pale, drawn face, his anxious gaze fixed upon Holmes, and his thin hands clasped convulsively together. His pale lips quivered as he listened to the dreadful experience which had befallen his family, and his dark eyes seemed to reflect something of the horror of the scene.*

'Ask what you like, Mr Holmes,' said he, eagerly. 'It is a bad thing to speak of, but I will answer you the truth.'

'Tell me about last night.'

'Well, Mr Holmes, I supped there, as the vicar has said, and my elder brother George* proposed a game of whist afterwards. We sat down about nine o'clock. It was a quarter past ten when I moved to go. I left them all round the table, as merry as could be.'

'Who let you out?'

'Mrs Porter had gone to bed, so I let myself out. I shut the hall door behind me. The window of the room in which they sat was closed, but the blind was not drawn down. There was no change in door or window this morning, nor any reason to think that any stranger had been to the house. Yet there they sat, driven clean mad with terror, and Brenda lying dead of fright, with her head hanging over the arm of the chair. I'll never get the sight of that room out of my mind so long as I live.'

'The facts, as you state them, are certainly most remarkable,' said Holmes. 'I take it that you have no theory yourself which can in any way account for them?'

'It's devilish, Mr Holmes; devilish!' cried Mortimer Tregennis. 'It is not of this world. Something has come into that room which has dashed the light of reason from their minds. What human contrivance could do that?'

'I fear,' said Holmes, 'that if the matter is beyond humanity it is certainly beyond me. Yet we must exhaust all natural explanations before we fall back upon such a theory as this. As to yourself, Mr Tregennis, I take it you were divided in some way from your family, since they lived together and you had rooms apart?'

'That is so, Mr Holmes, though the matter is past and done with. We were a family of tin-miners at Redruth,* but we sold out our venture to a company, and so retired with enough to keep us. I won't deny that there was some feeling about the division of the money and it stood between us for a time, but it was all forgiven and forgotten, and we were the best of friends together.'

'Looking back at the evening which you spent together, does anything stand out in your memory as throwing any possible light upon the tragedy? Think carefully, Mr Tregennis, for any clue which can help me.'

'There is nothing at all, sir.'

'Your people were in their usual spirits?'

'Never better.'

'Were they nervous people? Did they ever show any apprehension of coming danger?'

'Nothing of the kind.'

'You have nothing to add then, which could assist me?'

Mortimer Tregennis considered earnestly for a moment.

'There is one thing occurs to me,' said he at last. 'As we sat at the table my back was to the window, and my brother George, he being my partner at cards, was facing it. I saw him once look hard over my shoulder, so I turned and looked also. The blind was up and the window shut, but I could just make out the bushes on the lawn, and it seemed to me for a moment that I saw something moving among them. I couldn't even say if it were man or animal, but I just thought there was something there. When I asked him what he was looking at, he told me that he had the same feeling. That is all that I can say.'

'Did you not investigate?'

'No; the matter passed as unimportant.'

'You left them, then, without any premonition of evil?'

'None at all.'

'I am not clear how you came to hear the news so early this morning.'

'I am an early riser, and generally take a walk before breakfast. This morning I had hardly started when the doctor in his carriage overtook me. He told me that old Mrs Porter had sent a boy down with an urgent message. I sprang in beside him and we drove on. When we got there we looked into that dreadful room. The candles and the fire must have burned out hours before, and they had been sitting there in the dark until dawn had broken. The doctor said Brenda must have been dead at least six hours. There were no signs of violence. She just lay across the arm of the chair with that look on her face. George and Owen were singing snatches* of songs and gibbering like two great apes. Oh, it was awful to see! I couldn't stand it, and the doctor was as white as a sheet. Indeed, he fell into a chair in a sort of faint, and we nearly had him on our hands as well.'

'Remarkable—most remarkable!' said Holmes, rising and taking his hat. 'I think, perhaps, we had better go down to Tredannick Wartha without further delay. I confess that I have seldom known a case which at first sight presented a more singular problem.'

Our proceedings of that first morning did little to advance the investigation. It was marked, however, at the outset by an incident which left the most sinister impression upon my mind. The approach to the spot at which the tragedy occurred is down a narrow, winding, country lane. While we made our way along it we heard the rattle of a carriage coming towards us, and stood aside to let it pass. As it drove by us I caught a glimpse through the closed window of a horribly contorted, grinning face glaring out at us. Those staring eyes and gnashing teeth flashed past us like a dreadful vision.

'My brothers!' cried Mortimer Tregennis, white to the lips. 'They are taking them to Helston.'*

We looked with horror after the black carriage, lumbering upon its way. Then we turned our steps towards this ill-omened house in which they had met their strange fate.

It was a large and bright dwelling, rather a villa than a cottage, with a considerable garden which was already, in that Cornish air, well filled with spring flowers. Towards this garden the window of the sitting-room fronted, and from it, according to Mortimer Tregennis, must have come that thing of evil which had by sheer horror in a single instant blasted their minds. Holmes walked slowly and thoughtfully among the flower-plots* and along the path before we entered the porch. So absorbed was he in his thoughts, I remember, that he stumbled over the watering-pot, upset its contents, and deluged both our feet and the garden path. Inside the house we were met by the elderly Cornish housekeeper, Mrs Porter, who, with the aid of a young girl, looked after the wants of the family. She readily answered all Holmes's questions. She had heard nothing in the night. Her employers had all been in excellent spirits lately, and she had never known them more cheerful and prosperous. She had fainted with horror upon entering the room in the morning and seeing that dreadful company round the table. She had, when she recovered, thrown open the window to let the morning air in, and had run down to the lane, whence she sent a farm-lad for the doctor. The lady was on her bed upstairs, if we cared to see her. It took four strong men to get the brothers into the asylum carriage. She would not herself stay in the house another day, and was starting that very afternoon to rejoin her family at St Ives.*

We ascended the stairs and viewed the body. Miss Brenda Tregennis had been a very beautiful girl, though now verging upon middle age. Her dark, clear-cut face was handsome, even in death, but there still lingered upon it something of that convulsion of horror which had been her last human emotion. From her bedroom we descended to the sitting-room where this strange tragedy had actually occurred. The charred ashes of the overnight fire lay in the grate. On the table were the four guttered and burned-out candles, with the cards scattered over its surface. The chairs had been moved back against the walls, but all else was as it had been the night before. Holmes paced with light, swift steps about the room; he sat in the various chairs, drawing them up and reconstructing their positions. He tested how much of the garden was visible; he examined the floor, the ceiling, and the fireplace; but never once did I see that sudden brightening of his eyes and tightening of his lips which would have told me that he saw some gleam of light in this utter darkness.

'Why a fire?' he asked once. 'Had they always a fire in this small room on a spring evening?'

Mortimer Tregennis explained that the night was cold and damp. For that reason, after his arrival, the fire was lit. 'What are you going to do now, Mr Holmes?' he asked.

My friend smiled and laid his hand upon my arm. 'I think, Watson, that I shall resume that course of tobacco-poisoning which you have so often and so justly condemned,' said he. 'With your permission, gentlemen, we will now return to our cottage, for I am not aware that any new factor is likely to come to our notice here. I will turn the facts over in my mind, Mr Tregennis, and should anything occur to me I will certainly communicate with you and the vicar. In the meantime I wish you both good morning.'

It was not until long after we were back in Poldhu Cottage that Holmes broke his complete and absorbed silence. He sat coiled in his armchair, his haggard and ascetic face hardly visible amid the blue swirl of his tobacco smoke, his black brows drawn down, his forehead contracted, his eyes vacant and far away. Finally, he laid down his pipe and sprang to his feet.

'It won't do, Watson!' said he, with a laugh. 'Let us walk along the cliffs together and search for flint arrows. We are more likely to find them than clues to this problem. To let the brain work without sufficient material is like racing an engine. It racks itself to pieces. The sea air, sunshine, and patience, Watson—all else will come.

'Now, let us calmly define our position, Watson,' he continued, as we skirted the cliffs together. 'Let us get a firm grip of the very little which we *do* know, so that when fresh facts arise we may be ready to fit them into their places. I take it, in the first place, that neither of us is prepared to admit diabolical intrusions into the affairs of men. Let us begin by ruling that entirely out of our minds. Very good. There remain three persons who have been grievously stricken by some conscious or unconscious human agency.

That is firm ground. Now, when did this occur? Evidently, assuming his narrative to be true, it was immediately after Mr Mortimer Tregennis had left the room. That is a very important point. The presumption is that it was within a few minutes afterwards. The cards still lay upon the table. It was already past their usual hour for bed. Yet they had not changed their position or pushed back their chairs. I repeat, then, that the occurrence was immediately after his departure, and not later than eleven o'clock last night.

'Our next obvious step is to check, so far as we can, the movements of Mortimer Tregennis after he left the room. In this there is no difficulty, and they seem to be above suspicion. Knowing my methods as you do, you were, of course, conscious of the somewhat clumsy water-pot expedient by which I obtained a clearer impress of his foot than might otherwise have been possible. The wet, sandy path took it admirably. Last night was also wet, you will remember, and it was not difficult—having obtained a sample print—to pick out his track among others and to follow his movements. He appears to have walked away swiftly in the direction of the vicarage.

'If, then, Mortimer Tregennis disappeared from the scene, and yet some outside person affected the card-players, how can we reconstruct that person, and how was such an impression of horror conveyed? Mrs Porter may be eliminated. She is evidently harmless. Is there any evidence that someone crept up to the garden window and in some manner produced so terrific an effect that he drove those who saw it out of their senses? The only suggestion in this direction comes from Mortimer Tregennis himself, who says that his brother spoke about some movement in the garden. That is certainly remarkable, as the night was rainy, cloudy, and dark. Anyone who had the design to alarm these people would be compelled to place his very face against the glass before he could be seen. There is a three-foot flower-border outside this window, but no indication of a foot-mark. It is difficult to imagine, then, how an outsider could have made so terrible an impression upon the company, nor have we found any possible motive for so strange and elaborate an attempt. You perceive our difficulties, Watson?'

'They are only too clear,' I answered, with conviction.

'And yet, with a little more material, we may prove that they are not insurmountable,' said Holmes. 'I fancy that among your extensive archives, Watson, you may find some which were nearly as obscure. Meanwhile, we shall put the case aside until more accurate data are available, and devote the rest of our morning to the pursuit of neolithic man.'

I may have commented upon my friend's power of mental detachment, but never have I wondered at it more than upon that spring morning in Cornwall when for two hours he discoursed upon celts,* arrowheads, and shards, as lightly as if no sinister mystery was waiting for his solution. It was not until we had returned in the afternoon to our cottage that we found a visitor awaiting us, who soon brought our minds back to the matter in hand. Neither of us needed to be told who that visitor was. The huge body, the craggy and deeply-seamed face with the fierce eyes and hawk-like nose, the grizzled hair which nearly brushed our cottage ceiling, the beard—golden at the fringes and white near the lips, save for the nicotine stain from his perpetual cigar—all these were as well known in London as in Africa, and could only be associated with the tremendous personality of Dr Leon Sterndale,* the great lion-hunter and explorer.

We had heard of his presence in the district, and had once or twice caught sight of his tall figure upon the moorland paths. He made no advances to us, however, nor would we have dreamed of doing so to him, as it was well known that it was his love of seclusion which caused him to spend the greater part of the intervals between his journeys in a small bungalow buried in the lonely wood of Beauchamp Arriance.* Here, amid his books and his maps, he lived an absolutely lonely life, attending to his own simple wants, and paying little apparent heed to the affairs of his neighbours. It was a surprise to me, therefore, to hear him asking Holmes in an eager voice, whether he had made any advance in his reconstruction of this mysterious episode.

'The county police are utterly at fault,' said he; 'but perhaps your wider experience has suggested some conceivable explanation. My only claim to being taken into your confidence is that during my many residences here I have come to know this family of Tregennis very well—indeed, upon my Cornish mother's side I could call them cousins—and their strange fate has naturally been a great shock to me. I may tell you that I had got as far as Plymouth upon my way to Africa, but the news reached me this morning, and I came straight back again to help in the inquiry.'

Holmes raised his eyebrows.

'Did you lose your boat through it?'

'I will take the next.'

'Dear me! that is friendship indeed.'

'I tell you they were relatives.'

'Quite so—cousins of your mother. Was your baggage aboard the ship?'

'Some of it, but the main part at the hotel.'

'I see. But surely this event could not have found its way into the Plymouth morning papers?'

'No, sir; I had a telegram.'

'Might I ask from whom?'

A shadow passed over the gaunt face of the explorer.

'You are very inquisitive, Mr Holmes.'

'It is my business.'

With an effort, Dr Sterndale recovered his ruffled composure.

'I have no objection to telling you,' he said. 'It was Mr Roundhay, the vicar, who sent me the telegram which recalled me.'

'Thank you,' said Holmes. 'I may say in answer to your original question, that I have not cleared my mind entirely on the subject of this case, but that I have every hope of reaching some conclusion. It would be premature to say more.'

'Perhaps you would not mind telling me if your suspicions point in any particular direction?'

'No, I can hardly answer that.'

'Then I have wasted my time, and need not prolong my visit.' The famous doctor strode out of our cottage in considerable ill-humour, and within five minutes Holmes had followed him. I saw him no more until the evening, when he returned with a slow step and haggard face which assured me that he had made no great progress with his investigation. He glanced at a telegram which awaited him, and threw it into the grate.

'From the Plymouth hotel, Watson,' he said. 'I learned the name of it from the vicar, and I wired to make certain that Dr Leon Sterndale's account was true. It appears that he did indeed spend last night there, and that he has actually allowed some of his baggage to go on to Africa, while he returned to be present at this investigation. What do you make of that, Watson?'

'He is deeply interested.'*

'Deeply interested—yes. There is a thread here which we have not yet grasped, and which might lead us through the tangle. Cheer up, Watson, for I am very sure that our material has not yet all come to hand. When it does, we may soon leave our difficulties behind us.'

Little did I think how soon the words of Holmes would be realized, or how strange and sinister would be that new development which opened up an entirely fresh line of investigation. I was shaving at my window in the morning when I heard the rattle of hoofs, and, looking up, saw a dogcart coming at a gallop down the road. It pulled up at our door, and our friend the vicar sprang from it and rushed up our garden path. Holmes was already dressed, and we hastened down to meet him.

Our visitor was so excited that he could hardly articulate, but at last in gasps and bursts his tragic story came out of him.

'We are devil-ridden, Mr Holmes! My poor parish is devil-ridden!' he cried. 'Satan himself is loose in it! We are given over into his hands!' He danced about in his agitation, a ludicrous object if it were not for his ashy face and startled eyes. Finally he shot out his terrible news.

'Mr Mortimer Tregennis died during the night, and with exactly the same symptoms as the rest of his family.'

Holmes sprang to his feet, all energy in an instant.

'Can you fit us both into your dogcart?'

'Yes, I can.'

'Then, Watson, we will postpone our breakfast. Mr Round-hay, we are entirely at your disposal. Hurry—hurry, before things get disarranged.'

The lodger occupied two rooms at the vicarage, which were in an angle by themselves, the one above the other. Below was a large sitting-room; above, his bedroom. They looked out upon a croquet-lawn which came up to the windows. We had arrived before the doctor or the police, so that everything was absolutely undisturbed. Let me describe exactly the scene as we saw it upon that misty March morning. It has left an impression which can never be effaced from my mind.

The atmosphere of the room was of a horrible and depressing stuffiness. The servant who had first entered had thrown up the window, or it would have been even more intolerable. This might partly be due to the fact that a lamp* stood flaring and smoking on the centre table. Beside it sat the dead man, leaning back in his chair, his thin beard projecting, his spectacles pushed up on to his forehead, and his lean, dark face turned towards the window and twisted into the same distortion of terror which had marked the features of his dead sister. His limbs were convulsed and his fingers contorted as though he had died in a very paroxysm of fear. He was fully clothed, though there were signs that his dressing had been done in a hurry. We had already learned that his bed had been slept in, and that the tragic end had come to him in the early morning.

One realised the red-hot energy which underlay Holmes's phlegmatic exterior when one saw the sudden change which came over him from the moment that he entered the fatal apartment. In an instant he was tense and alert, his eyes shining, his face set, his limbs quivering with eager activity. He was out on the lawn, in through the window, round the room, and up into the bedroom, for all the world like a dashing foxhound drawing a cover.* In the bedroom he made a rapid cast around, and ended by throwing open the window, which appeared to give him some fresh cause for excitement, for he leaned out of it with loud ejaculations of interest and delight. Then he rushed down the stair, out through the open window, threw himself upon his face on the lawn, sprang up and into the room once more, all with the energy of the hunter who is at the very heels of his quarry. The lamp, which was an ordinary standard,* he examined with minute care, making certain measurements upon its bowl. He carefully scrutinized with his lens the talc shield* which covered the top of the chimney, and scraped off some ashes which adhered to its upper surface, putting some of them into an envelope, which he placed in his pocket-book. Finally, just as the doctor and the official police put in an appearance, he beckoned to the vicar and we all three went out upon the lawn.

'I am glad to say that my investigation has not been entirely barren,' he remarked. 'I cannot remain to discuss the matter with the police, but I should be exceedingly obliged, Mr Roundhay, if you would give the inspector my compliments and direct his attention to the bedroom window and to the sitting-room lamp. Each is suggestive, and together they are almost conclusive. If the police would desire further information I shall be happy to see any of them at the cottage. And now, Watson, I think that, perhaps, we shall be better employed elsewhere.'

It may be that the police resented the intrusion of an amateur, or that they imagined themselves to be upon some hopeful line of investigation; but it is certain that we heard nothing from them for the next two days. During this time Holmes spent some of his time smoking and dreaming in the cottage; but a greater portion in country walks which he undertook alone, returning after many hours without remark as to where he had been. One experiment served to show me the line of his investigation. He had bought a lamp which was the duplicate of the one which had burned in the room of Mortimer Tregennis on the morning of the tragedy. This he filled with the same oil as that used at the vicarage, and he carefully timed the period which it would take to be exhausted. Another experiment which he made was of a more unpleasant nature, and one which I am not likely ever to forget.*

'You will remember, Watson,' he remarked one afternoon, 'that there is a single common point of resemblance in the varying reports which have reached us. This concerns the effect of the atmosphere of the room in each case upon those who had first entered it. You will recollect that Mortimer Tregennis, in describing the episode of his last visit to his brothers' house, remarked that the doctor on entering the room fell into a chair? You had forgotten? Well, I can answer for it that it was so. Now, you will remember also that Mrs Porter, the housekeeper, told us that she herself fainted upon entering the room and had afterwards opened the window. In the second case—that of Mortimer Tregennis himself—you cannot have forgotten the horrible stuffiness of the room when we arrived, though the servant had thrown open the window. That servant, I found upon inquiry, was so ill that she had gone to her bed. You will admit, Watson, that these facts are very suggestive. In each case, there is evidence of a poisonous atmosphere. In each case, also, there is combustion* going on in the room—in the one case a fire, in the other a lamp. The fire was needed, but the lamp was lit—as a comparison of the oil consumed will show—long after it was broad daylight. Why? Surely because there is some connection between three things—the burning, the stuffy atmosphere, and, finally, the madness or death of those unfortunate people. That is clear, is it not?'

'It would appear so.'

'At least we may accept it as a working hypothesis. We will suppose, then, that something was burned in each case which produced an atmosphere causing strange toxic effects.* Very good. In the first instance—that of the Tregennis family—this substance was placed in the fire. Now the window was shut, but the fire would naturally carry fumes to some extent up the chimney. Hence one would expect the effects of the poison to be less than in the second case, where there was less escape for the vapour. The result seems to indicate that it was so, since in the first case only the woman, who had presumably the more sensitive organism, was killed, the others exhibiting that temporary or permanent lunacy which is evidently the first effect of the drug. In the second case the result was complete. The facts, therefore, seem to bear out the theory of a poison which worked by combustion.

'With this train of reasoning in my head I naturally looked about in Mortimer Tregennis's room to find some remains of this substance. The obvious place to look was the talc shield or smoke-guard of the lamp. There, sure enough, I perceived a number of flaky ashes, and round the edges a fringe of brownish powder, which had not yet been consumed. Half of this I took, as you saw, and I placed it in an envelope.'

'Why half, Holmes?'

'It is not for me, my dear Watson, to stand in the way of the official police force. I leave them all the evidence which I found. The poison still remained upon the talc, had they the wit to find it. Now, Watson, we will light our lamp; we will, however, take the precaution to open our window to avoid the premature decease of two deserving members of society, and you will seat yourself near that open window in an arm-chair, unless, like a sensible man, you determine to have nothing to do with the affair. Oh, you will see it out, will you? I thought I knew my Watson. This chair I will place opposite yours, so that we may be the same distance from the poison, and face to face. The door we will leave ajar. Each is now in a position to watch the other and to bring the experiment to an end should the symptoms seem alarming. Is that all clear? Well, then, I take our powder—or what remains of it—from the envelope, and I lay it above the burning lamp. So! Now, Watson, let us sit down and await developments.'

They were not long in coming. I had hardly settled in my chair before I was conscious of a thick, musky odour, subtle and nauseous. At the very first whiff of it my brain and my imagination were beyond all control. A thick, black cloud swirled before my eyes, and my mind told me that in this cloud, unseen as yet, but about to spring out upon my appalled senses, lurked all that was vaguely horrible, all that was monstrous and inconceivably wicked in the universe. Vague shapes swirled and swam amid the dark cloud-bank, each a menace and a warning of something coming, the advent of some unspeakable dweller upon the threshold, whose very shadow would blast my soul. A freezing horror took possession of me. I felt that my hair was rising, that my eyes were protruding, that my mouth was opened, and my tongue like leather. The turmoil within my brain was such that something must surely snap. I tried to scream, and was vaguely aware of some hoarse croak which was my own voice, but distant and detached from myself. At the same moment, in some effort of escape, I broke through that cloud of despair, and had a glimpse of Holmes's face, white, rigid, and drawn with horror—the very look which I had seen upon the features of the dead. It was that vision which gave me an instant of sanity and of strength. I dashed from my chair, threw my arms round Holmes, and together we lurched through the door, and an instant afterwards had thrown ourselves down upon the grass plot and were lying side by side, conscious only of the glorious sunshine which was bursting its way through the hellish cloud of terror which had girt us in. Slowly it rose from our souls like the mists from a landscape, until peace and reason had returned, and we were sitting upon the grass, wiping our clammy foreheads, and looking with apprehension at each other to mark the last traces of that terrific experience which we had undergone.

'Upon my word, Watson!' said Holmes at last, with an unsteady voice, 'I owe you both my thanks and an apology. It was an unjustifiable experiment even for oneself, and doubly so for a friend. I am really very sorry.'

'You know,' I answered, with some emotion, for I had never seen so much of Holmes's heart before, 'that it is my greatest joy and privilege to help you.'

He relapsed at once into the half-humorous, half-cynical vein which was his habitual attitude to those about him. 'It would be superfluous to drive us mad, my dear Watson,' said he. 'A candid observer would certainly declare that we were so already before we embarked upon so wild an experiment. I confess that I never imagined that the effect could be so sudden and so severe.' He dashed into the cottage, and, reappearing with the burning lamp held at full arm's length, he threw it among a bank of brambles. 'We must give the room a little time to clear. I take it, Watson, that you have no longer a shadow of a doubt as to how these tragedies were produced?'

'None whatever.'

'But the cause remains as obscure as before. Come into the arbour here, and let us discuss it together. That villainous stuff seems still to linger round my throat. I think we must admit that all the evidence points to this man, Mortimer Tregennis, having been the criminal in the first tragedy, though he was the victim in the second one. We must remember, in the first place, that there is some story of a family quarrel, followed by a reconciliation. How bitter that quarrel may have been, or how hollow the reconciliation, we cannot tell. When I think of Mortimer Tregennis, with the foxy face and the small, shrewd, beady eyes behind the spectacles, he is not a man whom I should judge to be of a particularly forgiving disposition. Well, in the next place, you will remember that this idea of someone moving in the garden, which took our attention for a moment from the real cause of the tragedy, emanated from him. He had a motive in misleading us. Finally, if he did not throw this substance into the fire at the moment of leaving the room, who did do so? The affair happened immediately after his departure. Had anyone else come in, the family would certainly have risen from the table. Besides, in peaceful Cornwall, visitors do not arrive after ten o'clock at night. We may take it, then, that all the evidence points to Mortimer Tregennis as the culprit.'

'Then his own death was suicide!'

'Well, Watson, it is on the face of it a not impossible supposition. The man who had the guilt upon his soul of having brought such a fate upon his own family might well be driven by remorse to inflict it upon himself. There are, however, some cogent reasons against it. Fortunately, there is one man in England who knows all about it, and I have made arrangements by which we shall hear the facts this afternoon from his own lips. Ah! he is a little before his time. Perhaps you would kindly step this way, Dr Leon Sterndale. We have been conducting a chemical experiment indoors which has left our little room hardly fit for the reception of so distinguished a visitor.'

I had heard the click of the garden gate, and now the majestic figure of the great African explorer appeared upon the path. He turned in some surprise towards the rustic arbour in which we sat.

'You sent for me, Mr Holmes. I had your note about an hour ago, and I have come, though I really do not know why I should obey your summons.'

'Perhaps we can clear the point up before we separate,' said Holmes. 'Meanwhile, I am much obliged to you for your courteous acquiescence. You will excuse this informal reception in the open air, but my friend Watson and I have nearly furnished an additional chapter to what the papers call the Cornish Horror, and we prefer a clear atmosphere for the present. Perhaps, since the matters which we have to discuss will affect you personally in a very intimate fashion, it is as well that we should talk where there can be no eavesdropping.'

The explorer took his cigar from his lips and gazed sternly at my companion.

'I am at a loss to know, sir,' he said, 'what you can have to speak about which affects me personally in a very intimate fashion.'

'The killing of Mortimer Tregennis,' said Holmes.

For a moment I wished that I were armed. Sterndale's fierce face turned to a dusky red, his eyes glared, and the knotted, passionate veins started out in his forehead, while he sprang forward with clenched hands towards my companion. Then he stopped, and with a violent effort he resumed a cold, rigid calmness which was, perhaps, more suggestive of danger than his hot-headed outburst.

'I have lived so long among savages and beyond the law,' said he, 'that I have got into the way of being a law to myself. You would do well, Mr Holmes, not to forget it, for I have no desire to do you an injury.'

'Nor have I any desire to do you an injury, Dr Sterndale. Surely the clearest proof of it is that, knowing what I know, I have sent for you and not for the police.'

Sterndale sat down with a gasp, overawed for, perhaps, the first time in his adventurous life. There was a calm assurance of power in Holmes's manner which could not be withstood. Our visitor stammered for a moment, his great hands opening and shutting in his agitation.

'What do you mean?' he asked, at last. 'If this is bluff upon your part, Mr Holmes, you have chosen a bad man for your experiment. Let us have no more beating about the bush. What *do* you mean?'

'I will tell you,' said Holmes, 'and the reason why I tell you is that I hope frankness may beget frankness. What my next step may be will depend entirely upon the nature of your own defence.'

'My defence?'

'Yes, sir.'

'My defence against what?'

'Against the charge of killing Mortimer Tregennis.'

Sterndale mopped his forehead with his handkerchief. 'Upon my word, you are getting on,' said he. 'Do all your successes depend upon this prodigious power of bluff?'

'The bluff', said Holmes, sternly, 'is upon your side, Dr Leon Sterndale, and not upon mine. As proof I will tell you some of the facts upon which my conclusions are based. Of your return from Plymouth, allowing much of your property to go on to Africa, I will say nothing save that it first informed me that you were one of the factors which had to be taken into account in reconstructing this drama—'

'I came back—'

'I have heard your reasons and regard them as unconvincing and inadequate. We will pass that. You came down here to ask me whom I suspected. I refused to answer you. You then went to the vicarage, waited outside it for some time, and finally returned to your cottage.'

'How do you know that?'

'I followed you.'

'I saw no one.'

'That is what you may expect to see when I follow you. You spent a restless night at your cottage, and you formed certain plans, which in the early morning you proceeded to put into execution. Leaving your door just as day was breaking, you filled your pocket with some reddish gravel* that was lying heaped beside your gate.'

Sterndale gave a violent start and looked at Holmes in amazement.

'You then walked swiftly for the mile which separated you from the vicarage. You were wearing, I may remark, the same pair of ribbed tennis shoes which are at the present moment upon your feet. At the vicarage you passed through the orchard and the side hedge, coming out under the window of the lodger Tregennis. It was now daylight, but the household was not yet stirring. You drew some of the gravel from your pocket, and you threw it up at the window above you—'

Sterndale sprang to his feet.

'I believe that you are the devil himself!' he cried.

Holmes smiled at the compliment. 'It took two, or possibly three, handfuls before the lodger came to the window. You beckoned him to come down. He dressed hurriedly and descended to his sitting-room. You entered by the window. There was an interview—a short one—during which you walked up and down the room. Then you passed out and closed the window, standing on the lawn outside smoking a cigar and watching what occurred. Finally, after the death of Tregennis, you withdrew as you had come. Now, Dr Sterndale, how do you justify such conduct, and what were the motives for your actions? If you prevaricate or trifle with me, I give you my assurance that the matter will pass out of my hands for ever.'

Our visitor's face had turned ashen grey as he listened to the words of his accuser. Now he sat for some time in thought with his face sunk in his hands. Then, with a sudden impulsive gesture, he plucked a photograph from his breast-pocket and threw it on the rustic table before us.

'That is why I have done it,' said he.

It showed the bust and face of a very beautiful woman. Holmes stooped over it.

'Brenda Tregennis,' said he.

'Yes, Brenda Tregennis,' repeated our visitor. 'For years I have loved her. For years she has loved me. There is the secret of that Cornish seclusion which people have mar-velled at. It has brought me close to the one thing on earth that was dear to me. I could not marry her, for I have a wife who has left me for years and yet whom, by the deplorable laws of England, I could not divorce.* For years Brenda waited. For years I waited. And this is what we have waited for.' A terrible sob shook his great frame, and he clutched his throat under his brindled beard. Then with an effort he mastered himself and spoke on.

'The vicar knew. He was in our confidence. He would tell you that she was an angel upon earth. That was why he telegraphed to me and I returned. What was my baggage or Africa to me when I learned that such a fate had come upon my darling? There you have the missing clue to my action, Mr Holmes.'

'Proceed,' said my friend.

Dr Sterndale drew from his pocket a paper packet and laid it upon the table. On the outside was written, '*Radix pedis diaboli*' with a red poison label beneath it. He pushed it towards me. 'I understand that you are a doctor, sir. Have you ever heard of this preparation?'

'Devil's-foot root! No, I have never heard of it.'

'It is no reflection upon your professional knowledge,' said he, 'for I believe that, save for one sample in a laboratory at Buda,* there is no other specimen in Europe. It has not yet found its way either into the pharmacopoeia* or into the literature of toxicology.* The root is shaped like a foot, half human, half goat-like; hence the fanciful name given by a botanical missionary. It is used as an ordeal* poison by the medicine-men in certain districts of West Africa, and is kept as a secret among them. This particular specimen I obtained under very extraordinary circumstances in the Ubanghi* country.' He opened the paper as he spoke, and disclosed a heap of reddish-brown, snuff-like powder.

'Well, sir?' asked Holmes, sternly.

'I am about to tell you, Mr Holmes, all that actually occurred, for you already know so much that it is clearly to my interest that you should know all. I have already explained the relationship in which I stood to the Tregennis family. For the sake of the sister I was friendly with the brothers. There was a family quarrel about money which estranged this man Mortimer, but it was supposed to be made up, and I afterwards met him as I did the others. He was a sly, subtle, scheming man, and several things arose which gave me a suspicion of him, but I had no cause for any positive quarrel.

'One day, only a couple of weeks ago, he came down to my cottage and I showed him some of my African curiosities. Among other things I exhibited this powder, and I told him of its strange properties, how it stimulates those brain centres which control the emotion of fear, and how either madness or death is the fate of the unhappy native who is subjected to the ordeal by the priest of his tribe. I told him also how powerless European science would be to detect it. How he took it I cannot say, for I never left the room, but there is no doubt that it was then, while I was opening cabinets and stooping to boxes, that he managed to abstract some of the devil's-foot root. I well remember how he plied me with questions as to the amount and the time that was needed for its effect, but I little dreamed that he could have a personal reason for asking.

'I thought no more of the matter until the vicar's telegram reached me at Plymouth. This villain had thought that I would be at sea before the news could reach me, and that I should be lost for years in Africa. But I returned at once. Of course, I could not listen to the details without feeling assured that my poison had been used. I came round to see you on the chance that some other explanation had suggested itself to you. But there could be none. I was convinced that Mortimer Tregennis was the murderer; that for the sake of money, and with the idea, perhaps, that if the other members of his family were all insane he would be the sole guardian of their joint property, he had used the devil's-foot powder upon them, driven two of them out of their senses, and killed his sister Brenda, the one human being whom I have ever loved or who has ever loved me. There was his crime; what was to be his punishment?

'Should I appeal to the law? Where were my proofs? I knew that the facts were true, but could I hope to make a jury of countrymen believe so fantastic a story? I might or I might not. But I could not afford to fail. My soul cried out for revenge. I have said to you once before, Mr Holmes, that I have spent much of my life outside the law, and that I have come at last to be a law to myself. So it was now. I determined that the fate which he had given to others should be shared by himself. Either that, or I would do justice upon him with my own hand. In all England there can be no man who sets less value upon his own life than I do at the present moment.

'Now I have told you all. You have yourself supplied the rest. I did, as you say, after a restless night, set off early from my cottage. I foresaw the difficulty of arousing him, so I gathered some gravel from the pile which you have mentioned, and I used it to throw up to his window. He came down and admitted me through the window of the sitting-room. I laid his offence before him. I told him that I had come both as judge and executioner. The wretch sank into a chair paralysed at the sight of my revolver. I lit the lamp, put the powder above it, and stood outside the window, ready to carry out my threat to shoot him should he try to leave the room. In five minutes he died. My God! how he died! But my heart was flint, for he endured nothing which my innocent darling had not felt before him. There is my story, Mr Holmes. Perhaps, if you loved a woman, you would have done as much yourself. At any rate, I am in your hands. You can take what steps you like. As I have already said, there is no man living who can fear death less than I do.'

Holmes sat for some little time in silence.

'What were your plans?' he asked, at last.

'I had intended to bury myself in Central Africa. My work there is but half finished.'

'Go and do the other half,' said Holmes. 'I, at least, am not prepared to prevent you.'

Dr Sterndale raised his giant figure, bowed gravely, and walked from the arbour. Holmes lit his pipe and handed me his pouch.

'Some fumes which are not poisonous would be a welcome change,' said he. 'I think you must agree, Watson, that it is not a case in which we are called upon to interfere. Our investigation has been independent, and our action shall be so also. You would not denounce the man?'

'Certainly not,' I answered.

'I have never loved, Watson, for if I did and if the woman I loved had met such an end, I might act even as our lawless lion-hunter has done. Who knows? Well, Watson, I will not offend your intelligence by explaining what is obvious. The gravel upon the window-sill was, of course, the starting-point of my research. It was unlike anything in the vicarage garden. Only when my attention had been drawn to Dr Sterndale and his cottage did I find its counterpart. The lamp shining in broad daylight and the remains of powder upon the shield were successive links in a fairly obvious chain. And now, my dear Watson, I think we may dismiss the matter from our mind, and go back with a clear conscience to the study of those Chaldean roots which are surely to be traced in the Cornish branch* of the great Celtic speech.'

The Red Circle

I

'WELL, Mrs Warren, I cannot see that you have any particular cause for uneasiness, nor do I understand why I, whose time is of some value, should interfere in the matter. I really have other things to engage me.' So spoke Sherlock Holmes, and turned back to the great scrap-book in which he was arranging and indexing some of his recent material.

But the landlady had the pertinacity, and also the cunning, of her sex. She held her ground firmly.

'You arranged an affair for a lodger of mine last year,' she said—'Mr Fairdale Hobbs.'

'Ah, yes—a simple matter.'

'But he would never cease talking of it—your kindness, sir, and the way in which you brought light into the darkness. I remembered his words when I was in doubt and darkness myself. I know you could if you only would.'

Holmes was accessible upon the side of flattery, and also, to do him justice, upon the side of kindliness. The two forces made him lay down his gum-brush with a sigh of resignation and push back his chair.

'Well, well, Mrs Warren, let us hear about it, then. You don't object to tobacco, I take it? Thank you, Watson—the matches! You are uneasy, as I understand, because your new lodger remains in his rooms and you cannot see him. Why, bless you, Mrs Warren, if I were your lodger you often would not see me for weeks on end.'

'No doubt, sir; but this is different. It frightens me, Mr Holmes. I can't sleep for fright. To hear his quick step moving here and moving there from early morning to late at night, and yet never to catch so much as a glimpse of him—it's more than I can stand. My husband is as nervous over it as I am, but he is out at his work all day, while I get no rest from it. What is he hiding for? What has he done? Except for the girl,* I am all alone in the house with him, and it's more than my nerves can stand.'

Holmes leaned forward and laid his long, thin fingers upon the woman's shoulder. He had an almost hypnotic power of soothing when he wished. The scared look faded from her eyes, and her agitated features smoothed into their usual commonplace. She sat down in the chair which he had indicated.

'If I take it up I must understand every detail,' said he. 'Take time to consider. The smallest point may be the most essential. You say that the man came ten days ago, and paid you for a fortnight's board and lodging?'

'He asked my terms, sir. I said fifty shillings* a week. There is a small sitting-room and bedroom, and all complete, at the top of the house.'

'Well?'

'He said, "I'll pay you five pounds a week if I can have it on my own terms." I'm a poor woman, sir, and Mr Warren earns little, and the money meant much to me. He took out a ten-pound note, and he held it out to me then and there. "You can have the same every fortnight for a long time to come if you keep the terms," he said. "If not, I'll have no more to do with you." '

'What were the terms?'

'Well, sir, they were that he was to have a key of the house. That was all right. Lodgers often have them. Also, that he was to be left entirely to himself, and never, upon any excuse, to be disturbed.'

'Nothing wonderful in that, surely?'

'Not in reason, sir. But this is out of all reason. He has been there for ten days, and neither Mr Warren, nor I, nor the girl has once set eyes upon him. We can hear that quick step of his pacing up and down, up and down, night, morning, and noon; but except on that first night he has never once gone out of the house.'

'Oh, he went out the first night, did he?'

'Yes, sir, and returned very late—after we were all in bed. He told me after he had taken the rooms that he would do so, and asked me not to bar the door. I heard him come up the stair after midnight.'

'But his meals?'

'It was his particular direction that we should always, when he rang, leave his meal upon a chair outside his door. Then he rings again when he has finished, and we take it down from the same chair. If he wants anything else he prints it on a slip of paper and leaves it.'

'Prints it?'

'Yes, sir; prints it in pencil. Just the word, nothing more. Here's one I brought to show you—SOAP. Here's another— MATCH. This is one he left the first morning—DAILY GAZETTE.* I leave that paper with his breakfast every morning.'

'Dear me, Watson,' said Holmes, staring with great curiosity at the slips of foolscap which the landlady had handed to him, 'this is certainly a little unusual. Seclusion I can understand; but why print? Printing is a clumsy process. Why not write? What would it suggest, Watson?'

'That he desired to conceal his handwriting.'

'But why? What can it matter to him that his landlady should have a word of his writing? Still, it may be as you say. Then, again, why such laconic messages?'

'I cannot imagine.'

'It opens a pleasing field for intelligent speculation. The words are written with a broad-pointed, violet-tinted pencil of a not unusual pattern. You will observe that the paper is torn away at the side here after the printing was done, so that the S of SOAP is partly gone. Suggestive, Watson, is it not?'

'Of caution?'

'Exactly. There was evidently some mark, some thumb-print,* something which might give a clue to the person's identity. Now, Mrs Warren, you say that the man was of middle size, dark, and bearded. What age would he be?'

'Youngish, sir—not over thirty.'

'Well, can you give me no further indications?'

'He spoke good English, sir, and yet I thought he was a foreigner by his accent.'

'And he was well dressed?'

'Very smartly dressed, sir—quite the gentleman. Dark clothes—nothing you would note.'

'He gave no name?'

'No, sir.'

'And has had no letters or callers?'

'None.'

'But surely you or the girl enter his room of a morning?'

'No, sir; he looks after himself entirely.'

'Dear me! that is certainly remarkable. What about his luggage?'

'He had one big brown bag with him—nothing else.'

'Well, we don't seem to have much material to help us. Do you say nothing has come out of that room—absolutely nothing?'

The landlady drew an envelope from her bag; from it she shook out two burnt matches and a cigarette-end upon the table.

'They were on his tray this morning. I brought them because I had heard that you can read great things out of small* ones.'

Holmes shrugged his shoulders.

'There is nothing here,' said he. 'The matches have, of course, been used to light cigarettes. That is obvious from the shortness of the burnt end. Half the match is consumed in lighting a pipe or cigar.* But, dear me! this cigarette stub is certainly remarkable. The gentleman was bearded and moustached, you say?'

'Yes, sir.'

'I don't understand that. I should say that only a clean-shaven man could have smoked this. Why, Watson, even your modest moustache would have been singed.'

'A holder?' I suggested.

'No, no; the end is matted. I suppose there could not be two people in your rooms, Mrs Warren?'

'No, sir. He eats so little that I often wonder it can keep life in one.'

'Well, I think we must wait for a little more material. After all, you have nothing to complain of. You have received your rent, and he is not a troublesome lodger, though he is certainly an unusual one. He pays you well, and if he chooses to lie concealed it is no direct business of yours. We have no excuse for an intrusion upon his privacy until we have some reason to think that there is a guilty reason for it. I've taken up the matter, and I won't lose sight of it. Report to me if anything fresh occurs, and rely upon my assistance if it should be needed.

'There are certainly some points of interest in this case, Watson,' he remarked, when the landlady had left us. 'It may, of course, be trivial—individual eccentricity; or it may be very much deeper than appears on the surface. The first thing that strikes one is the obvious possibility that the person now in the rooms may be entirely different from the one who engaged them.'

'Why should you think so?'

'Well, apart from this cigarette-end, was it not suggestive that the only time the lodger went out was immediately after his taking the rooms? He came back—or someone came back—when all witnesses were out of the way. We have no proof that the person who came back was the person who went out. Then, again, the man who took the rooms spoke English well. This other, however, prints "match" when it should have been "matches". I can imagine that the word was taken out of a dictionary, which would give the noun but not the plural. The laconic style may be to conceal the absence of knowledge of English. Yes, Watson, there are good reasons to suspect that there has been a substitution of lodgers.'

'But for what possible end?'

'Ah! there lies our problem. There is one rather obvious line of investigation.' He took down the great book in which, day by day, he filed the agony columns of the various London journals. 'Dear me!' said he, turning over the pages, 'what a chorus of groans, cries, and bleatings! What a

99

rag-bag of singular happenings! But surely the most valuable hunting-ground that ever was given to a student of the unusual! This person is alone, and cannot be approached by letter without a breach of that absolute secrecy which is desired. How is any news or any message to reach him from without? Obviously by advertisement through a newspaper. There seems no other way, and fortunately we need concern ourselves with the one paper only. Here are the *Daily Gazette* extracts of the last fortnight. "Lady with a black boa at Prince's Skating Club"—that we may pass. "Surely Jimmy will not break his mother's heart"—that appears to be irrelevant. "If the lady who fainted in the Brixton bus"—she does not interest me. "Every day my heart longs—" Bleat, Watson—unmitigated bleat! Ah! this is a little more possible. Listen to this: "Be patient. Will find some sure means of communication. Meanwhile, this column.—G." That is two days after Mrs Warren's lodger arrived. It sounds plausible, does it not? The mysterious one could understand English, even if he could not print it. Let us see if we can pick up the trace again. Yes, here we are—three days later. "Am making successful arrangements. Patience and prudence. The clouds will pass.—G." Nothing for a week after that. Then comes something much more definite: "The path is clearing. If I find chance signal message remember code agreed—one A, two B, and so on. You will hear soon.—G." That was in yesterday's paper, and there is nothing in to-day's.* It's all very appropriate to Mrs Warren's lodger. If we wait a little, Watson, I don't doubt that the affair will grow more intelligible.'

So it proved; for in the morning I found my friend standing on the hearthrug with his back to the fire, and a smile of complete satisfaction upon his face.

'How's this, Watson?' he cried, picking up the paper from the table. ' "High red house with white stone facings. Third floor. Second window left. After dusk.—G." That is definite enough. I think after breakfast we must make a little reconnaissance of Mrs Warren's neighbourhood. Ah, Mrs Warren! what news do you bring us this morning?'

Our client had suddenly burst into the room with an explosive energy which told of some new and momentous development.

'It's a police matter, Mr Holmes!' she cried. 'I'll have no more of it! He shall pack out of that with his baggage.* I would have gone straight up and told him so, only I thought it was but fair to you to take your opinion first. But I'm at the end of my patience, and when it comes to knocking my old man* about—'

'Knocking Mr Warren about?'

'Using him roughly, anyway.'

'But who used him roughly?'

'Ah! that's what we want to know! It was this morning, sir. Mr Warren is a time-keeper at Morton and Waylight's, in Tottenham Court Road.* He has to be out of the house before seven. Well, this morning he had not got ten paces down the road when two men came up behind him, threw a coat over his head, and bundled him into a cab that was beside the kerb. They drove him an hour, and then opened the door and shot him out. He lay in the roadway so shaken in his wits that he never saw what became of the cab. When he picked himself up he found he was on Hampstead Heath;* so he took a bus home, and there he lies now on the sofa, while I came straight round to tell you what had happened.'

'Most interesting,' said Holmes. 'Did he observe the appearance of these men—did he hear them talk?'

'No; he is clean dazed. He just knows that he was lifted up as if by magic and dropped as if by magic. Two at least were in it, and maybe three.'

'And you connect this attack with your lodger?'

'Well, we've lived there fifteen years and no such happenings ever came before. I've had enough of him. Money's not everything. I'll have him out of my house before the day is done.'

'Wait a bit, Mrs Warren. Do nothing rash. I begin to think that this affair may be very much more important than appeared at first sight. It is clear now that some danger is threatening your lodger. It is equally clear that his enemies, lying in wait for him near your door, mistook your husband for him in the foggy morning light. On discovering their mistake they released him. What they would have done had it not been a mistake, we can only conjecture.'

'Well, what am I to do, Mr Holmes?'

'I have a great fancy to see this lodger of yours, Mrs Warren.'

'I don't see how that is to be managed, unless you break in the door. I always hear him unlock it as I go down the stair after I leave the tray.'

'He has to take the tray in. Surely we could conceal ourselves and see him do it.'

The landlady thought for a moment.

'Well, sir, there's the box-room opposite. I could arrange a looking-glass, maybe, and if you were behind the door—'

'Excellent!' said Holmes. 'When does he lunch?'

'About one, sir.'

'Then Dr Watson and I will come round in time. For the present, Mrs Warren, good-bye.'

At half-past twelve we found ourselves upon the steps of Mrs Warren's house—a high, thin, yellow-brick edifice in Great Orme Street, a narrow thoroughfare at the north-east side of the British Museum. Standing as it does near the corner of the street, it commands a view down Howe Street,* with its more pretentious houses. Holmes pointed with a chuckle to one of these, a row of residential flats, which projected so that they could not fail to catch the eye.

'See, Watson!' said he. ' "High red house with stone facings." There is the signal station all right. We know the place, and we know the code; so surely our task should be simple. There's a "To Let" card in that window. It is evidently an empty flat to which the confederate has access. Well, Mrs Warren, what now?'

'I have it all ready for you. If you will both come up and leave your boots below on the landing, I'll put you there now.'

It was an excellent hiding-place which she had arranged. The mirror was so placed that, seated in the dark, we could very plainly see the door opposite. We had hardly settled down in it, and Mrs Warren left us, when a distant tinkle announced that our mysterious neighbour had rung. Presently the landlady appeared with the tray, laid it down upon a chair beside the closed door, and then, treading heavily, departed. Crouching together in the angle of the door, we kept our eyes fixed upon the mirror. Suddenly, as the landlady's footsteps died away, there was the creak of a turning key, the handle revolved, and two thin hands darted out and lifted the tray from the chair. An instant later it was hurriedly replaced, and I caught a glimpse of a dark, beautiful, horrified face glaring at the narrow opening of the box-room. Then the door crashed to, the key turned once more, and all was silence. Holmes twitched my sleeve, and together we stole down the stair.

'I will call again in the evening,' said he to the expectant landlady. 'I think, Watson, we can discuss this business better in our own quarters.'

'My surmise, as you saw, proved to be correct,' said he, speaking from the depths of his easy-chair. 'There has been a substitution of lodgers. What I did not foresee is that we should find a woman, and no ordinary woman, Watson.'

'She saw us.'

'Well, she saw something to alarm her. That is certain. The general sequence of events is pretty clear, is it not? A couple seek refuge in London from a very terrible and instant danger. The measure of that danger is the rigour of their precautions. The man, who has some work which he must do, desires to leave the woman in absolute safety while he does it. It is not an easy problem, but he solved it in an original fashion, and so effectively that her presence was not even known to the landlady who supplies her with food. The printed messages, as is now evident, were to prevent her sex being discovered by her writing. The man cannot come near the woman, or he will guide their enemies to her. Since he cannot communicate with her direct, he has recourse to the agony column of a paper. So far all is clear.'

'But what is at the root of it?'

'Ah, yes, Watson—severely practical, as usual! What is at the root of it all? Mrs Warren's whimsical problem enlarges somewhat and assumes a more sinister aspect as we proceed. This much we can say: that it is no ordinary love escapade. You saw the woman's face at the sign of danger. We have heard, too, of the attack upon the landlord, which was undoubtedly meant for the lodger. These alarms, and the desperate need for secrecy, argue that the matter is one of life or death. The attack upon Mr Warren further shows that the enemy, whoever they are, are themselves not aware of the substitution of the female lodger for the male. It is very curious and complex, Watson.'

'Why should you go further in it? What have you to gain from it?'

'What indeed? It is Art for Art's sake,* Watson. I suppose when you doctored you found yourself studying cases without thought of a fee?'

'For my education, Holmes.'

'Education never ends, Watson. It is a series of lessons with the greatest for the last.* This is an instructive case. There is neither money nor credit in it, and yet one would wish to tidy it up. When dusk comes we should find ourselves one stage advanced in our investigation.'

When we returned to Mrs Warren's rooms, the gloom of a London winter evening had thickened into one grey curtain, a dead monotone of colour, broken only by the sharp yellow squares of the windows and the blurred haloes of the gas-lamps. As we peered from the darkened sitting-room of the lodging-house, one more dim light glimmered high up through the obscurity.

'Someone is moving in that room,' said Holmes in a whisper, his gaunt and eager face thrust forward to the window-pane. 'Yes, I can see his shadow. There he is again! He has a candle in his hand. Now he is peering across. He wants to be sure that she is on the look-out. Now he begins to flash. Take the message also, Watson, that we may check each other. A single flash—that is A, surely. Now, then. How many did you make it? Twenty. So did I. That should mean

T.* AT—that's intelligible enough! Another T. Surely this is the beginning of a second word. Now, then—TENTA. Dead stop. That can't be all, Watson? ATTENTA gives no sense. Nor is it any better as three words—AT. TEN. TA, unless T. A. are a person's initials. There it* goes again! What's that? ATTE—why, it is the same message over again. Curious, Watson, very curious! Now he is off once more! AT—why, he is repeating it for the third time. ATTENTA three times! How often will he repeat it? No, that seems to be the finish. He has withdrawn from the window. What do you make of it, Watson?'

'A cipher message, Holmes.'

My companion gave a sudden chuckle of comprehension. 'And not a very obscure cipher, Watson,' said he. 'Why, of course, it is Italian! That A means that it is addressed to a woman. "Beware! Beware! Beware!" How's that, Watson?'

'I believe you have hit it.'

'Not a doubt of it. It is a very urgent message, thrice repeated to make it more so. But beware of what? Wait a bit; he is coming to the window once more.'

Again we saw the dim silhouette of a crouching man and the whisk of the small flame across the window, as the signals were renewed. They came more rapidly than before—so rapid that it was hard to follow them.

'PERICOLO—Pericolo—Eh, what's that, Watson? Danger, isn't it? Yes, by Jove, it's a danger signal. There he goes again! PERI. Hullo, what on earth—'

The light had suddenly gone out, the glimmering square of window had disappeared, and the third floor formed a dark band round the lofty building, with its tiers of shining casements. That last warning cry had been suddenly cut short. How, and by whom? The same thought occurred on the instant to us both. Holmes sprang up from where he crouched by the window.

'This is serious, Watson,' he cried. 'There is some devilry going forward! Why should such a message stop in such a way? I should put Scotland Yard in touch with this business—and yet, it is too pressing for us to leave.'

'Shall I go for the police?'

'We must define the situation a little more clearly. It may bear some more innocent interpretation. Come, Watson, let us go across ourselves and see what we can make of it.'

2

As we walked rapidly down Howe Street I glanced back at the building which we had left. There, dimly outlined at the top window, I could see the shadow of a head, a woman's head, gazing tensely, rigidly, out into the night, waiting with breathless suspense for the renewal of that interrupted message. At the doorway of the Howe Street flats a man, muffled in a cravat and great-coat, was leaning against the railing. He started as the hall-light fell upon our faces.

'Holmes!' he cried.

'Why, Gregson!' said my companion, as he shook hands with the Scotland Yard detective. 'Journeys end with lovers' meetings.* What brings you here?'

'The same reasons that bring you, I expect,' said Gregson. 'How you got on to it I can't imagine.'

'Different threads, but leading up to the same tangle. I've been taking the signals.'

'Signals?'

'Yes, from that window. They broke off in the middle. We came over to see the reason. But since it is safe in your hands I see no object in continuing the business.'

'Wait a bit!' cried Gregson, eagerly. 'I'll do you this justice, Mr Holmes, that I was never in a case yet that I didn't feel stronger for having you on my side.* There's only the one exit to these flats, so we have him safe.'

'Who is he?'

'Well, well, we score over you for once, Mr Holmes. You must give us best this time.' He struck his stick sharply upon the ground, on which a cabman, his whip in his hand, sauntered over from a four-wheeler which stood on the far side of the street. 'May I introduce you to Mr Sherlock

Holmes?' he said to the cabman. 'This is Mr Leverton, of Pinkerton's American Agency.'

'The hero of the Long Island Cove mystery?'* said Holmes. 'Sir, I am pleased to meet you.'

The American, a quiet, businesslike young man, with a clean-shaven, hatchet face, flushed up at the words of commendation. 'I am on the trail of my life now, Mr Holmes,' said he. 'If I can get Gorgiano—'*

'What! Gorgiano of the Red Circle?'

'Oh, he has a European fame, has he? Well, we've learned all about him in America. We *know* he is at the bottom of fifty murders, and yet we have nothing positive we can take him on. I tracked him over from New York, and I've been close to him for a week in London, waiting for some excuse to get my hand on his collar. Mr Gregson and I ran him to ground in that big tenement house, and there's only the one door, so he can't slip us. There's three folk come out since he went in, but I'll swear he wasn't one of them.'

'Mr Holmes talks of signals,' said Gregson. 'I expect, as usual, he knows a good deal that we don't.'

In a few clear words Holmes explained the situation as it had appeared to us. The American struck his hands together with vexation.

'He's on to us!' he cried.

'Why do you think so?'

'Well, it figures out that way, does it not? Here he is, sending out messages to an accomplice—there are several of his gang in London. Then suddenly, just as by your own account he was telling them that there was danger, he broke short off. What could it mean except that from the window he had suddenly either caught sight of us in the street, or in some way come to understand how close the danger was, and that he must act right away if he was to avoid it? What do you suggest, Mr Holmes?'

'That we go up at once and see for ourselves.'

'But we have no warrant for his arrest.'

'He is in unoccupied premises under suspicious circumstances,' said Gregson. 'That is good enough for the moment.

When we have him by the heels we can see if New York can't help us to keep him. I'll take the responsibility of arresting him now.'

Our official detectives may blunder in the matter of intelligence, but never* in that of courage. Gregson climbed the stair to arrest this desperate murderer with the same absolutely quiet and businesslike bearing with which he would have ascended the official staircase of Scotland Yard. The Pinkerton man had tried to push past him, but Gregson had firmly elbowed him back. London dangers were the privilege of the London force.

The door of the left-hand flat upon the third landing was standing ajar. Gregson pushed it open. Within, all was absolute silence and darkness. I struck a match, and lit the detective's lantern. As I did so, and as the flicker steadied into a flame, we all gave a gasp of surprise. On the deal boards of the carpetless floor there was outlined a fresh track of blood. The red steps pointed towards us, and led away from an inner room, the door of which was closed. Gregson flung it open and held his light full blaze in front of him, whilst we all peered eagerly over his shoulders.

In the middle of the floor of the empty room was huddled the figure of an enormous man, his clean-shaven, swarthy face grotesquely horrible in its contortion, and his head encircled by a ghastly crimson halo of blood, lying in a broad wet circle upon the white woodwork. His knees were drawn up, his hands thrown out in agony, and from the centre of his broad, brown, upturned throat there projected the white haft of a knife driven blade-deep into his body. Giant as he was, the man must have gone down like a pole-axed* ox before that terrific blow. Beside his right hand a most formidable horn-handled, two-edged dagger lay upon the floor, and near it a black kid glove.

'By George! it's Black Gorgiano himself!' cried the American detective. 'Someone has got ahead of us this time.'

'Here is the candle in the window, Mr Holmes,' said Gregson. 'Why, whatever are you doing?'

Holmes had stepped across, had lit the candle, and was passing it backwards and forwards across the window-panes. Then he peered into the darkness, blew the candle out, and threw it on the floor.

'I rather think that will be helpful,' said he. He came over and stood in deep thought while the two professionals were examining the body. 'You say that three people came out from the flat while you were waiting downstairs,' said he, at last. 'Did you observe them closely?'

'Yes, I did.'

'Was there a fellow about thirty, black-bearded, dark, of middle size?'

'Yes; he was the last to pass me.'

'That is your man, I fancy. I can give you his description, and we have a very excellent outline of his footmark. That should be enough for you.'

'Not much, Mr Holmes, among the millions of London.'

'Perhaps not. That is why I thought it best to summon this lady to your aid.'

We all turned round at the words. There, framed in the doorway, was a tall and beautiful woman—the mysterious lodger of Bloomsbury. Slowly she advanced, her face pale and drawn with a frightful apprehension, her eyes fixed and staring, her terrified gaze riveted upon the dark figure on the floor.

'You have killed him!' she muttered. 'Oh, *Dio mio*,* you have killed him!' Then I heard a sudden sharp intake of her breath, and she sprang into the air with a cry of joy. Round and round the room she danced, her hands clapping, her dark eyes gleaming with delighted wonder, and a thousand pretty Italian exclamations pouring from her lips. It was terrible and amazing to see such a woman so convulsed with joy at such a sight. Suddenly she stopped and gazed at us all with a questioning stare.

'But you! You are police, are you not? You have killed Giuseppe Gorgiano. Is it not so?'

'We are police, madam.'

She looked round into the shadows of the room.

'But where, then, is Gennaro?' she asked. 'He is my husband, Gennaro Lucca. I am Emilia Lucca, and we are both from New York. Where is Gennaro? He called me this moment from this window, and I ran with all my speed.'

'It was I who called,' said Holmes.

'You! How could you call?'

'Your cipher was not difficult, madam. Your presence here was desirable. I knew that I had only to flash "*Vieni*"* and you would surely come.'

The beautiful Italian looked with awe at my companion.

'I do not understand how you know these things,' she said. 'Giuseppe Gorgiano—how did he—' She paused, and then suddenly her face lit up with pride and delight. 'Now I see it! My Gennaro! My splendid, beautiful Gennaro, who has guarded me safe from all harm, he did it, with his own strong hand he killed the monster! Oh, Gennaro, how wonderful you are! What woman could ever be worthy of such a man?'

'Well, Mrs Lucca,' said the prosaic Gregson, laying his hand upon the lady's sleeve with as little sentiment as if she were a Notting Hill hooligan,* 'I am not very clear yet who you are or what you are; but you've said enough to make it very clear that we shall want you at the Yard.'

'One moment, Gregson,' said Holmes. 'I rather fancy that this lady may be as anxious to give us information as we can be to get it. You understand, madam, that your husband will be arrested and tried for the death of the man who lies before us? What you say may be used in evidence. But if you think that he has acted from motives which are not criminal, and which he would wish to have known, then you cannot serve him better than by telling us the whole story.'

'Now that Gorgiano is dead we fear nothing,' said the lady. 'He was a devil and a monster, and there can be no judge in the world who would punish my husband for having killed him.'

'In that case,' said Holmes, 'my suggestion is that we lock this door, leave things as we found them, go with this lady to her room, and form our opinion after we have heard what it is that she has to say to us.'

Half an hour later we were seated, all four, in the small sitting-room of Signora Lucca, listening to her remarkable narrative of those sinister events, the ending of which we had chanced to witness. She spoke in rapid and fluent but very unconventional English, which, for the sake of clearness, I will make grammatical.

'I was born in Posilippo, near Naples,' said she, 'and was the daughter of Augusto Barelli, who was the chief lawyer and once the deputy of that port.* Gennaro was in my father's employment, and I came to love him, as any woman must. He had neither money nor position—nothing but his beauty and strength and energy—so my father forbade the match. We fled together, were married at Bari, and sold my jewels to gain the money which would take us to America. This was four years ago, and we have been in New York ever since.

'Fortune was very good to us at first. Gennaro was able to do a service to an Italian gentleman—he saved him from some ruffians in the place called the Bowery,* and so made a powerful friend. His name was Tito Castalotte, and he was the senior partner of the great firm of Castalotte and Zamba, who are the chief fruit importers of New York. Signor Zamba is an invalid, and our new friend Castalotte has all power within the firm, which employs more than three hundred men. He took my husband into his employment, made him head of a department, and showed his goodwill towards him in every way. Signor Castalotte was a bachelor, and I believe that he felt as if Gennaro was his son, and both my husband and I loved him as if he were our father. We had taken and furnished a little house in Brooklyn,* and our whole future seemed assured, when that black cloud appeared which was soon to overspread our sky.

'One night, when Gennaro returned from his work, he brought a fellow-countryman back with him. His name was Gorgiano, and he had come also from Posilippo. He was a huge man, as you can testify, for you have looked upon his corpse. Not only was his body that of a giant, but everything about him was grotesque, gigantic, and terrifying. His voice was like thunder in our little house. There was scarce room for the whirl of his great arms as he talked. His thoughts, his emotions, his passions, all were exaggerated and monstrous. He talked, or rather roared, with such energy that others could but sit and listen, cowed with the mighty stream of words. His eyes blazed at you and held you at his mercy. He was a terrible and wonderful man. I thank God that he is dead!

'He came again and again. Yet I was aware that Gennaro was no more happy than I was in his presence. My poor husband would sit pale and listless, listening to the endless raving upon politics and upon social questions which made up our visitor's conversation. Gennaro said nothing, but I who knew him so well could read in his face some emotion which I had never seen there before. At first I thought that it was dislike. And then, gradually, I understood that it was more than dislike. It was fear—a deep, secret, shrinking fear. That night—the night that I read his terror—I put my arms round him and I implored him by his love for me and by all that he held dear to hold nothing from me, and to tell me why this huge man overshadowed him so.

'He told me, and my own heart grew cold as ice as I listened. My poor Gennaro, in his wild and fiery days, when all the world seemed against him and his mind was driven half mad by the injustices of life, had joined a Neapolitan society, the Red Circle, which was allied to the old Carbonari.* The oaths and secrets of this brotherhood were frightful; but once within its rule no escape was possible. When we had fled to America Gennaro thought that he had cast it all off for ever. What was his horror one evening to meet in the streets the very man who had initiated him in Naples, the giant Gorgiano, a man who had earned the name of "Death" in the South of Italy, for he was red to the elbow in murder! He had come to New York to avoid the Italian police, and he had already planted a branch of this dreadful society in his new home. All this Gennaro told me, and showed me a summons which he had received that very day, a Red Circle drawn upon the head of it, telling him that a lodge* would be held upon a certain date, and that his presence at it was required and ordered.

'That was bad enough, but worse was to come. I had noticed for some time that when Gorgiano came to us, as he constantly did, in the evening, he spoke much to me; and even when his words were to my husband, those terrible, glaring, wild-beast eyes of his were always turned upon me. One night his secret came out. I had awakened what he called "love" within him—the love of a brute—a savage. Gennaro had not yet returned when he came. He pushed his way in, seized me in his mighty arms, hugged me in his bear's embrace, covered me with kisses, and implored me to come away with him. I was struggling and screaming when Gennaro entered and attacked him. He struck Gennaro senseless and fled from the house which he was never more to enter. It was a deadly enemy that we made that night.

'A few days later came the meeting. Gennaro returned from it with a face which told me that something dreadful had occured. It was worse than we could have imagined possible. The funds of the society were raised by blackmailing rich Italians and threatening them with violence should they refuse the money. It seems that Castalotte, our dear friend and benefactor, had been approached. He had refused to yield to threats, and he had handed the notices to the police. It was resolved now that such an example should be made of him as would prevent any other victim from rebelling. At the meeting it was arranged that he and his house should be blown up with dynamite. There was a drawing of lots as to who should carry out the deed. Gennaro saw our enemy's cruel face smiling at him as he dipped his hand in the bag. No doubt it had been prearranged in some fashion, for it was the fatal disc with the Red Circle upon it, the mandate for murder, which lay upon his palm. He was to kill his best friend, or he was to expose himself and me to the vengeance of his comrades. It was part of their fiendish system to punish those whom they feared or hated by injuring not only their own persons, but those whom they loved, and it was the knowledge of this which hung as a terror over my poor Gennaro's head and drove him nearly crazy with apprehension.

'All that night we sat together, our arms round each other, each strengthening each for the troubles that lay before us. The very next evening had been fixed for the attempt. By midday my husband and I were on our way to London, but not before he had given our benefactor full warning of his danger, and had also left such information for the police as would safeguard his life for the future.

'The rest, gentlemen, you know for yourselves. We were sure that our enemies would be behind us like our own shadows. Gorgiano had his private reasons for vengeance, but in any case we knew how ruthless, cunning, and untiring he could be. Both Italy and America are full of stories of his dreadful powers. If ever they were exerted it would be now. My darling made use of the few clear days which our start had given us in arranging for a refuge for me in such a fashion that no possible danger could reach me. For his own part, he wished to be free that he might communicate both with the American and with the Italian police. I do not myself know where he lived, or how. All that I learned was through the columns of a newspaper. But once, as I looked through my window, I saw two Italians watching the house, and I understood that in some way Gorgiano had found out our retreat. Finally Gennaro told me, through the paper, that he would signal to me from a certain window, but when the signals came they were nothing but warnings, which were suddenly interrupted. It is very clear to me now that he knew Gorgiano to be close upon him, and that, thank God! he was ready for him when he came. And now, gentlemen, I would ask you whether we have anything to fear from the Law, or whether any judge upon earth would condemn my Gennaro for what he has done?'

'Well, Mr Gregson,' said the American, looking across at the official, 'I don't know what your British point of view may be, but I guess that in New York this lady's husband will receive a pretty general vote of thanks.'

'She will have to come with me and see the Chief,' Gregson answered. 'If what she says is corroborated, I do not think she or her husband has much to fear. But what I can't make head or tail of, Mr Holmes, is how on earth *you* got yourself mixed up in the matter.'

'Education, Gregson, education. Still seeking knowledge at the old university.* Well, Watson, you have one more specimen of the tragic and grotesque to add to your collection. By the way, it is not eight o'clock, and a Wagner night at Covent Garden!* If we hurry, we might be in time for the second act.'

The Disappearance of Lady Frances Carfax

'BUT why Turkish?' asked Mr Sherlock Holmes, gazing fixedly at my boots. I was reclining in a cane-backed chair at the moment, and my protruded feet had attracted his ever-active attention.

'English,' I answered, in some surprise. 'I got them at Latimer's, in Oxford Street.'*

Holmes smiled with an expression of weary patience.

'The bath!' he said; 'the bath! Why the relaxing and expensive Turkish rather than the invigorating home-made article?'

'Because for the last few days I have been feeling rheumatic and old. A Turkish bath is what we call an alterative in medicine—a fresh starting-point, a cleanser of the system.

'By the way, Holmes,' I added, 'I have no doubt the connection between my boots and a Turkish bath is a perfectly self-evident one to a logical mind, and yet I should be obliged to you if you would indicate it.'

'The train of reasoning is not very obscure, Watson,' said Holmes, with a mischievous twinkle. 'It belongs to the same elementary class of deduction which I should illustrate if I were to ask you who shared your cab in your drive this morning.'

'I don't admit that a fresh illustration is an explanation,' said I, with some asperity.

'Bravo, Watson! A very dignified and logical remonstrance. Let me see, what were the points? Take the last one first—the cab. You observe that you have some splashes on the left sleeve and shoulder of your coat. Had you sat in the centre of a hansom you would probably have had no splashes, and if you had they would certainly have been symmetrical. Therefore it is clear that you sat at the side. Therefore it is equally clear that you had a companion.'*

'That is very evident.'

'Absurdly commonplace, is it not?'

'But the boots and the bath?'

'Equally childish. You are in the habit of doing up your boots in a certain way. I see them on this occasion fastened with an elaborate double bow, which is not your usual method of tying them. You have, therefore, had them off. Who has tied them? A bootmaker—or the boy at the bath. It is unlikely that it is the bootmaker, since your boots are nearly new. Well, what remains? The bath. Absurd, is it not? But, for all that, the Turkish bath has served a purpose.'

'What is that?'

'You say that you have had it because you need a change. Let me suggest that you take one. How would Lausanne do, my dear Watson—first-class tickets and all expenses paid on a princely scale?'

'Splendid! But why?'

Holmes leaned back in his armchair and took his notebook from his pocket.

'One of the most dangerous classes in the world,' said he, 'is the drifting and friendless woman. She is the most harmless, and often the most useful of mortals, but she is the inevitable inciter of crime in others. She is helpless. She is migratory. She has sufficient means to take her from country to country and from hotel to hotel. She is lost, as often as not, in a maze of obscure *pensions* and boarding-houses. She is a stray chicken in a world of foxes. When she is gobbled up she is hardly missed. I much fear that some evil has come to the Lady Frances Carfax.'*

I was relieved at this sudden descent from the general to the particular. Holmes consulted his notes.

'Lady Frances,' he continued, 'is the sole survivor of the direct family of the late Earl of Rufton. The estates went, as you may remember, in the male line. She was left with limited means, but with some very remarkable old Spanish jewellery of silver and curiously-cut diamonds to which she was fondly attached—too attached, for she refused to leave them with her banker and always carried them* about with her. A rather pathetic figure, the Lady Frances, a beautiful woman, still in fresh middle age, and yet, by a strange chance, the last derelict of what only twenty years ago was a goodly fleet.'

'What has happened to her, then?'

'Ah, what has happened to the Lady Frances? Is she alive or dead? There is our problem. She is a lady of precise habits, and for four years it has been her invariable custom to write every second week to Miss Dobney, her old governess, who has long retired, and lives in Camberwell. It is this Miss Dobney who consulted me. Nearly five weeks have passed without a word. The last letter was from the Hôtel National at Lausanne.* Lady Frances seems to have left there and given no address. The family* are anxious, and, as they are exceedingly wealthy, no sum will be spared if we can clear the matter up.'

'Is Miss Dobney the only source of information? Surely she had other correspondents?'

'There is one correspondent who is a sure draw, Watson. That is the bank. Single ladies must live, and their passbooks are compressed diaries. She banks at Silvester's. I have glanced over her account. The last cheque but one paid her bill at Lausanne, but it was a large one and probably left her with cash in hand. Only one cheque has been drawn since.'

'To whom, and where?'

'To Miss Marie Devine. There is nothing to show where the cheque was drawn. It was cashed at the Crédit Lyonnais at Montpellier* less than three weeks ago. The sum was fifty pounds.'

'And who is Miss Marie Devine?'

'That also I have been able to discover. Miss Marie Devine was the maid of Lady Frances Carfax. Why she should have paid her this cheque we have not yet determined. I have no doubt, however, that your researches will soon clear the matter up.'

'*My* researches!'

'Hence the health-giving expedition to Lausanne. You know that I cannot possibly leave London while old Abrahams is in such mortal terror of his life. Besides, on general principles it is best that I should not leave the country. Scotland Yard feels lonely without me, and it causes an unhealthy excitement among the criminal classes. Go, then, my dear Watson, and if my humble counsel can ever be valued at so extravagant a rate as twopence a word,* it waits your disposal night and day at the end of the Continental wire.'

Two days later found me at the National Hotel at Lausanne, where I received every courtesy at the hands of M. Moser, the well-known manager. Lady Frances, as he informed me, had stayed there for several weeks. She had been much liked by all who met her. Her age was not more than forty. She was still handsome, and bore every sign of having in her youth been a very lovely woman. M. Moser knew nothing of any valuable jewellery, but it had been remarked by the servants that the heavy trunk in the lady's bedroom was always scrupulously locked. Marie Devine, the maid, was as popular as her mistress. She was actually engaged to one of the head waiters in the hotel, and there was no difficulty in getting her address. It was 11, Rue de Trajan, Montpellier. All this I jotted down, and felt that Holmes himself could not have been more adroit in collecting his facts.

  Only one corner still remained in the shadow. No light which I possessed could clear up the cause for the lady's sudden departure. She was very happy at Lausanne. There was every reason to believe that she intended to remain for the season in her luxurious rooms overlooking the lake. And yet she had left at a single day's notice, which involved her in the useless payment of a week's rent. Only Jules Vibart, the lover of the maid, had any suggestion to offer. He connected the sudden departure with the visit to the hotel a day or two before of a tall, dark, bearded man. '*Un sauvage—un véritable sauvage!*'* cried Jules Vibart. The man had rooms somewhere in the town. He had been seen talking earnestly to madame on the promenade by the lake. Then he had called. She had refused to see him. He was English, but of his name there was no record. Madame had left the place immediately afterwards. Jules Vibart, and, what was of more importance, Jules Vibart's sweetheart, thought that this call and this departure were cause and effect. Only one thing Jules could not discuss. That was the reason why Marie had left her mistress. Of that he could or would say nothing. If I wished to know, I must go to Montpellier and ask her.

So ended the first chapter of my inquiry. The second was devoted to the place which Lady Frances Carfax had sought when she left Lausanne. Concerning this there had been some secrecy, which confirmed the idea that she had gone with the intention of throwing someone off her track. Otherwise why should not her luggage have been openly labelled for Baden? Both she and it reached the Rhenish spa by some circuitous route. Thus much I gathered from the manager of Cook's local office. So to Baden I went, after dispatching to Holmes an account of all my proceedings, and receiving in reply a telegram of half-humorous commendation.

At Baden the track was not difficult to follow. Lady Frances had stayed at the Englischer Hof* for a fortnight. Whilst there she had made the acquaintance of a Dr Shlessinger and his wife, a missionary from South America. Like most lonely ladies, Lady Frances found her comfort and occupation in religion. Dr Shlessinger's remarkable personality, his whole-hearted devotion, and the fact that he was recovering from a disease contracted in the exercise of his apostolic duties, affected her deeply. She had helped Mrs Shlessinger in the nursing of the convalescent saint. He spent his day, as the manager described it to me, upon a lounge-chair on the veranda, with an attendant lady upon either side of him. He was preparing a map of the Holy Land, with special reference to the kingdom of the Midianites,* upon which he was writing a monograph. Finally, having improved much in health, he and his wife had returned to London, and Lady Frances had started thither in their company. This was just three weeks before, and the manager had heard nothing since. As to the maid, Marie, she had gone off some days beforehand in floods of tears, after informing the other maids that she was leaving service for ever. Dr Shlessinger had paid the bill of the whole party before his departure.

'By the way,' said the landlord, in conclusion, 'you are not the only friend of Lady Frances Carfax who is inquiring after her just now. Only a week or so ago we had a man here upon the same errand.'

'Did he give a name?' I asked.

'None; but he was an Englishman, though of an unusual type.'

'A savage?' said I, linking my facts after the fashion of my illustrious friend.

'Exactly. That describes him very well. He is a bulky, bearded, sunburned fellow, who looks as if he would be more at home in a farmers' inn than in a fashionable hotel. A hard, fierce man, I should think, and one whom I should be sorry to offend.'

Already the mystery began to define itself, as figures grow clearer with the lifting of a fog. Here was this good and pious lady pursued from place to place by a sinister and unrelenting figure. She feared him, or she would not have fled from Lausanne. He had still followed. Sooner or later he would overtake her. Had he already overtaken her? Was *that* the secret of her continued silence? Could the good people who were her companions not screen her from his violence or his blackmail? What horrible purpose, what deep design, lay behind this long pursuit? There was the problem which I had to solve.

To Holmes I wrote showing how rapidly and surely I had got down to the roots of the matter. In reply I had a telegram asking for a description of Dr Shlessinger's left ear. Holmes's ideas of humour are strange and occasionally offensive, so I took no notice of his ill-timed jest—indeed, I had already reached Montpellier in my pursuit of the maid, Marie, before his message came.

I had no difficulty in finding the ex-servant and in learning all that she could tell me. She was a devoted creature, who had only left her mistress because she was sure that she was in good hands, and because her own approaching marriage made a separation inevitable in any case. Her mistress had, as she confessed with distress, shown some irritability of temper towards her during their stay in Baden, and had even questioned her once as if she had suspicions of her honesty, and this had made the parting easier than it would otherwise have been. Lady Frances had given her fifty pounds as a wedding-present. Like me, Marie viewed with deep distrust the stranger who had driven her mistress from Lausanne. With her own eyes she had seen him seize the lady's wrist with great violence on the public promenade by the lake. He was a fierce and terrible man. She believed that it was out of dread of him that Lady Frances had accepted the escort of the Shlessingers to London. She had never spoken to Marie about it, but many little signs had convinced the maid that her mistress lived in a state of continual nervous apprehension. So far she had got in her narrative, when suddenly she sprang from her chair and her face was convulsed with surprise and fear. 'See!' she cried. 'The miscreant follows still! There is the very man of whom I speak.'

Through the open sitting-room window I saw a huge, swarthy man with a bristling black beard walking slowly down the centre of the street and staring eagerly at the numbers of the houses. It was clear that, like myself, he was on the track of the maid. Acting upon the impulse of the moment, I rushed out and accosted him.

'You are an Englishman,' I said.

'What if I am?' he asked, with a most villainous scowl.

'May I ask what your name is?'

'No, you may not,' said he, with decision.

The situation was awkward, but the most direct way is often the best.

'Where is the Lady Frances Carfax?' I asked.

He stared at me in amazement.

'What have you done with her? Why have you pursued her? I insist upon an answer!' said I.

The fellow gave a bellow of anger and sprang upon me like a tiger. I have held my own in many a struggle, but the man had a grip of iron and the fury of a fiend. His hand was on my throat and my senses were nearly gone before an unshaven French *ouvrier*, in a blue blouse, darted out from a *cabaret* opposite, with a cudgel in his hand, and struck my assailant a sharp crack over the forearm, which made him leave go his hold. He stood for an instant fuming with rage and uncertain whether he should not renew his attack. Then, with a snarl of anger, he left me and entered the cottage from which I had just come. I turned to thank my preserver, who stood beside me in the roadway.

'Well, Watson,' said he, 'a very pretty hash* you have made of it! I rather think you had better come back with me to London by the night express.'

An hour afterwards Sherlock Holmes, in his usual garb and style, was seated in my private room at the hotel. His explanation of his sudden and opportune appearance was simplicity itself, for, finding that he could get away from London, he determined to head me off at the next obvious point of my travels. In the disguise of a working-man he had sat in the *cabaret* waiting for my appearance.

'And a singularly consistent investigation you have made, my dear Watson,' said he. 'I cannot at the moment recall any possible blunder which you have omitted. The total effect of your proceedings has been to give the alarm* everywhere and yet to discover nothing.'

'Perhaps you would have done no better,' I answered, bitterly.

'There is no "perhaps" about it. I *have* done better. Here is the Hon. Philip Green, who is a fellow-lodger with you in this hotel, and we may find in him the starting-point for a more successful investigation.'

A card had come up on a salver, and it was followed by the same bearded ruffian who had attacked me in the street. He started when he saw me.

'What is this, Mr Holmes?' he asked. 'I had your note and I have come. But what has this man to do with the matter?'

'This is my old friend and associate, Dr Watson, who is helping us in this affair.'

The stranger held out a huge, sunburned hand, with a few words of apology.

'I hope I didn't harm you. When you accused me of hurting her I lost my grip of myself. Indeed, I'm not responsible in these days. My nerves are like live wires. But this situation is beyond me. What I want to know, in the first place, Mr Holmes, is, how in the world you came to hear of my existence at all.'

'I am in touch with Miss Dobney, Lady Frances's governess.'

'Old Susan Dobney with the mob cap!* I remember her well.'

'And she remembers you. It was in the days before—before you found it better to go to South Africa.'*

'Ah, I see you know my whole story. I need hide nothing from you. I swear to you, Mr Holmes, that there never was in this world a man who loved a woman with a more whole-hearted love than I had for Frances. I was a wild youngster, I know—not worse than others of my class.* But her mind was pure as snow.* She could not bear a shadow of coarseness. So, when she came to hear of things that I had done, she would have no more to say to me. And yet she loved me—that is the wonder of it!—loved me well enough to remain single all her sainted days just for my sake alone. When the years had passed and I had made my money at Barberton* I thought perhaps I could seek her out and soften her. I had heard that she was still unmarried. I found her at Lausanne, and tried all I knew. She weakened, I think, but her will was strong, and when next I called she had left the town. I traced her to Baden, and then after a time heard that her maid was here. I'm a rough fellow, fresh from a rough life, and when Dr Watson spoke to me as he did I lost hold of myself for a moment. But for God's sake tell me what has become of the Lady Frances.'

'That is for us to find out,' said Sherlock Holmes, with peculiar gravity. 'What is your London address, Mr Green?'

'The Langham Hotel* will find me.'

'Then may I recommend that you return there and be on hand in case I should want you? I have no desire to encourage false hopes, but you may rest assured that all that can be done will be done for the safety of Lady Frances. I can say no more for the instant. I will leave you this card so that you may be able to keep in touch with us. Now, Watson, if you will pack your bag I will cable to Mrs Hudson to make one of her best efforts for two hungry travellers at seven-thirty tomorrow.'

A telegram was awaiting us when we reached our Baker Street rooms, which Holmes read with an exclamation of interest and threw across to me. 'Jagged or torn,' was the message, and the place of origin Baden.

'What is this?' I asked.

'It is everything,' Holmes answered. 'You may remember my seemingly irrelevant question as to this clerical gentleman's left ear. You did not answer it.'

'I had left Baden, and could not inquire.'

'Exactly. For this reason I sent a duplicate to the manager of the Englischer Hof, whose answer lies here.'

'What does it show?'

'It shows, my dear Watson, that we are dealing with an exceptionally astute and dangerous man. The Rev. Dr Shlessinger, missionary from South America, is none other than Holy Peters, one of the most unscrupulous rascals that Australia has ever evolved—and for a young country it has turned out some very finished types. His particular speciality is the beguiling of lonely ladies by playing upon their religious feelings, and his so-called wife, an Englishwoman named Fraser, is a worthy helpmate. The nature of his tactics suggested his identity to me, and this physical peculiarity—he was badly bitten in a saloon-fight at Adelaide* in '89—confirmed my suspicion. This poor lady is in the hands of a most infernal couple, who will stick at nothing, Watson. That she is already dead is a very likely supposition. If not, she is undoubtedly in some sort of confinement, and unable to write to Miss Dobney or her other friends. It is always possible that she never reached London, or that she has passed through it, but the former is improbable, as, with their system of registration,* it is not easy for foreigners to play tricks with the Continental police; and the latter is also unlikely, as these rogues could not hope to find any other place where it would be as easy to keep a person under restraint. All my instincts tell me that she is in London, but, as we have at present no possible means of telling where, we can only take the obvious steps, eat our dinner, and possess our souls in patience.* Later in the evening I will stroll down and have a word with friend Lestrade at Scotland Yard.'

But neither the official police nor Holmes's own small, but very efficient, organization* sufficed to clear away the mystery. Amid the crowded millions of London the three persons we sought were as completely obliterated as if they had never lived. Advertisements were tried, and failed. Clues were followed, and led to nothing. Every criminal resort which Shlessinger might frequent was drawn in vain. His old associates were watched, but they kept clear of him. And then suddenly, after a week of helpless suspense, there came a flash of light. A silver-and-brilliant* pendant of old Spanish design had been pawned at Bevington's,* in Westminster Road. The pawner was a large, clean-shaven man of clerical appearance. His name and address were demonstrably false. The ear had escaped notice, but the description was surely that of Shlessinger.

Three times had our bearded friend from the Langham called for news—the third time within an hour of this fresh development. His clothes were getting looser on his great body. He seemed to be wilting away in his anxiety. 'If you will only give me something to do!' was his constant wail. At last Holmes could oblige him.

'He has begun to pawn the jewels. We should get him now.'

'But does this mean that any harm has befallen the Lady Frances?'

Holmes shook his head very gravely.

'Supposing that they have held her prisoner up to now, it is clear that they cannot let her loose without their own destruction. We must prepare for the worst.'

'What can I do?'

'These people do not know you by sight?'

'No.'

'It is possible that he will go to some other pawnbroker in the future. In that case, we must begin again. On the other hand, he has had a fair price and no questions asked, so if he is in need of ready money he will probably come back to Bevington's. I will give you a note to them, and they will let you wait in the shop. If the fellow comes you will follow him home. But no indiscretion, and, above all, no violence. I put you on your honour that you will take no step without my knowledge and consent.'*

For two days the Hon. Philip Green (he was, I may mention, the son of the famous admiral of that name who commanded the Sea of Azof fleet in the Crimean War)* brought us no news. On the evening of the third he rushed into our sitting-room, pale, trembling, with every muscle of his powerful frame quivering with excitement.

'We have him! We have him!' he cried.

He was incoherent in his agitation. Holmes soothed him with a few words, and thrust him into an arm-chair.

'Come, now, give us the order of events,' said he.

'She came only an hour ago. It was the wife, this time, but the pendant she brought was the fellow of the other. She is a tall, pale woman, with ferret eyes.'*

'That is the lady,' said Holmes.

'She left the office and I followed her. She walked up the Kennington Road, and I kept behind her. Presently she went into a shop. Mr Holmes, it was an undertaker's.'

My companion started. 'Well?' he asked, in that vibrant voice which told of the fiery soul behind the cold, grey face.

'She was talking to the woman behind the counter. I entered as well. "It is late," I heard her say, or words to that effect. The woman was excusing herself. "It should be there before now," she answered. "It took longer, being out of the ordinary." They both stopped and looked at me, so I asked some question and then left the shop.'

'You did excellently well. What happened next?'

'The woman came out, but I had hid myself in a doorway. Her suspicions had been aroused, I think, for she looked round her. Then she called a cab and got in. I was lucky enough to get another and so to follow her. She got down at last at No. 36, Poultney Square, Brixton. I drove past, left my cab at the corner of the square, and watched the house.'

'Did you see anyone?'

'The windows were all in darkness save one on the lower floor. The blind was down, and I could not see in. I was standing there, wondering what I should do next, when a covered van drove up with two men in it. They descended, took something out of the van, and carried it up the steps to the hall door. Mr Holmes, it was a coffin.'

'Ah!'

'For an instant I was on the point of rushing in. The door had been opened to admit the men and their burden. It was the woman who had opened it. But as I stood there she caught a glimpse of me, and I think that she recognized me. I saw her start, and she hastily closed the door. I remembered my promise to you, and here I am.'

'You have done excellent work,' said Holmes scribbling a few words upon a half-sheet of paper. 'We can do nothing legal without a warrant, and you can serve the cause best by taking this note down to the authorities and getting one. There may be some difficulty, but I should think that the sale of the jewellery should be sufficient. Lestrade will see to all details.'

'But they may murder her in the meanwhile. What could the coffin mean, and for whom could it be but for her?'

'We will do all that can be done, Mr Green. Not a moment will be lost. Leave it in our hands. Now, Watson,' he added, as our client hurried away, 'he will set the regular forces on the move. We are, as usual, the irregulars, and we must take our own line of action. The situation strikes me as so desperate that the most extreme measures are justified. Not a moment is to be lost in getting to Poultney Square.

'Let us try to reconstruct the situation,' said he, as we drove swiftly past the Houses of Parliament and over Westminster Bridge. 'These villains have coaxed this unhappy lady to London, after first alienating her from her faithful maid. If she has written any letters they have been intercepted. Through some confederate they have engaged a furnished house. Once inside it, they have made her a prisoner, and they have become possessed of the valuable jewellery which has been their object from the first. Already they have begun to sell part of it, which seems safe enough to them, since they have no reason to think that anyone is interested in the lady's fate. When she is released she will, of course, denounce them. Therefore, she must not be released. But they cannot keep her under lock and key for ever. So murder is their only solution.'

'That seems very clear.'

'Now we will take another line of reasoning. When you follow two separate chains of thought, Watson, you will find some point of intersection which should approximate to the truth. We will start now, not from the lady, but from the coffin, and argue backwards. That incident proves, I fear, beyond all doubt that the lady is dead. It points also to an orthodox burial with proper accompaniment of medical certificate and official sanction. Had the lady been obviously murdered, they would have buried her in a hole in the back garden. But here all is open and regular. What does that mean? Surely that they have done her to death in some way which has deceived the doctor, and simulated a natural end—poisoning, perhaps. And yet how strange that they should ever let a doctor approach her unless he were a confederate, which is hardly a credible proposition.'

'Could they have forged a medical certificate?'

'Dangerous, Watson, very dangerous. No, I hardly see them doing that. Pull up, cabby! This is evidently the undertaker's, for we have just passed the pawnbroker's. Would you go in, Watson? Your appearance inspires confidence.

Ask what hour the Poultney Square funeral takes place tomorrow.'

The woman in the shop answered me without hesitation that it was to be at eight o'clock in the morning.

'You see, Watson, no mystery; everything above-board! In some way the legal forms have undoubtedly been complied with, and they think that they have little to fear. Well, there's nothing for it now but a direct frontal attack. Are you armed?'

'My stick!'

'Well, well, we shall be strong enough. "Thrice is he armed who hath his quarrel just."* We simply can't afford to wait for the police, or to keep within the four corners of the law. You can drive off, cabby. Now, Watson, we'll just take our luck together, as we have occasionally done in the past.'

He had rung loudly at the door of a great dark house in the centre of Poultney Square. It was opened immediately, and the figure of a tall woman was outlined against the dim-lit hall.

'Well, what do you want?' she asked, sharply, peering at us through the darkness.

'I want to speak to Dr Shlessinger,' said Holmes.

'There is no such person here,' she answered, and tried to close the door, but Holmes had jammed it with his foot.

'Well, I want to see the man who lives here, whatever he may call himself,' said Holmes firmly.

She hesitated. Then she threw open the door. 'Well, come in!' said she. 'My husband is not afraid to face any man in the world.' She closed the door behind us, and showed us into a sitting-room on the right side of the hall, turning up the gas as she left us. 'Mr Peters will be with you in an instant,' she said.

Her words were literally true, for we had hardly time to look round the dusty and moth-eaten apartment in which we found ourselves before the door opened and a big, clean-shaven, bald-headed man stepped lightly into the room. He had a large red face, with pendulous cheeks, and a general air of superficial benevolence which was marred by a cruel, vicious mouth.

'There is surely some mistake here, gentlemen,' he said, in an unctuous, make-everything-easy voice. 'I fancy that you have been misdirected. Possibly if you tried farther down the street—'

'That will do; we have no time to waste,' said my companion, firmly. 'You are Henry Peters, of Adelaide, late the Rev. Dr Shlessinger, of Baden and South America. I am as sure of that as that my own name is Sherlock Holmes.'

Peters, as I will now call him, started and stared hard at his formidable pursuer. 'I guess your name does not frighten me, Mr Holmes,' said he, coolly. 'When a man's conscience is easy, you can't rattle him.* What is your business in my house?'

'I want to know what you have done with the Lady Frances Carfax, whom you brought away with you from Baden.'

'I'd be very glad if you could tell me where that lady may be,' Peters answered, coolly. 'I've a bill against her for nearly a hundred pounds, and nothing to show for it but a couple of trumpery pendants that the dealer would hardly look at. She attached herself to Mrs Peters and me at Baden (it is a fact that I was using another name at the time), and she stuck on to us until we came to London. I paid her bill and her ticket. Once in London, she gave us the slip, and, as I say, left these out-of-date jewels to pay her bills. You find her, Mr Holmes, and I'm your debtor.'

'I *mean* to find her,' said Sherlock Holmes. 'I'm going through this house till I do find her.'

'Where is your warrant?'

Holmes half drew a revolver from his pocket. 'This will have to serve till a better one comes.'

'Why, you are a common burglar.'

'So you might describe me,' said Holmes, cheerfully. 'My companion is also a dangerous ruffian. And together we are going through your house.'

Our opponent opened the door.

'Fetch a policeman, Annie!' said he. There was a whisk of feminine skirts down the passage, and the hall door was opened and shut.

'Our time is limited, Watson,' said Holmes. 'If you try to stop us, Peters, you will most certainly get hurt. Where is that coffin which was brought into your house?'

'What do you want with the coffin? It is in use. There is a body in it.'

'I must see that body.'

'Never with my consent.'

'Then without it.' With a quick movement Holmes pushed the fellow to one side and passed into the hall. A door half open stood immediately before us. We entered. It was the dining-room. On the table, under a half-lit chandelier, the coffin was lying. Holmes turned up the gas and raised the lid. Deep down in the recesses of the coffin lay an emaciated figure. The glare from the lights above beat down upon an aged and withered face. By no possible process of cruelty, starvation, or disease could this worn-out wreck be the still beautiful Lady Frances. Holmes's face showed his amazement, and also his relief.

'Thank God!' he muttered. 'It's someone else.'

'Ah, you've blundered badly for once, Mr Sherlock Holmes,' said Peters, who had followed us into the room.

'Who is this dead woman?'

'Well, if you really must know, she is an old nurse of my wife's, Rose Spender her name, whom we found in the Brixton Workhouse Infirmary.* We brought her round here, called in Dr Horsom, of 13, Firbank Villas—mind you take the address, Mr Holmes—and had her carefully tended, as Christian folk should. On the third day she died—certificate says senile decay—but that's only the doctor's opinion, and, of course, you know better. We ordered her funeral to be carried out by Stimson and Co., of the Kennington Road, who will bury her at eight o'clock tomorrow morning. Can you pick any hole in that, Mr Holmes? You've made a silly blunder, and you may as well own up to it. I'd give something for a photograph of your gaping, staring face when you pulled aside that lid expecting to see the Lady Frances Carfax, and only found a poor old woman of ninety.'

Holmes's expression was as impassive as ever under the jeers of his antagonist, but his clenched hands betrayed his acute annoyance.

'I am going through your house,' said he.

'Are you, though!' cried Peters, as a woman's voice and heavy steps sounded in the passage. 'We'll soon see about that. This way, officers, if you please. These men have forced their way into my house, and I cannot get rid of them. Help me to put them out.'

A sergeant and a constable stood in the doorway. Holmes drew his card from his case.

'This is my name and address. This is my friend, Dr Watson.'

'Bless you, sir, we know you very well,' said the sergeant, 'but you can't stay here without a warrant.'

'Of course not. I quite understand that.'

'Arrest him!' cried Peters.

'We know where to lay our hands on this gentleman if he is wanted,' said the sergeant, majestically, 'but you'll have to go, Mr Holmes.'

'Yes, Watson, we shall have to go.'

A minute later we were in the street once more. Holmes was as cool as ever, but I was hot with anger and humiliation. The sergeant had followed us.

'Sorry, Mr Holmes, but that's the law.'

'Exactly, sergeant; you could not do otherwise.'

'I expect there was good reason for your presence there. If there is anything I can do—'

'It's a missing lady, sergeant, and we think she is in that house. I expect a warrant presently.'

'Then I'll keep my eye on the parties, Mr Holmes. If anything comes along, I will surely let you know.'

It was only nine o'clock, and we were off full cry upon the trail at once. First we drove to Brixton Workhouse Infirmary, where we found that it was indeed the truth that a charitable couple had called some days before, that they had claimed an imbecile old woman as a former servant, and that they had obtained permission to take her away with them. No surprise was expressed at the news that she had since died.

The doctor was our next goal. He had been called in, had found the woman dying of pure senility, had actually seen her pass away, and had signed the certificate in due form. 'I assure you that everything was perfectly normal and there was no room for foul play in the matter,' said he. Nothing in the house had struck him as suspicious, save that for people of their class it was remarkable that they should have no servant.* So far and no farther went the doctor.

Finally, we found our way to Scotland Yard. There had been difficulties of procedure in regard to the warrant. Some delay was inevitable. The magistrate's signature might not be obtained until next morning. If Holmes would call about nine he could go down with Lestrade and see it acted upon. So ended the day, save that near midnight our friend, the sergeant, called to say that he had seen flickering lights here and there in the windows of the great dark house, but that no one had left it and none had entered. We could but pray for patience, and wait for the morrow.

Sherlock Holmes was too irritable for conversation and too restless for sleep. I left him smoking hard, with his heavy, dark brows knotted together, and his long, nervous fingers tapping upon the arms of his chair, as he turned over in his mind every possible solution of the mystery. Several times in the course of the night I heard him prowling about the house. Finally, just after I had been called in the morning, he rushed into my room. He was in his dressing-gown, but his pale, hollow-eyed face told me that his night had been a sleepless one.

'What time was the funeral? Eight, was it not?' he asked, eagerly. 'Well, it is seven-twenty now. Good heavens, Watson, what has become of any brains that God has given me? Quick, man, quick! It's life or death—a hundred chances on death to one on life. I'll never forgive myself, never, if we are too late!'

Five minutes had not passed before we were flying in a hansom down Baker Street. But even so it was twenty-five to eight as we passed Big Ben, and eight struck as we tore down the Brixton Road. But others were late as well as we. Ten minutes after the hour the hearse was still standing at the door of the house, and even as our foaming horse came to a halt the coffin, supported by three men, appeared on the threshold. Holmes darted forward and barred their way.

'Take it back!' he cried, laying his hand on the breast of the foremost. 'Take it back this instant!'

'What the devil do you mean? Once again I ask you, where is your warrant?' shouted the furious Peters, his big red face glaring over the farther end of the coffin.

'The warrant is on its way. This coffin shall remain in the house until it comes.'

The authority in Holmes's voice* had its effect upon the bearers. Peters had suddenly vanished into the house, and they obeyed these new orders. 'Quick, Watson, quick! Here is a screw-driver!' he shouted as the coffin was replaced upon the table. 'Here's one for you, my man! A sovereign* if the lid comes off in a minute! Ask no questions—work away! That's good! Another! And another! Now pull all together! It's giving! It's giving! Ah, that does it at last!'

With a united effort we tore off the coffin-lid. As we did so there came from the inside a stupefying and overpowering smell of chloroform. A body lay within, its head all wreathed in cotton-wool, which had been soaked in the narcotic. Holmes plucked it off and disclosed the statuesque face of a handsome and spiritual woman of middle age. In an instant he had passed his arm round the figure and raised her to a sitting position.

'Is she gone, Watson? Is there a spark left? Surely we are not too late!'

For half an hour it seemed that we were.* What with actual suffocation, and what with the poisonous fumes of the chloroform, the Lady Frances seemed to have passed the last point of recall. And then, at last, with artificial respiration, with injected ether, with every device that science could suggest, some flutter of life, some quiver of the eyelids, some dimming of a mirror, spoke of the slowly returning life. A cab had driven up, and Holmes, parting the blind, looked out at it. 'Here is Lestrade with his warrant,' said he. 'He will find that his birds have flown. And here,' he added, as a heavy step hurried along the passage, 'is someone who has a better right to nurse this lady than we have. Good morning, Mr Green; I think that the sooner we can move the Lady Frances the better. Meanwhile, the funeral may proceed, and the poor old woman who still lies in that coffin may go to her last resting-place alone.'

'Should you care to add the case to your annals, my dear Watson,' said Holmes that evening, 'it can only be as an example of that temporary eclipse to which even the best-balanced mind may be exposed. Such slips are common to all mortals, and the greatest is he who can recognize and repair them. To this modified credit I may, perhaps, make some claim. My night was haunted by the thought that somewhere a clue, a strange sentence, a curious observation, had come under my notice and had been too easily dismissed. Then, suddenly, in the grey of the morning, the words came back to me. It was the remark of the undertaker's wife, as reported by Philip Green. She had said, "It should be there before now. It took longer, being out of the ordinary." It was the coffin of which she spoke. It had been out of the ordinary. That could only mean that it had been made to some special measurement. But why? Why? Then in an instant I remembered the deep sides, and the little wasted figure at the bottom. Why so large a coffin for so small a body? To leave room for another body. Both would be buried under the one certificate. It had all been so clear, if only my own sight had not been dimmed. At eight the Lady Frances would be buried. Our one chance was to stop the coffin before it left the house.

'It was a desperate chance that we might find her alive, but it *was* a chance, as the result showed. These people had never, to my knowledge, done a murder. They might shrink from actual violence at the last. They could bury her with no sign of how she met her end, and even if she were exhumed there was a chance for them. I hoped that such considerations might prevail with them. You can reconstruct the scene well enough. You saw the horrible den upstairs, where the poor lady had been kept so long. They rushed in and overpowered her with their chloroform, carried her down, poured more into the coffin to insure against her waking, and then screwed down the lid. A clever device, Watson. It is new to me in the annals of crime.* If our ex-missionary friends escape the clutches of Lestrade, I shall expect to hear of some brilliant incidents in their future career.'

The Dying Detective

M RS HUDSON, the landlady of Sherlock Holmes, was a long-suffering woman. Not only was her first-floor flat invaded at all hours by throngs of singular and often undesirable characters, but her remarkable lodger showed an eccentricity and irregularity in his life which must have sorely tried her patience. His incredible untidiness, his addiction to music at strange hours, his occasional revolver practice within doors, his weird and often malodorous scientific experiments, and the atmosphere of violence and danger which hung around him made him the very worst tenant in London. On the other hand his payments were princely.* I have no doubt that the house might have been purchased at the price which Holmes paid for his rooms during the years that I was with him.

The landlady stood in the deepest awe of him, and never dared to interfere with him, however outrageous his proceedings might seem. She was fond of him too, for he had a remarkable gentleness and courtesy in his dealings with women. He disliked and distrusted the sex but he was always a chivalrous opponent. Knowing how genuine was her regard for him I listened earnestly to her story when she came to my rooms in the second year of my married life,* and told me of the sad condition to which my poor friend was reduced.

'He's dying, Dr Watson,' said she. 'For three days he has been sinking and I doubt if he will last the day. He would not let me get a doctor. This morning when I saw his bones sticking out of his face and his great bright eyes looking at me I could stand no more of it. "With your leave or without it, Mr Holmes, I am going for a doctor this very hour," said I. "Let it be Watson then," said he. I wouldn't waste an hour in coming to him, sir, or you may not see him alive.'

I was horrified, for I had heard nothing of his illness. I need not say that I rushed for my coat and my hat. As we drove back I asked for the details.

'There is little I can tell you, sir. He has been working at a case down at Rotherhithe* in an alley near the river and he has brought this illness back with him. He took to his bed on Wednesday afternoon and has never moved since. For these three days neither food nor drink have* passed his lips.'

'Good God! Why did you not call in a doctor?'

'He wouldn't have it, sir. You know how masterful he is. I didn't dare to disobey him. But he's not long for this world as you'll see for yourself the moment that you set eyes on him.'

He was indeed a deplorable spectacle. In the dim light of a foggy November day the sick-room was a gloomy spot, but it was that gaunt wasted face staring at me from the bed which sent a chill to my heart. His eyes had the brightness of fever, there was a hectic flush upon either cheek, and dark crusts clung to his lips. The thin hands upon the coverlet twitched incessantly. His voice was croaking and spasmodic. He lay listlessly as I entered the room but the sight of me brought a gleam of recognition to his eyes.

'Well, Watson, we seem to have fallen upon evil days,' said he in a feeble voice but with something of his old carelessness of manner.

'My dear fellow—' I cried, approaching him.

'Stand back! Stand right back!' said he, with the sharp imperiousness which I had associated only with moments of crisis. 'If you approach me, Watson, I shall order you out of the house.'

'But why?'

'Because it is my desire. Is that not enough?'*

Yes, Mrs Hudson was right. He was more masterful than ever. It was pitiful however to see his exhaustion.

'I only wished to help' I explained.

'Exactly You will help best by doing what you are told.'

'Certainly, Holmes.'

He relaxed the austerity of his manner.

'You are not angry?' he asked, gasping for breath.

Poor devil, how could I be angry when I saw him lying in such a plight before me?

'It's for your own sake, Watson,' he croaked.

'For *my* sake?'

'I know what is the matter with me. It is a Coolie disease from Sumatra*—a thing that the Dutch know more about than we, though they have made little of it up to date. One thing only is certain. It is infallibly deadly and it is horribly contagious.'

He spoke now with a feverish energy, the long hands twitching and jerking as he motioned me away.

'Contagious by touch, Watson—that's it, by touch. Keep your distance and all is well.'

'Good heavens, Holmes, do you suppose that such a consideration weighs with me for an instant? It would not affect me in the case of a stranger. Do you imagine it would prevent me from doing my duty to so old a friend?'*

Again I advanced, but he repulsed me with a look of furious anger.

'If you will stand there I will talk. If you do not you must leave the room.'

I have so deep a respect for the extraordinary qualities of Holmes that I have always deferred to his wishes even when I least understood them. But now all my professional instincts were aroused. Let him be my master elsewhere, I at least was his in a sick-room.

'Holmes,' said I, 'you are not yourself. A sick man is but a child and so I will treat you. Whether you like it or not, I will examine your symptoms and treat you for them.'

He looked at me with venomous eyes.

'If I am to have a doctor whether I will or not, let me at least have something in which* I have confidence,' said he.

'Then you have none in me?'

'In your friendship certainly. But facts are facts, Watson, and after all you are only a general practitioner with very limited experience and mediocre qualifications. It is painful to have to say these things but you leave me no choice.'

I was bitterly hurt.

'Such a remark is unworthy of you, Holmes. It shows me very clearly the state of your own nerves. But if you have no confidence in me I would not intrude my services. Let me bring Sir Jasper Meek or Penrose Fisher or any of the best men in London. But someone you *must* have, and that is final. If you think that I am going to stand here and see you die without either helping you myself or bringing anyone else to help you, then you have mistaken your man.'

'You mean well, Watson!* said the sick man, with something between a sob and a groan. 'Shall I demonstrate your own ignorance? What do you know pray of Tapanuli fever? What do you know of the black Formosa corruption?'*

'I have never heard of either.'*

'There are many problems of disease,* many strange pathological possibilities, in the East, Watson.' He paused after each sentence to collect his failing strength. 'I have learned as* much during some recent researches which have a medico-criminal aspect.* It was in the course of them that I contracted this complaint.* You can do nothing.'

'Possibly not. But I happen to know that Dr Ainstree, the greatest living authority upon tropical disease is now in London. All remonstrance is useless, Holmes. I am going this instant to fetch him.' I turned resolutely to the door.

Never have I had such a shock. In an instant with a tiger-spring the dying man had intercepted me. I heard the sharp snap of a twisted key. The next moment he had staggered back to his bed exhausted and panting after his one tremendous outflame of energy.

'You won't take the key from me by force, Watson. I've got you, my friend. Here you are and here you will stay until I will otherwise. But I'll humour you.' (All this in little gasps with terrible struggles for breath between.) 'You've only my own good at heart. Of course I know that very well. You shall have your way. But give me time to get my strength. Not now, Watson—not now. It's four o'clock. At six you can go.'

'This is insanity, Holmes.'

'Only two hours, Watson, I promise you will go at six. Are you content to wait?'

'I seem to have no choice.'

'None in the world, Watson. Thank you I need no help in arranging the clothes. You will please keep your distance. Now, Watson, there is one other condition that I would make. You will seek help not from the man you mention* but from the one that I choose.'

'By all means.'

'The first three sensible words that you have uttered since you entered this room, Watson.* You will find some books over there. I am somewhat exhausted. I wonder how a battery feels when it pours electricity into a non-conductor. At six, Watson, we resume our conversation.'

But it was destined to be resumed long before that hour and under* circumstances which gave me a shock hardly second to that caused by his spring* to the door. I had stood for some minutes looking at the silent figure in the bed.* His face was almost covered by the clothes and he appeared to be asleep. Then, unable to settle down to reading, I walked slowly round the room, examining the pictures of celebrated criminals with which every wall was adorned.* Finally, in my aimless perambulation, I came to the mantelpiece. A litter of pipes, tobacco-pouches, syringes, penknives, revolver cartridges, and other debris was scattered over it. In the midst of these was a small black and white ivory box with a sliding lid. It was a neat little thing, and I had stretched out my hand to examine it more closely, when—

It was a dreadful cry that he gave—a yell which might have been heard down the street. My skin went cold and my hair bristled at that horrible scream. As I turned I caught a glimpse of a convulsed face and frantic eyes. I stood paralysed, with the little box in my hand.

'Put it down! Down, this instant, Watson, this instant, I say!' His head sank back upon the pillow and he gave a deep sigh of relief as I replaced the box upon the mantelpiece. 'I hate to have my things touched, Watson. You know that I hate it. You fidget me beyond endurance. You a doctor—you are enough to drive a patient into an asylum. Sit down, man, and let me have my rest!'

The incident left a most unpleasant impression upon my mind. The violent and causeless excitement, followed by this brutality of speech, so far removed from his usual suavity, showed me how deep was the disorganization of his mind. Of all ruins that of a noble mind is the most deplorable.* I sat in silent dejection until the stipulated time had passed. He seemed to have been watching the clock, as well as I, for it was hardly six before he began to talk with the same feverish animation as before.

'Now, Watson,' said he. 'Have you any change in your pocket?'

'Yes.'

'Any silver?'

'A good deal.'

'How many half-crowns?'*

'I have five.'

'Ah, too few! too few! How very unfortunate, Watson! However such as they are you can put them in your watch-pocket. And all the rest of your money in your left trowser-pocket.* Thank you. It will balance you so much better* like that.'

This was raving insanity. He shuddered and again made a sound* between a cough and a sob.

'You will now light the gas, Watson, but you will be very careful that not for one instant shall it be more than half on. I implore you to be careful, Watson. Thank you, that is excellent. No, you need not draw the blind. Now you will have the kindness to place some letters and papers upon this table within my reach. Thank you. Now some of that litter from the mantelpiece. Excellent, Watson! There is a sugar-tongs there. Kindly raise that small ivory box with its assistance. Place it here among the papers. Good! You can now go and fetch Mr Culverton Smith* of 13 Lower Burke Street.'*

To tell the truth my desire to fetch a doctor had somewhat weakened, for poor Holmes was so obviously delirious that it seemed dangerous to leave him. However, he was as eager now to consult the person named as he had been obstinate in refusing.

'I never heard the name,' said I.

'Possibly not, my good Watson. It may surprise you to know that the man upon earth who is best versed in this disease is not a medical man but a planter. Mr Culverton Smith is a well-known resident of Sumatra,* now visiting London. An outbreak of the disease upon his plantation which was far absent from medical aid, caused him to study it himself with some rather far-reaching consequences.* He is a very methodical person and I did not desire you to start before six because I was well aware that you would not find him in his study.* If you could persuade him to come here and give us the benefit of his unique experience of this disease, the investigation of which has been his dearest hobby, I cannot doubt that he could help me.'

I give Holmes's remarks as a consecutive whole and will not attempt to indicate how they were interrupted by gaspings for breath and those clutchings of his hands which indicated the pain from which he was suffering. His appearance had changed for the worse during the few hours that I had been with him. Those hectic spots were more pronounced, the eyes shone more brightly out of darker hollows, and a cold sweat glimmered upon his brow. He still retained however the jaunty gallantry of his speech. To the last gasp he would always be the master.

'You will tell him exactly how you have left me,' said he. 'You will convey the very impression which is in your own mind. A dying man—a dying and delirious man. Indeed I cannot think why the whole bed of the ocean is not one solid mass of oysters,* so prolific the creatures seem. Ah, I am wandering! Strange how the brain controls the brain! What was I saying, Watson?'

'My directions for Mr Culverton* Smith.'

'Ah yes, I remember. My life depends upon it. Plead with him, Watson. There is no good feeling between us.* His nephew, Watson—I had suspicions of foul play and I allowed him to see it. The boy died horribly. He has a grudge against

me. You will soften him, Watson. Beg him, pray him, get
him here by any means. He can save me—only he.'

'I will bring him in a cab, if I have to carry him down to it.'*

'You will do nothing of the sort. You will persuade him to
come. And then you will return in front of him. Make any
excuse so as not to come with him.* Don't forget, Watson.
You won't fail me. You never did fail me. No doubt there
are natural enemies which limit the increase of the creatures. You and I, Watson, we have done our part. Shall the
world then be overrun by oysters. No, no, horrible! You'll
convey all that is in your mind.'

I left him full of the image of this magnificent intellect
babbling like a foolish child. He had handed me the key and
with a happy thought* I took it with me lest he should lock
himself in. Mrs Hudson was waiting trembling and weeping in the passage. Behind me as I passed from the flat I
heard Holmes's high thin voice in some delirious chant.
Below as I stood whistling for a cab a man came on me
through the fog.

'How is Mr Holmes, sir?' he asked.

It was an old acquaintance, Inspector Morton of Scotland
Yard, dressed in unofficial tweeds.*

'He is very ill,' I answered.

He looked at me in a most singular fashion. Had it not
been too fiendish* I could have imagined that the gleam of
the fanlight showed exultation* in his face.

'I heard some rumour of it,' said he. The cab had driven
up and I left him.

Lower Burke Street* proved to be a line of fine houses
lying in the vague borderland between Notting Hill and
Kensington. The particular one at which my cabman pulled
up had an air of smug and demure respectability in its old-
fashioned iron railings, its massive folding-door and its
shining brasswork. All was in keeping with a solemn butler
who appeared framed in the pink radiance of a tinted
electric light behind him.*

'Yes, Mr Culverton Smith is in.* Dr Watson! Very good,
sir,* I will take up your card.'

My humble name and title did not appear to impress Mr Culverton Smith. Through the half-open door I heard a high, petulant, penetrating voice.

'Who is this person? What does he want? Dear me, Staples, how often have I said that I am not to be disturbed in my hours of study!'

There came a gentle flow of soothing explanation from the butler.

'Well I won't see him, Staples. I can't have my work interrupted like this. I am not at home. Say so. Tell him to come in the morning if he really must see me.'

Again the gentle murmur.

'Well, well, give him that message. He can come in the morning, or he can stay away. My work must not be hindered.'

I thought of Holmes tossing upon his bed of sickness, and counting the minutes perhaps until I should* bring help to him. It was not a time to stand upon ceremony. His life depended upon my promptness. Before the apologetic butler had delivered his message I had pushed past him and was in the room.

With a shrill cry* of anger a man rose from a reclining chair beside the fire. I saw a great yellow face, coarse-grained and greasy, with heavy, double chins,* and two sullen* menacing grey eyes, which glared at me from under tufted and sandy brows. A high bald head had a small velvet smoking-cap poised coquettishly upon one side of its pink curve. The skull was of enormous capacity, and yet as I looked down I saw to my amazement that the figure of the man was small and frail, twisted in the shoulders and back like one who has suffered from rickets in his childhood.

'What's this?' he cried in a high screaming voice. 'What is the meaning of this intrusion? Didn't I send you word* that I would see you to-morrow morning?'

'I am sorry,' said I, 'but the matter cannot be delayed. Mr Sherlock Holmes—'

The mention of my friend's name had an extraordinary effect upon the little man. The look of anger passed in an instant from his face. His features became tense and alert.

'Have you come from Holmes?' he asked.

'I have just left him.'

'What about Holmes? How is he?'

'He is desperately ill. That is why I have come.'

The man motioned me* to a chair, and turned to resume his own. As he did so I caught a glimpse of his face in the mirror over the mantelpiece. I could have sworn that it was set in a malicious and abominable smile. Yet I persuaded myself that it must have been some nervous contraction which I had surprised, for he turned to me an instant later with genuine concern upon his features.

'I am sorry to hear this,' said he. 'I only know Mr Holmes through some business dealings which we have had, but I have every respect for his talents and his character. He is an amateur of crime, as I am of disease. For him the villain, for me the microbe. There are my prisons,' he continued, pointing to a row of bottles and jars which stood upon a side table. 'Among these gelatine cultivations* some of the very worst offenders in the world are now doing time.'

'It was on account of your special knowledge that Mr Holmes desired to see you. He has a high opinion of you and thought that you were the one man in London who could help him.'

The little man started, and the jaunty smoking-cap slid to the floor.

'Why?' he asked. 'Why should Mr Holmes think that I could help him in his trouble?'

'Because of your knowledge of Eastern diseases.'

'But why should be think that this disease which he has contracted is Eastern?'

'Because in some professional inquiry he has been working among Chinese sailors down in the Docks.'

Mr Culverton Smith smiled pleasantly and picked up his smoking-cap.

'Oh, that's it, is it?' said he. 'I trust the matter is not so grave as you suppose. How long has he been ill?'

147

'About three days.'

'Is he delirious?'

'Occasionally.'

'Tut, tut! This sounds serious. It would be inhuman not to answer his call. I very much resent any interruption to my work, Dr Watson, but this case is certainly exceptional. I will come with you at once.'

I remembered Holmes's injunction.

'I have another appointment,'* said I.

'Very good. I will go alone.* I have a note of Mr Holmes's address. You can rely upon my being there within half an hour at most.'*

It was with a sinking heart* that I re-entered Holmes's bedroom. For all that I knew the worst might have happened in my absence. To my enormous relief he had improved greatly in the interval. His appearance* was as ghastly as ever, but all trace of delirium had left him and he spoke* in a feeble voice it is true but with even more than his usual crispness and lucidity.

'Well, did you see him, Watson?'

'Yes, he is coming.'

'Admirable, Watson, Admirable! You are the best of messengers.'

'He wished to return with me.'

'That would never do, Watson. That would be obviously impossible. Did he ask what ailed me?'

'I told him about the Chinese in the East-end.'

'Exactly. Well, Watson, you have done all that a good friend could. You can now disappear from the scene.'

'I must wait and hear his opinion, Holmes.'

'Of course you must. But I have reasons to suppose that this opinion would be very much more frank and valuable if he imagines that we are alone. There is just room behind the head of my bed, Watson.'

'My dear Holmes!'

'I fear there is no alternative, Watson. The room does not lend itself to concealment which is as well as it is the less likely to arouse suspicion. But just there, Watson, I fancy that it could be done.' Suddenly he sat up with a rigid intentness upon his haggard face.* 'There are the wheels, Watson. Quick man, if you love me! And don't budge, whatever happens—whatever happens, do you hear? Don't speak! Don't move! Just listen with all your ears.' Then in an instant his sudden access of strength departed* and his masterful purposeful talk droned away* into the low vague murmurings of a semi-delirious man.

From the hiding-place* into which I had been so swiftly hustled I heard the footfalls* upon the stair, with the opening and the closing of the bedroom door. Then to my surprise there came a long silence broken only by the heavy breathings and gaspings of the sick man. I could imagine that our visitor was standing by the bedside and looking down at the sufferer. At last that strange hush was broken.

'Holmes!' he cried. 'Holmes!' in the insistent* tone of one who awakens a sleeper. 'Can't you hear me,* Holmes!' There was a rustling as if he had shaken the sick man roughly by the shoulder.

'Is that you, Mr Smith?' Holmes whispered. 'I hardly dared hope that you would come.'

The other laughed.

'I should imagine not,' he said. 'And yet, you see, I am here. Coals of fire,* Holmes—coals of fire!'

'It is very good of you—very noble of you. I appreciate your special knowledge.'

Our visitor sniggered.

'You do. You are fortunately the only man in London who does.* Do you know what is the matter with you?'

'The same,' said Holmes.

'Ah, you recognize the symptoms?'

'Only too well.'

'Well, I shouldn't be surprised, Holmes—I shouldn't be surprised if it *were* the same. A bad look-out for you if it is. Poor Victor was a dead man on the fourth day—a strong hearty young fellow. It was certainly, as you said, very surprising that he should have contracted an out-of-the-way

Asiatic disease in the heart of London—a disease too of which I had made such a very special study.* Singular coincidence, Holmes. Very smart of you to notice it, but rather uncharitable to suggest that it was cause and effect.'

'I knew that you did it.'

'Oh you did, did you? Well, you couldn't prove it anyhow. But what do you think of yourself spreading reports about me like that, and then crawling to me for help the moment you are in trouble? What sort of a game is that—eh?'

I heard the rasping laboured breathing of the sick man.* 'Give me the water!' he gasped.

'You're precious near your end, my friend, but I don't want you to go till I have had a word with you.* That's why I give you water. There, don't slop it about! That's right. Can you understand what I say?'

Holmes groaned.

'Do what you can for me. Let bygones be bygones' he whispered.* 'I'll put the words out of my head—I swear I will. Only cure me and I'll forget it.'

'Forget what?'

'Well, about Victor Savage's death. You as good as admitted just now* that you had done it. I'll forget it.'

'You can forget it or remember it, just as you like. I don't see you in the witness box. Quite another shaped box, my good Holmes, I assure you. It matters nothing to me that you should know how my nephew died. It's not him we are talking about. It's you.'

'Yes, yes.'

'The fellow who came for me—I've forgotten his name— said that you contracted it down in the East-end* among the sailors.'

'I could only account for it so.'

'You are proud of your brains, Holmes, are you not? Think yourself smart, don't you? You came across* someone who was smarter this time. Now cast your mind back, Holmes. Can you think of no other way you could have got this thing?'

'I can't think. My mind is gone. For heavens sake help me!'

'Yes, I will help you. I'll help you to understand just where you are and how you got there. I'd like you to know before you die.'

'Give me something to ease my pain.'

'Painful is it? Yes, the coolies used to do some squealing towards the end. Takes you as cramp, I fancy.'

'Yes, yes, it is cramp.'

'Well, you can hear what I say anyhow. Listen now. Can you remember any unusual incident in your life just about the time your symptoms began?'

'No, no, nothing.'

'Think again.'

'I'm too ill to think.'

'Well then, I'll help you. Did anything come by post?'

'By post?'

'A box by chance?'

'I'm fainting. I'm gone.'

'Listen, Holmes!' There was a sound as if he was shaking the dying man, and it was all that I could do to hold myself quiet in my hiding-place. 'You must hear me. You *shall* hear me.* Do you remember a box—an ivory box? It came on Wednesday. You opened it—do you remember?'

'Yes, yes, I opened it. There was a sharp spring inside it. Some joke—'

'It was no joke as you will find to your cost. You fool, you would have it and you have got it. Who asked you to cross my path?* If you had left me alone I would not have hurt you.'

'I remember,' Holmes gasped. 'The spring! It drew blood.* This box—this on the table.'

'The very one, by George, and it may as well leave the room in my pocket. There goes your last shred of evidence. But you have the truth now, Holmes, and you can die with the knowledge that I killed you. You knew too much of the fate of Victor Savage, so I have sent you to share it. You are very near your end, Holmes. I will sit here and I will watch you die.'

Holmes's voice had sunk to an almost inaudible whisper.

'What is that?' said Smith. 'Turn up the gas. Ah, the shadows begin to fall, do they? Yes, I will turn it up, that I may see you the better.' He crossed the room and the light suddenly brightened. 'Is there any other little service that I can do you, my friend?'

'A match and a cigarette.'

I nearly called out in my joy and my amazement. He was speaking in his natural voice—a little weak perhaps but the very voice I knew. There was a long pause and I felt that Culverton Smith was standing in silent amazement looking down at his companion.

'What's the meaning of this?' I heard him say at last in a dry rasping tone.

'The best way of successfully acting a part is to be it,' said Holmes. 'I give you my word that for three days I have tasted neither food, nor drink,* until you were good enough to pour me out that glass of water. But it is the tobacco which I find most irksome.* Ah, here *are* some cigarettes.' I heard the striking of a match. 'That is very much better. Hullo, hullo, do I hear the step of a friend?'

There were footfalls outside, the door opened and Inspector Morton appeared.

'All is in order and this is your man' said Holmes.

The officer gave the usual cautions.*

'I arrest you on the charge of the murder of one Victor Savage,' he concluded.

'And you might add of the attempted murder of one Sherlock Holmes' remarked my friend with a chuckle. 'To save an invalid trouble, Inspector, Mr Culverton Smith was good enough to give our signal by turning up the gas.* By the way the prisoner has a small box in the right-hand pocket of his coat which it would be as well to remove. Thank you! I would handle it gingerly if I were you. Put it down here. It may play its part in the trial.'

There was a sudden rush and a scuffle, followed by the clash of iron and a cry of pain.

'You'll only get yourself hurt,' said the Inspector. 'Stand still, will you?' There was the click of the closing handcuffs.

'A nice trap!' cried the high snarling voice. 'It will bring *you* into the dock, Holmes, not me.* He asked me to come here to cure him. I was sorry for him and I came. Now he will pretend no doubt that I have said anything which he may invent which will corroborate his insane suspicions. You can lie as you like, Holmes. My word is always as good as yours.'

'Good heavens!' cried Holmes. 'I had totally forgotten him. My dear Watson, I owe you a thousand apologies. To think that I should have overlooked you! I need not introduce you to Mr Culverton Smith* since I understand that you met somewhat earlier in the evening. Have you the cab below.* I will follow you when I am dressed for I may be of some use at the Station.'

'I never needed it more,' said Holmes, as he refreshed himself with a glass of claret and some biscuits in the intervals of his toilet. 'However, as you know, my habits are irregular, and such a feat means less to me than to most men. It was very essential that I should impress Mrs Hudson with the reality of my condition since she was to convey it to you, and you in turn to him. You won't be offended, Watson. You will realize that among your many talents dissimulation finds no place, and that if you had shared my secret you would never have been able to impress Smith with the urgent necessity of his presence, which was the vital point of the whole scheme. Knowing his vindictive nature I was perfectly certain that he would come to look upon his handiwork.'

'But your appearance, Holmes—your ghastly face?'

'Three days of absolute fast does not improve one's beauty, Watson. For the rest there is nothing which a sponge may not cure. With vaseline* upon one's forehead, belladonna* in one's eyes, rouge over the cheek-bones, and crusts of beeswax round one's lips a very satisfying effect can be produced. Malingering is a subject upon which I have sometimes thought of writing a monograph.* A little occasional talk about half-crowns, oysters, or any other extraneous subject produces a pleasing effect of delirium.'

'But why would you not let me near you since there was in truth no infection?'

'Can you ask, my dear Watson? Do you imagine that I have no respect for your medical talents? Could I fancy that your astute judgment would pass a dying man who, however weak, had no rise of pulse or temperature? At four yards I could deceive you. If I failed to do so who would bring my Smith within my grasp? No, Watson, I would not touch that box. You can just see if you look at it sideways where the sharp spring like a viper's tooth emerges as you open it. I dare say it was by some such device that poor Savage, who stood between this monster and a reversion,* was done to death. My correspondence however is, as you know, a varied one, and I am somewhat upon my guard against any packages which reach me. It was clear to me however that by pretending that he had really succeeded in his design I might surprise a confession. That pretence I have carried out with the thoroughness of the true artist.* Thank you, Watson, you must help me on with my coat. When we have finished at the police-station I think that something nutritious at Simpson's would not be out of place.'*

His Last Bow

AN EPILOGUE OF SHERLOCK HOLMES*

I T was nine o'clock at night upon the second of August—
the most terrible August in the history of the world.* One
might have thought already that God's curse hung heavy
over a degenerate earth,* for there was an awesome hush
and a feeling of vague expectancy in the sultry and stagnant
air. The sun had long set, but one blood-red gash, like an
open wound, lay low in the distant west. Above, the stars
were shining brightly; and below, the lights of the shipping
glimmered in the bay.* The two famous Germans stood
beside the stone parapet of the garden walk, with the long,
low, heavily-gabled house behind them, and they looked
down upon the broad sweep of the beach at the foot of the
great chalk cliff* on which Von Bork, like some wandering
eagle, had perched himself four years before. They stood
with their heads close together, talking in low, confidential
tones. From below, the two glowing ends of their cigars
might have been the smouldering eyes of some malignant
fiend looking down in the darkness.

A remarkable man this Von Bork—a man who could
hardly be matched among all the devoted agents of the
Kaiser.* It was his talents which had first recommended him
for the English mission, the most important mission of all,
but since he had taken it over those talents had become
more and more manifest to the half-dozen people in the
world who were really in touch with the truth. One of these
was his present companion, Baron Von Herling,* the Chief
Secretary of the legation,* whose huge 100-horse-power Benz
car* was blocking the country lane as it waited to carry* its
owner back to London.

'Things are moving very fast now and quite in accordance
with the time-table.* So far as I can judge the trend of
events, you will probably be back in Berlin within the week,'

155

the secretary was saying. 'When you get there, my dear Von Bork, I think you will be surprised at the warm* welcome you will receive. I happen to know what is thought in the All-Highest* quarters of your work in this country.' He was a huge man, the secretary, deep, broad, and tall, with a slow, heavy fashion of speech which had been his main asset in his political career.*

Von Bork laughed in a deprecating way.*

'They are not very hard to deceive, these Englanders,'* he remarked. 'A more docile, simple folk could not be imagined.'

'I don't know about that,' said the other, thoughtfully. 'They have strange, unexpected* limits and one must learn to allow for* them. It is that surface simplicity of theirs which makes a trap for the stranger. One's first impression is that they are entirely soft. Then you come* suddenly upon something very hard, and you know that you have reached the limit, and must adapt yourself to the fact. They have, for example, their insular* conventions which simply *must* be observed.'

'Meaning "good form" and "playing the game" and* that sort of thing?' Von Bork sighed as one who had suffered much.

'Meaning British prejudice and convention,* in all its queer manifestations. As an example I may quote one of my own worst blunders—I can afford to talk of my blunders, for you know my work well enough to be aware of my successes. It was on my first arrival. I was invited to a week-end gathering at the country-house of a Cabinet Minister. The conversation was amazingly indiscreet.'

Von Bork nodded. 'I've been there,' said he, dryly.

'Exactly. Well, I naturally sent a *résumé* of the information to Berlin. Unfortunately, our good Chancellor is a little heavy-handed in these matters,* and he transmitted a remark which showed that he was aware of what had been said. This, of course, took the trail straight up to me. You've no idea the harm that it did me. There was nothing soft about our British hosts on that occasion, I can assure you. I was two years living it down. Now you, with this sporting pose of yours—'

'No, no, don't call it a pose. A pose is an artificial thing. This is quite natural. I am a born sportsman. I enjoy it.'

'Well, that makes it the more effective. You yacht against them, you hunt with them, you play polo, you match them in every game. Your four-in-hand takes the prize at Olympia*—I have even heard that you go to the length of boxing with the young officers. What is the result? Nobody takes you seriously. You are a "good old sport", "quite a decent fellow for a German", a hard-drinking, night-club, knock-about-town, devil-may-care young fellow. And all the time this quiet country-house of yours is the centre of half the mischief in England, and the sporting squire—the most astute secret-service man in Europe. Genius, my dear Van Bork—genius!'

'You flatter me, Baron. But certainly I may claim that my four years in this country have not been unproductive. I've never shown you my little store. Would you mind stepping in for a moment?'

The door of the study opened straight on to the terrace. Von Bork pushed it back, and, leading the way, he clicked the switch of the electric light. He then closed the door behind the bulky form which followed him, and carefully adjusted the heavy curtain over the latticed window. Only when all these precautions had been taken and tested did he turn his sun-burned, aquiline face to his guest.

'Some of my papers have gone,' said he. 'When my wife and the household left yesterday for Flushing* they took the less important with them. I must, of course, claim the protection of the Embassy for the others.'

'Everything has been most carefully arranged.* Your name has already been filed as one of the personal suite.* There will be no difficulties for you or your baggage. Of course, it is just possible that we may not have to go. England may leave France to her fate. We are sure that there is no binding treaty between them.'*

'And Belgium?' He stood listening intently for the answer.*

'Yes, and Belgium, too.'

Von Bork shook his head. 'I don't see how that could be. There is a definite treaty there. It would be the end of her—and what an end!* She could never recover from such a humiliation.'

'She would at least have peace for the moment.'

'But her honour?'

'Tut, my dear sir, we live in a utilitarian age. Honour is a mediaeval conception. Besides, England is not ready. It is an inconceivable thing, but even our special war-tax of fifty millions, which one would think made our purpose as clear as if we had advertised it on the front page of *The Times*, has not roused these people from their slumbers. Here and there one hears a question. It is my business to find an answer. Here and there also there is irritation. It is my business to soothe it. But I can assure you that so far as the essentials go—the storage of munitions, the preparation for submarine attack, the arrangements for making high explosives—nothing is prepared. How then can England come in, especially when we have stirred her up such a devil's brew of Irish civil war,* window-breaking furies,* and God knows what to keep her thoughts at home?'

'She must think of her future.'

'Ah, that is another matter. I fancy that in the future we have our own very definite plans about England, and that your information will be very vital to us. It is to-day or to-morrow with Mr John Bull.* If he prefers to-day we are perfectly ready. If it is to-morrow we shall be more ready still. I should think they would be wiser to fight with allies than without them, but that is their own affair. This week is their week of destiny. But let us get away from speculation and back to *real-politik*.* You were speaking of your papers.'

He sat in the armchair with the light shining upon his broad, bald head, while he puffed sedately at his cigar and watched the movements of his companion.*

The large oak-panelled, book-lined room had a curtain hung in the further corner. When this was drawn it disclosed a large brass-bound safe. Von Bork detached a small key

from his watch-chain, and after some considerable manipulation of the lock he swung open the heavy door.

'Look!' said he, standing clear, with a wave of his hand.

The light shone vividly into the opened safe, and the
secretary of the Embassy gazed with an absorbed interest at
the rows of stuffed pigeon-holes with which it was furnished.
Each pigeon-hole had its label, and his eyes, as he glanced
along them, read a long series of such titles as 'Fords',*
'Harbour-Defences',* 'Aeroplanes',* 'Ireland',* 'Egypt',*
'Portsmouth Forts',* 'The Channel',* 'Rosyth',* and a score
of others. Each compartment was bristling with papers and
plans.

'Colossal!' said the secretary. Putting down his cigar he
softly clapped his fat hands.

'And all in four years, Baron. Not such a bad show for the
hard-drinking, hard-riding country squire. But the gem of
my collection is coming and there is the setting all ready for
it.' He pointed to a space over which 'Naval Signals'* was
printed.

'But you have a good *dossier* there already?'

'Out of date and waste paper. The Admiralty in some way
got the alarm and every code has been changed. It was a
blow, Baron—the worst set-back in my whole campaign. But
thanks to my cheque-book and the good Altamont, all will
be well to-night.'

The Baron looked at his watch, and gave a guttural
exclamation of disappointment.

'Well, I really can wait no longer. You can imagine that
things are moving at present in Carlton House Terrace* and
that we have all to be at our posts. I had hoped to be able
to bring news of your great *coup*. Did Altamont name no
hour?'

Von Bork pushed over a telegram.

'Will come without fail to-night and bring new sparking-
plugs.* ALTAMONT.'

'Sparking-plugs, eh?'

'You see, he poses as a motor expert and I keep a full
garage. In our code everything likely to come up is named

after some spare part. If he talks of a radiator it is a battleship, of an oil-pump a cruiser, and so on. Sparking-plugs are naval signals.'

'From Portsmouth at midday,' said the secretary, examining the superscription. 'By the way, what do you give him?'

'Five hundred pounds for this particular job. Of course, he has a salary as well.'

'The greedy rogue. They are useful, these traitors, but I grudge them their blood-money.'

'I grudge Altamont nothing. He is a wonderful worker. If I pay him well, at least he delivers the goods, to use his own phrase. Besides, he is not a traitor. I assure you that our most Pan-Germanic Junker* is a sucking dove in his feelings towards England as compared with a real bitter Irish-American.'

'Oh, an Irish-American?'

'If you heard him talk you would not doubt it. Sometimes I assure you I can hardly understand him. He seems to have declared war on the King's English as well as on the English King. Must you really go? He may be here any moment.'

'No; I'm sorry, but I have already over-stayed my time. We shall expect you early to-morrow, and when you get that signal-book through the little door on the Duke of York's steps* you can put a triumphant *Finis* to your record in England. What! Tokay!'* He indicated a heavily-sealed, dust-covered bottle which stood with two high glasses upon a salver.

'May I offer you a glass before your journey?'

'No, thanks. But it looks like revelry.'

'Altamont has a nice taste in wines, and he took a fancy to my Tokay. He is a touchy fellow and needs humouring in small things. He is absolutely vital to my plans, and* I have to study him,* I assure you.' They had strolled out on to the terrace again, and along it to the farther end, where, at a touch from the Baron's chauffeur, the great car shivered and chuckled.* 'Those are the lights of Harwich,* I suppose,' said the secretary, pulling on his dust coat. 'How still and peaceful it all seems! There may be other lights within the week, and the English coast a less tranquil place! The heavens, too, may not be quite so peaceful, if all that the good Zeppelin* promises us comes true. By the way, who is that?'

Only one window showed a light behind them. In it there stood a lamp, and beside it, seated at a table, was a dear old ruddy-faced woman in a country cap. She was bending over her knitting and stopping occasionally to stroke a large black cat upon a stool beside her.

'That is Martha,* the only servant I have left.'

The secretary chuckled.

'She might almost personify Britannia,' said he, 'with her complete self-absorption and general air of comfortable somnolence. Well, *au revoir*, Von Bork!'* With a final wave of his hand he sprang into the car, and a moment later the two golden cones from the headlights shot forward through the darkness. The secretary lay back in the cushions of the luxurious limousine, with his thoughts full of the impending European tragedy, and hardly observing that* as his car swung round the village street it nearly passed over a little Ford* coming in the opposite direction.

Von Bork walked slowly back to the study when the last gleams of the motor lamps had faded into the distance. As he passed he observed that his old housekeeper had put out her lamp and retired. It was a new experience to him, the silence and darkness of his widespread house, for his family and household had been a large one. It was a relief to him, however, to think that they were all in safety, and that, but for that one old woman who lingered* in the kitchen, he had the whole place to himself. There was a good deal of tidying up to do inside his study and he set himself to do it until his keen, handsome face was flushed with the heat of the burning papers. A leather valise* stood beside his table, and into this he began to pack very neatly and systematically the precious contents of his safe. He had hardly got started with the work, however, when his quick ears caught the sound of a distant car. Instantly he gave an exclamation of satisfaction, strapped up the valise, shut the safe, locked it, and hurried out on to the terrace. He was just in time to see the lights of a small car come to a halt at the gate. A passenger sprang out of it and advanced swiftly towards him, while the chauffeur, a heavily-built, elderly man, with a grey moustache, settled down like one who resigns himself to a long vigil.

'Well?' asked Von Bork eagerly, running forward to meet his visitor.

For answer the man waved a small brown-paper parcel triumphantly above his head.

'You can give me the glad hand* tonight, mister,' he cried. 'I'm bringin' home the bacon at last.'

'The signals?'

'Same as I said in my cable.* Every last one of them semaphore, lamp-code, Marconi*—a copy, mind you, not the original. The sucker that sold it would have handed over the book itself.* That was too dangerous. But it's the real goods, and you can lay to that.'* He slapped the German upon the shoulder with a rough familiarity from which the other winced.

'Come in,' he said. 'I'm all alone in the house. I was only waiting for this. Of course, a copy is better than the original. If an original were missing they would change the whole thing. You think it's all safe about this copy?'*

The Irish-American had entered the study and stretched his long limbs from the arm-chair. He was a tall, gaunt man of sixty, with clear-cut features and a small goatee beard which gave him a general resemblance to the caricatures of Uncle Sam.* A half-smoked sodden cigar hung from the corner of his mouth, and as he sat down he struck a match and relit it. 'Makin' ready for a move?' he remarked, as he looked round him. 'Say, mister,' he added, as his eyes fell upon the safe from which the curtain was now removed, 'you don't tell me you keep your papers in that?'

'Why not?'

'Gosh, in a wide-open contraption like that! And they reckon you to be some spy. Why, a Yankee crook would be into that with a can-opener.* If I'd known that any letter of mine was goin' to lie loose in a thing like that I'd have been a mutt* to write to you at all.'

'It would puzzle any of your crooks* to force that safe,' Von Bork answered. 'You won't cut that metal with any tool.'

'But the lock?'

'No; it's a double combination lock. You know what that is?'

'Search me,' said the American.

'Well, you need a word as well as a set of figures before you can get the lock to work.' He rose and showed a double radiating disc round the keyhole. 'This outer one is for the letters, the inner one for the figures.'

'Well, well, that's fine.'

'So it's not quite as simple as you thought. It was four years ago that I had it made, and what do you think I chose for the word and figures?'

'It's beyond me.'

'Well, I chose 'August' for the word, and '1914' for the figures, and here we are.'

The American's face showed his surprise and admiration.

'My, but that was smart! You had it down to a fine thing.'

'Yes; a few of us even then could have guessed the date. Here it is, and I'm shutting down to-morrow morning.'

'Well, I guess you'll have to fix me up too.* I'm not stayin' in this goldarned* country all on my lonesome. In a week or less, from what I see, John Bull will be on his hind legs and fair rampin'. I'd rather watch him from over the water.'

'But you're an American citizen?'*

'Well, so was Jack James an American citizen, but he's doin' time in Portland* all the same. It cuts no ice with a British copper* to tell him you're an American citizen. "It's British law and order* over here," says he. By the way, mister, talking of Jack James, it seems to me you don't do much to cover your men.'

'What do you mean?' Von Bork asked, sharply.

'Well, you are their employer, ain't you? It's up to you to see that they don't fall down. But they do fall down and when did you ever pick them up? There's James—'

'It was James's own fault. You know that yourself. He was too self-willed for the job.'

'James was a bonehead—I give you that. Then there was Hollis.'

'The man was mad.'

'Well, he went a bit woozy* towards the end. It's enough to make a man bughouse* when he has to play a part from mornin' to night with a hundred guys all ready to set the coppers wise to him. But now there is Steiner—'

Von Bork started violently, and his ruddy face turned a shade paler.

'What about Steiner?'

'Well, they've pulled him,* that's all. They raided his store last night, and he and his papers are all in Portsmouth Jail. You'll go off and he, poor devil, will have to stand the racket, and lucky if he gets clear* with his life. That's why I want to get over the salt* water as soon as you do.'

Von Bork was a strong, self-contained man, but it was easy to see that the news had shaken him.

'How could they have got on to Steiner?' he muttered. 'That's the worst blow yet.'

'Well, you nearly had a darned sight* worse one, for I believe they are not far off me.'

'You don't mean that!'

'Sure thing. My landlady down Fratton way* had some inquiries, and when I heard of it I guessed it was time for me to hustle. But what I want to know, mister, is how the coppers know these things? Steiner is the fifth man you've lost since I signed on with you, and I know the name of the sixth if I don't get a move on. How do you explain it, and ain't you ashamed to see your men go down like this?'

Von Bork flushed crimson.

'How dare you speak in such a way!'

'If I didn't dare things, mister, I wouldn't be in your service. But I'll tell you straight what is in my mind. I've heard that with you German politicians, when an agent has done his work you are not very* sorry to see him put away where he can't talk too much.'*

Von Bork sprang to his feet.

'Do you dare to suggest that I have given away my own agents!'

'I don't stand for that, mister, but there's a stool pigeon or a cross* somewhere, and it's up to you to find out where it is. Anyhow, I am taking no more chances. It's me for little Holland, and the sooner the better.'

Von Bork had mastered his anger.

'We have been allies too long to quarrel now at the very hour of victory,' he said. 'You've done splendid work and taken big* risks and I can't forget it. By all means go to Holland, and you can get a boat from Rotterdam to New York. No other line will be safe a week from now when Von Tirpitz gets to work. But let us settle up, Altamont.* I'll take that book and pack it with the rest.'

The American held the small parcel in his hand, but made no motion to give it up.

'What about the dough?' he asked.

'The what?'

'The boodle. The reward. The five hundred pounds. The gunner turned durned* nasty at the last, and I had to square him with an extra hundred dollars or it would have been nitsky* for you and me. "Nothin' doin'!" says he, and he meant it too, but the last hundred did it. It's cost me two hundred pounds from first to last, so it isn't likely I'd give it up without gettin' my wad.'

Von Bork smiled with some bitterness. 'You don't seem to have a very high opinion of my honour,' said he; 'you want the money before you give up the book.'

'Well, mister, it is a business proposition.'

'All right. Have your way.' He sat down at the table and scribbled a cheque, which he tore from the book, but he refrained from handing it to his companion. 'After all, since we are to be on such terms, Mr Altamont,' said he, 'I don't see why I should trust you any more than you trust me. Do you understand?' he added, looking back over his shoulder at the American. 'There's the cheque upon the table. I claim the right to examine that parcel before you pick the money up.'

The American passed it over without a word. Von Bork undid a winding of string and two wrappers of paper. Then he sat gazing for a moment in silent amazement at a small blue book which lay before him. Across the cover was printed in golden letters *Practical Handbook of Bee Culture*. Only for one instant did the master-spy glare at this strangely-irrelevant* inscription. The next he was gripped at the back of his neck by a grasp of iron, and a chloroformed sponge was held in front of his writhing face.

'Another* glass, Watson?' said Mr Sherlock Holmes, as he extended the dusty* bottle of Imperial Tokay. 'We must drink to this joyous reunion.'*

The thickset chauffeur, who had seated himself by the table, pushed forward his glass with some eagerness.

'It is a good wine, Holmes,' he said, when he had drunk heartily to the sentiment.*

'A remarkable wine, Watson. Our noisy* friend upon the sofa has assured me that it is from Franz Joseph's special cellar at the Schoenbrunn Palace.* Might I trouble you to open the window, for chloroform vapour does not help the palate.'

The safe was ajar, and Holmes who was now* standing in front of it was removing *dossier* after *dossier*, swiftly examining each, and then packing it neatly in Von Bork's valise. The German lay upon the sofa sleeping stertorously, with a strap round his upper arms and another round his legs.

'We need not hurry ourselves, Watson. We are safe from interruption. Would you mind touching the bell? There is no one in the house except old Martha, who has played her part to admiration.* I got her the situation here when first I took the matter up. Ah, Martha, you will be glad to hear that all is well.'

The pleasant old lady had appeared in the doorway. She curtseyed with a smile to Mr Holmes, but glanced with some apprehension at the figure upon the sofa.

'It is all right, Martha. He has not been hurt at all.'

'I am glad of that, Mr Holmes. According to his lights he has been a kind master. He wanted me to go with his wife to Germany yesterday, but that would hardly have suited your plans, would it, sir?'

'No, indeed, Martha. So long as you were here I was easy in my mind. We waited some time for your signal to-night.'

'It was the secretary, sir; the stout gentleman from London.'*

'I know. His car passed ours. But for your excellent driving, Watson, we should have been the very type of Europe under the Prussian Juggernant. What more, Martha?'*

'I thought he would never go. I knew that it would not suit your plans, sir, to find him here.'

'No, indeed. Well, it only meant that we waited half an hour or so on the hill* until I saw your lamp go out and knew that the coast was clear. You can report to me to-morrow in London, Martha, at Claridge's Hotel.'*

'Very good, sir.'

'I suppose you have everything ready to leave?'

'Yes, sir. He posted seven letters to-day. I have the addresses, as usual. He received nine; I have these also.'*

'Very good, Martha. I will look into them tomorrow. Good-night. These papers,' he continued, as the old lady vanished, 'are not of very great importance for, of course, the information which they represent has been sent off long ago to the German Government. These are the originals which could not safely be got out of the country.'

'Then they are of no use?'

'I should not go so far as to say that, Watson. They will at least show our people what is known and what is not. I may say that a good many of these papers have come to him* through me, and I need not add are thoroughly untrustworthy. It would brighten my declining years to see a German cruiser navigating the Solent* according to the mine-field plans which I have furnished. But you, Watson'— he stopped his work and took his old friend by the shoulders—'I've hardly seen you in the light yet. How have the years used you? You look the same blithe boy as ever.'

'I feel twenty years younger, Holmes. I have seldom felt so happy as when I got your wire asking me to meet you at

Harwich with the car. But you, Holmes—you have changed very little—save for that horrible goatee.'

'These are the sacrifices one makes for one's country, Watson,' said Holmes, pulling at his little tuft. 'To-morrow it will be but a dreadful memory. With my hair cut and a few other superficial changes I shall no doubt reappear at Claridge's to-morrow as I was before this American stunt*— I beg your pardon, Watson; my well of English seems to be permanently defiled—before this American job came my way.'

'But you had retired, Holmes. We heard of you as living the life of a hermit among your bees and your books in a small farm upon the South Downs.'

'Exactly, Watson. Here is the fruit of my leisured ease, the *magnum opus** of my latter years!' He picked up the volume from the table and read out the whole title, '*Practical Handbook of Bee Culture, with some Observations upon the Segregation of the Queen.** Alone I did it.* Behold the fruit of pensive nights and laborious days, when I watched the little working gangs as once I watched the criminal world of London.'

'But how did you get to work again?'

'Ah! I have often marvelled at it myself. The Foreign Minister* alone I could have withstood, but when the Premier* also deigned to visit my humble roof—! The fact is, Watson, that this gentleman upon the sofa was a bit too good for our people. He was in a class by himself. Things were going wrong, and no one could understand why they were going wrong. Agents were suspected or even caught, but there was evidence of some strong and secret central force. It was absolutely necessary to expose it. Strong pressure was brought upon me to look into the matter. It has cost me two years, Watson, but they have not been devoid of excitement. When I say that I started my pilgrimage at Chicago,* graduated in an Irish secret society at Buffalo,* gave serious trouble to the constabulary* at Skibbereen* and so eventually caught the eye of a subordinate agent of Von Bork, who recommended me as a likely man, you will realize that the matter was complex. Since then I have been honoured by his confidence, which has not prevented most of his plans going subtly wrong and five of his best agents being in prison. I watched them, Watson, and I picked them as they ripened. Well, sir, I hope that you are none the worse?'

The last remark was addressed to Von Bork himself, who, after much gasping and blinking, had lain quietly listening to Holmes's statement. He broke out now into a furious stream of German invective, his face convulsed with passion. Holmes continued his swift investigation of documents, his long, nervous fingers opening and folding the papers* while his prisoner cursed and swore.

'Though unmusical, German is the most expressive of all languages,' he observed, when Von Bork had stopped from pure exhaustion. 'Hullo! Hullo!' he added, as he looked hard at the corner of a tracing before putting it in the box. 'This should put another bird in the cage. I had no idea that the paymaster* was such a rascal, though I have long had an eye upon him. Dear me,* Mister Von Bork, you have a great deal to answer for.'

The prisoner had raised himself with some difficulty upon the sofa and was staring with a strange mixture of amazement and hatred at his captor.

'I shall get level with you, Altamont,' he said, speaking with slow deliberation. 'If it takes me all my life I shall get level with you!'

'The old sweet song,'* said Holmes. 'How often have I heard it in days gone by! It was a favourite ditty of the late lamented Professor Moriarty.* Colonel Sebastian Moran has also been known* to warble it. And yet I live and keep bees upon the South Downs.'

'Curse you, you double traitor!' cried the German, straining against his bonds and glaring murder from his furious eyes.

'No, no, it is not so bad as that,' said Holmes, smiling. 'As my speech surely shows you, Mr Altamont of Chicago had no existence in fact. He was a concoction, a myth, an isolated strand from my bundle of personalities.* I used him and he is gone.'

'Then who are you?'

'It is really immaterial who I am, but since the matter seems to interest you, Mr Von Bork, I may say that this is not my first acquaintance with the members of your family. I have done a good deal of business in Germany in the past, and my name is probably familiar to you.'

'I would wish to know it,' said the Prussian grimly.

'It was I who brought about the separation between Irene Adler and the late King of Bohemia when your cousin Heinrich was the Imperial Envoy.* It was I also who saved from murder, by the Nihilist Klopman, Count Von und Zu Grafenstein,* who was your mother's elder brother. It was I—'

Von Bork sat up in amazement.

'There is only one man—' he cried.

'Exactly,' said Holmes.

Von Bork groaned and sank back on the sofa. 'And most of that information came through you!' he cried. 'What is it worth? What have I done? It is my ruin for ever!'

'It is certainly a little untrustworthy,' said Holmes. 'It will require some checking and you have little time to check it. Your admiral* may find the new guns rather larger than he expects, and the cruisers perhaps a trifle faster.'

Von Bork clutched at his own throat in despair.

'There are a good many other points of detail which will, no doubt, come to light in good time. But you have one quality which is very rare in a German, Mr Von Bork: you are a sportsman, and you will bear me no ill will when you realize that you, who have outwitted so many other people, have at last been outwitted yourself. After all, you have done your best for your country and I have done my best for mine, and what could be more natural? Besides,' he added, not unkindly, as he laid his hand upon the shoulder of the prostrate man, 'it is better than to fall before some more ignoble foe. These papers are now ready, Watson. If you will help me with our prisoner, I think that we may get started for London at once.'

It was no easy task to move Von Bork, for he was a strong and a desperate man. Finally, holding either arm, the two friends walked him very slowly down the garden path,* which he had trod with such proud confidence when he received the congratulations of the famous diplomatist only a few hours before. After a short final struggle he was hoisted, still bound hand and foot, into the spare seat of the little car. His precious valise was wedged in beside him.

'I trust that you are as comfortable as circumstances permit,' said Holmes, when the final arrangements were made. 'Should I be guilty of a liberty if I lit a cigar and placed it between your lips?'

But all amenities were wasted upon the angry German.

'I suppose you realize, Mr Sherlock Holmes,' said he, 'that if your Government bears you out in this treatment it becomes an act of war?'

'What about your Government and all this treatment?' said Holmes, tapping the valise.

'You are a private individual. You have no warrant for my arrest. The whole proceeding is absolutely illegal and outrageous.'

'Absolutely,' said Holmes.

'Kidnapping a German subject.'

'And stealing his private papers.'

'Well, you realize your position, you and your accomplice here. If I were to shout for help as we pass through the village—'

'My dear sir, if you did anything so foolish you would probably enlarge the too-limited titles of our village inns by giving us "The Dangling Prussian"* as a sign-post. The Englishman is a patient creature, but at present his temper is a little inflamed and it would be as well not to try him too far. No, Mr Von Bork, you will go with us in a quiet, sensible fashion to Scotland Yard, whence you can send for your friend Baron Von Herling and see if even now you may not fill that place which he has reserved for you in the Ambassadorial suite. As to you, Watson, you are joining up with your old service,* as I understand, so London won't be out of your way. Stand with me here upon the terrace, for it may be the last quiet talk that we shall ever have.'

The two friends chatted in intimate converse for a few minutes, recalling once again the days of the past whilst their prisoner vainly wriggled to undo the bonds that held him. As they turned to the car Holmes pointed back to the moonlit sea and shook a thoughtful head.

'There's an east wind coming, Watson.'*

'I think not, Holmes. It is very warm.'

'Good old Watson! You are the one fixed point in a changing age. There's an east wind coming all the same, such a wind as never blew on England yet. It will be cold and bitter, Watson, and a good many of us may wither* before its blast. But it's God's own wind none the less, and a cleaner, better, stronger land will lie in the sunshine when the storm has cleared.* Start her up, Watson,* for it's time that we were on our way. I have a cheque for five hundred pounds which should be cashed early, for the drawer is quite capable of stopping it, if he can.'*

EXPLANATORY NOTES

First English edn. of 10,684 copies published on 22 Oct. 1917 by John Murray. A Colonial issue of this edn. was published by G. Bell & Sons on the same date. First American edn. published by the George H. Doran Co. of New York in Oct. 1917. All the individual stories had been published in the *Strand Magazine*, as noted hereafter. This edn. follows the order of first publication which reflects the order in which the stories were composed.

3 *Preface*: the only point when Watson breaks from within the stories to address the reader, it enhances the theatrical metaphor implicit in the book-title, with the preface a form of presentation from Watson raising the curtain while on the title's indication Holmes at the close brings it down.

philosophy and agriculture: an allusion to Virgil's *Georgics*, whose agricultural preoccupations turn to specific discussion of bees in the last book, a work appropriate to Holmes after the conclusion of his Aeneid. ACD certainly read Virgil's *Aeneid* at Stonyhurst to the extent of a book or so, and would probably know the *Georgics* in synopsis and by extracts.

complete the volume: as originally completed, the volume carried 'The Adventure of the Cardboard Box', which had lain very long indeed in portfolio, having been printed in the *Strand* in Jan. 1893. Our series restores it to its proper place among *The Memoirs* whence it was removed (save for the first American edn.), primarily, it would seem, because ACD's father, Charles Altamont Doyle (1832–93), whose alcoholic dependence seems to have resembled in its progress and medical effect that of the murderer James Browner in 'The Cardboard Box', died in a mental home on 10 Oct. between magazine and book publication of *The Memoirs*. A quarter-century later was a sufficiently decent interval, and if ACD's mother, Mary Foley Doyle (1838–1921), had vetoed previous book publication her recent move near her son facilitated withdrawal of the prohibition.

WISTERIA LODGE

First published in the *Strand Magazine*, 36 (Sept.–Oct. 1908), 243–50, 363–73, with 10 illustrations by Arthur Twidle (subtitles for each month as here, but titled 'A Reminiscence of Mr Sherlock Holmes': present title substituted on first book publication). First American publication in *Collier's Weekly Magazine* (New York), 15 Aug. 1908, with 6 illustrations by Frederic Dorr Steele, the most famous American portrayer of Holmes. This was the first Sherlock Holmes short story with an English illustrator other than Sidney Paget, who had died on 29 Jan. 1908. Born in 1860, Paget had been married on 1 June 1893, on which day he received 'a beautiful silver cigarette case from "Sherlock Holmes"' as a wedding present from ACD. Paget continued drawing Holmes illustrations throughout his honeymoon, as what became *The Memoirs* was still running in the *Strand* until Dec. 1893. The illustrator of the present story, Arthur Twidle, also illustrated 'The Bruce-Partington Plans', but thereafter was never used again for a Holmes story, to the author's great regret.

5 *Wisteria*: hardy, climbing, deciduous shrub, bearing a blue-lilac flower, its other spelling 'wistaria' (from the American anatomist Caspar Wistar (1761–1818) by the botanist Thomas Nuttall (1786–1859), baptism 1818) having been used in *Strand* text: possibly ACD finally opted for 'wisteria' as combining 'weird', 'mysterious', and 'hysteria'.

1895: erroneously '1892' in all texts. Holmes's disappearance after Professor Moriarty's death is given in the appropriate stories ('The Final Problem' (*Memoirs*), 'The Empty House' (*Return*)) as from Apr. 1891 to Apr. 1894. The second case in *The Return*, 'The Norwood Builder', is reported as happening some months after Holmes's reappearance, 'the case of the papers of ex-President Murillo' falling in the interval. ACD, writing in Apr. 1908 (ACD to Herbert Greenhough Smith, 17 Apr. 1908, Metropolitan Toronto Library), had been refreshing himself on the Holmes stories (see next note below) and evidently decided on making flesh of the word as regards Murillo, but absently dated the event a year after 'The Final Problem' instead of a year after 'The Empty House' as he would have wished. He made no use of the Murillo 'papers' in the end.

red-headed men . . . five orange pips: both in *The Adventures*, 'The Red-headed League' having appeared in the *Strand* for Aug. 1891 and 'The Five Orange Pips' in that for Nov. 1891.

Post Office, Charing Cross: one of the oldest London post offices, situated at the cartographical centre of the London metropolis, open day and night.

a reply-paid telegram: a rapid-transit brief message whose cost rose with further wordage; women on either lower-paid jobs than men or man-dictated budgets would be daunted by the additional cost of covering a recipient's reply.

6 *Colonel Carruthers*: conflation of Colonel Moran ('The Empty House') and Robert Carruthers ('The Solitary Cyclist'), both in the *Return*.

spats: contraction of 'spatterdashes', short gaiters worn over the instep, covering ankle and shoe, fastened under the foot by strap and light buttons; in use for at least a century before this, but became identified with young dandies rather than old worthies after 1918. Compare their use by ACD's disciple P. G. Wodehouse. 'It is significant that Wodehouse could publish in 1936 a book entitled *Young Men in Spats*. For who was wearing spats at that date? They had gone out of fashion quite ten years earlier' (George Orwell, 'In Defence of P. G. Wodehouse', Feb. 1945).

toilet: grooming of hair and beard, to make oneself presentable.

7 *Mr Garcia's*: ACD had a fellow-pupil at Stonyhurst in the early 1870s named Henry Edmund Garcia, and the Jesuits made much of one of their earliest saints, Aloysius Gonzaga (1568–91), whose cult resulted in his being named (1926) the patron saint of Christian youth, whence this Garcia's first name. ACD had fellow-students of that Christian name, e.g. Alfred Aloysius Watson. ACD's 'The Confession' (*Star*, 17 Jan. 1898) has as hero a love-crossed Jesuit priest named Garcia, and it is the maiden name of Beryl Stapleton in *The Hound*. But its use here may also be prompted by a sinister reinterpretation of Elbert Hubbard's best-selling tract on devotion to duty *A Message to Garcia* (1899).

Wisteria Lodge: at a time when he was interviewing ACD, playing cricket for his team, and cheerfully paying homage to his master in the form of graceful pastiche and parodies in *Punch*, P[elham] G[renville] Wodehouse (1881–1975) had a non-Holmes sketch in the New Year *Punch* (30 Dec. 1903) shortly after Holmes's *Return*. It dealt with the return of Lord

Adalbert Perceval Cholmondley-Cholmondley to the London Smart Set in an imagined 1908 after his compulsion 'by financial troubles' in 1903 'to emigrate to Clapham'. To his horror, his old friends the Brabazon-Smiths prove to have forgotten the existence of bridge and to be devoted to cricket, boxing, football, Rugby, etc., wherefore 'In one of the larger oases on the Great Common you will see a simple red-brick hut. On its door-post are the words "Wistaria Villa". Enter, and you will be shown into the presence of Lord Adalbert Perceval Cholmondley-Cholmondley. He has returned to the wilds.' This may have supplied the title in its first form, the idea of suburban wilds, and the link—murderous as it proves—with a Common: the use of Wodehouse's 'The Prodigal' in the creation of 'Altamont' in 'His Last Bow' shows that the master was certainly reading his future chief disciple during this period.

7 *wrong end foremost*: 'People have often asked me whether I knew the end of a Holmes story before I started it. Of course I do. One could not possibly steer a course if one did not know one's destination. The first thing is to get your idea. Having got that key idea one's next task is to conceal it and lay emphasis upon everything which can make for a different explanation. Holmes, however, can see all the fallacies of the alternatives, and arrives more or less dramatically at the true solution by steps which he can describe and justify' (*Memories and Adventures*, 126).

Inspector Gregson: his revival here is further evidence of ACD's rereading, Gregson having been strongly established in *A Study in Scarlet*, after which 'The Greek Interpreter' (*Memoirs*) was his only other appearance until now. His first name is Tobias.

Lee: commuter town in Kent 7 miles from London where Neville St Clair lived so well off his alms as Hugh Boone ('The Man with the Twisted Lip', *Adventures*).

You traced him through the telegram: this has puzzled some commentators, but seems simple enough. Holmes has naturally realized from the presence of a Surrey detective that Wisteria Lodge is probably in that county; that Scott Eccles's grotesque experience is linked to a crime, however ignorant of that he may be; that the appearance also of a London detective means that a possible arrest is in contemplation; that Baynes has therefore found some clue linking Eccles with a visit to Wisteria Lodge on this night of singular happenings; that the clue has led to London in pursuit of Eccles for whom an obvious conceivable stopping-place on return to the metropolis railway terminus would have been an adjacent all-night telegraph office whence to communicate to a confederate or, as proved to be the case, to seek professional assistance. Having educated his readers to Holmesian methods, ACD now leaves such deductions to them, much as the deductions on Eccles himself are made by Watson with a confidence born of his years with Holmes.

9 *tête-à-tête*: limited to two persons. Scott Eccles, unshaven, bemused, pursuing detectives, and pursued by the police, nevertheless recovers his pompous genteelisms before all else.

11 *quarter-day is at hand*: Lady Day (25 Mar.) was traditionally the day on which payments fell due for the preceding quarter of the year. For all of his respectability, Eccles is evidently familiar with what ACD's native Edinburgh called 'a moonlicht flit', no doubt a necessary familiarity to reinforce self-approval at his own contrast from such proceedings and persons.

12 *dog-grate*: a fire-grate detached from the rear wall, standing within the fireplace on supports known as firedogs or andirons.

sealed with purple wax: letters, particularly those of an official or confidential nature, were frequently sealed by melting wax dropped on the flap and pressed down by a metal object, sometimes with a distinctive engraving.

perhaps: not in *Strand*.

sleeve-link: more recently styled 'cuff-link'; metal objects, possibly ornate or jewelled, connected by a tiny chain to do the work of wrist buttons. Holmes and Baynes, already scenting mutual rivalry, exchange observations but not inferences. A sleeve-link implies a man, as a nail-scissors implies a woman; the man probably is jacketless. An implication of a woman held by force is taking shape, a frequent theme in ACD, who worried about his sisters as governesses in Portugal in the 1880s. Alternatively, the woman might have prepared the message and the man the envelope in conspiratorial mutual incrimination (as did the Cunninghams in 'The Reigate Squire' (*Memoirs*)).

14 *a five-shilling reply*: Holmes's telegram provides for a long answer; even so, a shilling for a minimum of nine words and 4 shillings at 2 pence per word for another twenty-four would have cut it fine for the length of reply ultimately received (a shilling is 5 new pence in today's currency).

15 *I see no charm in the man*: counterpoint of Scott Eccles's self-description as 'being of a sociable turn'.

17 *possess our souls in patience*: 'In your patience possess ye your souls' (Luke 21:19); also in *The Valley of Fear*, ch. 7 and 'The Three Garridebs' (*Case-Book*), and p. 126 above.

Mr Hynes Hynes, JP: not, as has been supposed, a dittograph. Several such names were common among the landed gentry, the MP for Horsham 1885–93 during the time when ACD set 'The Five Orange Pips' (*Adventures*) there being Sir Walter Barttelot Barttelot, Bart. (1820–93). And there was, of course, ACD's friend who published several of his medical tales in the *Idler*, Jerome Klapka Jerome (1859–1927).

Mr Henderson, High Gable: the antecedent of Henderson's English residence, and to some extent Henderson himself, is clearly Juan Manuel [de] Rosas (1793–1877), the tyrant of Buenos Aires, who lived at Swaythling, Hants, near Southampton for a quarter-century until his peaceful death from 'indigestion'; his initial popularity in Argentina in the 1830s eroded into widespread hatred in response to his growing cruelty, capriciousness, vengefulness, and paranoid suspicion, terrorizing even his own family. A proverbial byword of liberal reproach, he expelled the Jesuits in 1847 for opposing his personal cult imposed on his subjects: anything ACD would have heard of him at Stonyhurst would therefore have been hostile, regardless of his later pamphleteering demands for a league of Christian nations presided over by the Pope. He seems to have had relatively little money, although he received a subsistence allowance from the ex-henchman who ousted him. ACD at Southsea from 1882 to 1890 could well have heard something of the ancient exile, a figure of striking appearance so recently living less than twenty miles away. There is a historiographical tradition in his favour for his work in laying the foundations of Argentinian federalism, of which F. García Calderón, *Latin America: Its Rise and Progress* (tr. Bernard Miall, 1913) was a leading exemplar in ACD's day, but the more usual view in Europe and the USA was probably that proclaimed in the title of the influential O. Martens, *Ein Caligula unseres Jahrhunderts* (Berlin, 1896). But the urgency of the portrait surely relates to Leopold and his Congo. Higham (p. 219) offers 'José Santos Zelaya, the heartless President of Nicaragua . . . [whose] departure for New York closely resembled the departure to Barcelona of the Tiger of San Pedro, Don Murileo [*sic*]': perhaps, but it took place in 1909.

18 *our tangled skein*: the title ACD first thought up for what became *A Study in Scarlet* was 'A Tangled Skein'.

the Bull: Baring-Gould noted that the hotel at Esher was 'The Bear'. Evidently ACD was amusing himself by this acknowledgement of the stockbroker belt.

San Pedro: imaginary Latin American country. An African despotism whose exiled perpetrator might pass for an English country gentleman would have been too obviously that of Leopold II (1835–1909), still reigning over the Belgians and now destined to receive his great pay-off for the Congo before the end of the year. ACD wanted quietly to assert the regime's Catholicism, hence the choice of the Spanish name for the first Pope, St Peter, combined with underlying paganism still uppermost in the minds of the exploited people.

20 *relic*: in Roman Catholic devotion, a first-class relic would be all or part of a saint's body; ACD symbolically applies a term from San Pedro's official religion to its unofficial one, voodoo. Voodoo was popularly if inaccurately rendered as 'hoodoo' at this time and Vachel Lindsay's 'The Congo' (1914) is suggestive here:

> Be careful what you do,
> Or Mumbo-Jumbo, God of the Congo,
> And all of the other
> Gods of the Congo,
> Mumbo-Jumbo will hoo-doo you.

21 *Au revoir*: very rare salutation in the Holmes saga, here used as declaration of chivalric rivalry based on mutual respect, so that Holmes v. Baynes takes on a touch of Sir Nigel Loring v. Bertrand du Guesclin (*The White Company*).

22 *the game was afoot*: used elsewhere in the Holmes canon, notably the opening to 'The Abbey Grange' (*Return*). Adapted from:

> I see you stand like greyhounds in the slips,
> Straining upon the start. The game's afoot:
> Follow your spirit, and, upon this charge
> Cry 'God for Harry! England and Saint George!'
> (Shakespeare, *Henry V*, III. i. 31–4)

22 *British Museum*: at this juncture the term was employed to indicate either the Museum itself, then as now at Great Russell Street, Bloomsbury, or its Reading Room, now designated as the 'British Library', where Holmes made researches on voodoo.

spud: not, of course, a potato in this instance, but the short spade employed in its culture and in those of other strongly rooted plants.

23 *mulatto*: extremely common expression of offensive racist meaning (but not necessarily offensive intention), to denote that the subject is from black and white parentage, the word being derived from the Portuguese diminutive of *mulo*, a mule product of mixed equine parentage. It was used synonymously with the more contemptuous 'half-breed', as employed above by Scott Eccles. There may be an association of ideas in that Sebastian Gomez, one of the leading pupils of the painter Bartolomé Esteban Murillo (1618–82) was known as 'Murillo's Mulatto'.

24 *something in . . . understand*: not his chosen status as rival of Sherlock Holmes, noted by both at the outset, but the inability of a man to recognize his own double—Baynes's methods are simply Holmes's, such as, in this instance, the plant of a newspaper error to lure the murderer into false security which was worked by Holmes in 'The Six Napoleons' (*Return*), duly codified in Holmes's aphorism 'The Press, Watson, is a most valuable institution, if you only know how to use it.'

27 *butlers, footmen . . . country-house*: Longman observes that 'Doyle is contrasting the relatively luxurious life of servants in English country houses with the poverty among the less securely employed or unemployed members of the working class'. To put the sentiments in the mouth of Holmes, a working and (at the beginning of his career) occasionally a destitute professional, gives a credible location to the anger.

29 *I shan't forget*: the *Strand* text has the more punctilious Victorian 'sha'n't'.

30 *Don Murillo*: Baynes in understandable ignorance of Latin usages fails to realize that 'Don Murillo' would be the Spanish equivalent of 'Sir Russell' (as Brigadier Gerard calls his English baronet friendly enemy (*Exploits of Brigadier Gerard*)). Correctly it would be 'Don Juan Murillo'.

31 *this man has stolen*: 'One may merely indicate the main points, that during the independent life of the Congo State all accounts have been kept secret . . . that sums amounting in the aggregate to several million pounds have been traced to the King, and that this money has been spent partly in buildings in Belgium, partly in land in the same country, partly in building on the Riviera, partly in the corruption of public men, and of the European and American Press (our own not being entirely untarnished, I fear), and, finally, in the expenses of such a private life as has made King Leopold's name notorious throughout Europe' (*The Crime of the Congo*, 115).

32 *Durando*: about the time the story was in proof ACD was much exercised about Dorando Pietri, who won the marathon at the London Olympic Games and was then disqualified (on the appeal of the runner-up) for having had water poured on him when he fainted just before the winning-tape. Having reported the ordeal of the gallant Italian waiter, ACD went on to propose means of honouring him (*Daily Mail*, 25 July 1908). (In the event, the race, though formally awarded to J. J. Hayes (USA), was thereafter popularly known as 'Dorando's Marathon'.) ACD, like more or less all of the British sporting public, referred to Pietri as 'Dorando' and he may have appropriated the name as a symbol of a Latin hero-martyr, making the substitution for some less dramatic original while revising proof. 'Victor' is the Latin for 'conqueror', especially in *victor ludorum* (the conqueror of the games). ACD returned to the memory of Dorando Pietri in his wartime *A Visit to Three Fronts* (1916): 'strong men gasped and women wept at his invincible but unavailing spirit . . . Durando's spirit is alive to-day' (pp. 33–4). Notice the mistaken 'Durando', and the Italian 'Signora' where the Spanish or Portuguese is required in the story.

would not let the matter rest: 'Surely there should be some punishment for those who by their injustice and violence have dragged Christianity and civilization in the dirt. Surely, also, there should compulsory compensation out of the swollen moneybags of the three hundred per cent concessionaires for the widows and the orphans, the maimed and the incapacitated. Justice cannot be satisfied with less' (*The Crime of the Congo*, 126).

34 *Guildford Assizes*: criminal offences of greater weight than a magistrate's court could support went to the local county town (if rural), and for Surrey that was Guildford. The principle meant that in this case the crime was handled further away from London at each stage, a reminder of the jealousy with which the shires viewed the metropolis, as Baynes himself symbolizes in his relations with Holmes.

The crime was ascribed to Nihilism: put like that, the Spanish police were really washing their hands of it, as Nihilism was confined to Russia. But in fact ACD, who had written 'A Night Among the Nihilists' (*London Society*, Apr. 1881), was presumably using the term as synonymous with Anarchism anywhere. Spanish Anarchism derived from the Russian Mikhail Bakunin (1814–76); Spain was the one great breeding-ground for his disciples.

35 *the strange creature . . . the creature*: the former relates to the fetish, the latter to its owner, but what seems like a clumsy and ill-directed repetition is on another level a deliberate atmospheric blurring of the distinction between them.

Eckermann's Voodooism and the Negroid Religions: the book is invented and the extract, while typical enough of that style of Edwardian anthropology, is spurious. Eckermann is famous as an authority on Goethe rather than on goats; ACD probably first encountered his name as a schoolboy in Germany, which explains the level of his current use of it. But Johann Peter Eckermann (1792–1854) in his *Conversations with Goethe* (1837, translated 1839) is certainly one of the originals of Dr Watson, as the use of Goethe in *The Sign of the Four* reminds us. Holmes's 'as I have had occasion to remark' is very Goethe-to-Eckermann.

36 *there is but one step . . . horrible*: 'there is but one step from the sublime to the ridiculous' (Napoleon to the Abbé du Pradt, Polish ambassador, on his recent retreat from Moscow, 1812). Napoleon plays something of Holmes's role in the Brigadier Gerard stories.

THE BRUCE-PARTINGTON PLANS

First published in the *Strand Magazine*, 36 (Dec. 1908), 689–705, with 6 illustrations by Arthur Twidle. Title as here but superscribed 'Reminiscences of Mr Sherlock Holmes (from the Diaries of his Friend John H. Watson, MD)'. First American publication in *Collier's Weekly Magazine* (New York), 12 Dec. 1908, with 5 illustrations by Frederic Dorr Steele.

37 *news of a revolution . . . Government*: to explain these seems somewhat subversive of the author's intent, as their effect is essentially impressionistic and Holmes's indifference to the genres rather than their instances is in question. But ACD was most unusually precise in dating the action of the story, and the events are at least as important as evidence of increasing international tension as background details for the story's plot. The revolution was the assassination of the Queen of Korea and imprisonment of the King on 8 Oct. 1895 under Japanese military encouragement, ACD being an interested observer of Japanese events through the residence in Japan of his friend Professor William K. Burton (1856–99, son of the historian John Hill Burton), as shown in the opening of his 'Jelland's Voyage' (1892, printed in *Round the Fire Stories*). The possible war arose from the massacres of Armenians in Turkey under the sultanate of Abdul Hamid II (1842–1918) (hence saluted in verse by Sir William Watson (1858–1935) as 'Abdul the Damned on his infernal throne'): Britain had sent a squadron to the Dardanelles, Austria had recommended international naval action against Turkey, Russia had drawn up plans to seize Stamboul, but France's unwillingness to risk general war held back military action. The change of government was in France, where the socialist Léon Bourgeois (1851–1925) formed a cabinet on 30 Oct. 1895 on the defeat of Alexandre Ribot (1842–1923).

38 *Brother Mycroft*: introduced in 'The Greek Interpreter' (*Memoirs*), seven years senior to Sherlock, more strongly endowed with faculties of observation and deduction, and partly a satire on non-practising medical and scientific specialists whose research, for all its brilliance, remains untested by field-work. In that case Mycroft's obsession with the problem and indifference to the human peril involved (a trait present, but less virulently, in Sherlock), costs one innocent life and puts that of the client under threat as well.

38 *Diogenes Club*: where Sherlock introduced Watson to Mycroft: named after the Greek philosopher Diogenes of Sinope, who lived in a tub like a dog (from which word in Greek came the name of his followers, 'Cynics') and was famous for his fruitless search for an honest man in the third century BC. 'No member is permitted to take the least notice of any other one. Save for the Strangers' Room, no talking is, under any circumstances, permitted.' The idea is in part an elaboration of the priestly status of the detective as depicted by the ex-Catholic ACD, Mycroft's exceptionally austere and specialist priesthood being given a secular milieu analagous to a Trappist monastery.

only once, he has been here: 'The Empty House' (*Return*) says that in Sherlock Holmes's absence from England after his supposed death in combat with Moriarty, Mycroft 'preserved my rooms and papers exactly as they had always been'; it appears that, eminently characteristically, he had accomplished this feat without going near them, the sole visit being that in 'The Greek Interpreter'.

39 *his specialism is omniscience*: Mycroft's specialism is an object of satire and his presence a signal of a strong satirical element in the ensuing story, but the satire may cut two ways and here ACD uses Mycroft as a means to deplore the absence of such specialism co-ordination in real life. The British official convention that 'foreign affairs' was a specialization (and rather a disreputable one) is also under fire.

Canada, and the bi-metallic question: in 1896, the year after these supposed events, William Jennings Bryan (1860–1925) was nominated presidential candidate for the Democratic and Populist parties of the United States on his evangelistically preached platform of silver as the currency basis alongside gold in a ratio of 16 to 1; the agitation strongly affected Canadian western states. Readers may amuse themselves working out the relevance of India and the Navy. Bryan was renominated in 1900 and 1908 for the Democrats; his third unsuccessful campaign was in full swing when ACD was writing this story.

Jupiter is descending to-day: i.e. the king of the gods leaves Olympus to walk among men, presumably as he did in the case of Philemon and Baucis, not as in those of Io, Latona,

Europa, Danaë, Alcmene, and Ganymede. The Baucis–Philemon episode would be the more appropriate as their reception of the gods in mendicant disguise preserved their security while their niggardly neighbours were subsequently reduced to submarine obliteration.

what is he to Mycroft?: Professor Clarke Olney, 'The Literacy of Sherlock Holmes' (*Sherlock Holmes Journal*, 2 (Winter 1955), 9–15), drew attention to the proximity of this to Hamlet's 'What's Hecuba to him or he to Hecuba, | That he should weep for her?' (II. ii. 593–4). The satirical note here has now extended beyond ACD's original use of Mycroft, to suggest satire from Sherlock at his brother's expense. 'The Greek Interpreter' having established Sherlock Holmes's inferiority complex respecting his elder brother, a hint of resentment is now added as part of the gradual humanization of Holmes (inspiring its own caricature when an apocryphal younger brother was given an omnipresent inferiority complex against Sherlock in Gene Wilder's *Sherlock Holmes' Smarter Brother* (1975), unrivalled among movies in its elegant acquaintance with ACD's life and works).

Underground: London's Underground railway is the oldest in the world, having been opened in 1862 to link Smithfield metropolitan station with the major railway termini of Euston, Paddington, and King's Cross. Earl's Court Underground station opened in 1871 as a converging point of the Wimbledon, Ealing, and Piccadilly lines, with direct links to Paddington. Liverpool Street Station was opened in 1874 primarily as a terminus but linked with the Underground.

40 *Woolwich Arsenal*: military arms store and factory on the south bank of the Thames, well beyond Greenwich and at this time in Kent, the place itself familiar to ACD by report from the 1880s from his conversations with the Southsea patient who greatly influenced his intellectual and literary development, Major-General Alfred Wilks Drayson, FRAS (1827–1901), who served at Woolwich in the intervals of his Indian and African sojourns, and whose *Experiences of a Woolwich Professor during Fifteen Years at the Royal Military Academy* appeared in 1886, the year his doctor was writing *A Study in Scarlet*: it says that 'When I was a cadet, the practical class was quartered in the Arsenal', on which he doubtless ensured ACD was an authority, however involuntary.

40 *a plate-layer*: a worker employed in laying and maintaining rails.

Aldgate Station: lying between Liverpool Street Station and Tower Hill in the present-day Circle line, geographically south-east of Liverpool Street and situated in the Whitechapel area.

41 *Metropolitan . . . Willesden*: the reference here is not to the specific Metropolitan railway line, now part of the Underground system, but of those lines lying within the metropolis as distinct from lines serving remoter suburbs and beyond.

Capital and Counties Bank: bank favoured by aspiring young men at this time, to the extent that in the year of this case, 1895, a Liverpool branch office had virtually to close its doors owing to the number of its officials who fled to the Continent when the Oscar Wilde scandal broke. It was ACD's own bank.

dress-circle: the lowest balcony of the theatre for which the wearing of evening dress was then obligatory, indicating that the purchaser wished to assert his gentlemanly status at some cost to his lowly salary.

42 *the present state of Siam*: officialese for 'the present state of Anglo-French rivalry over Siam'. The dispute was resolved in Jan. 1896 by the Anglo-French convention guaranteeing the independence of the portions of Siam as yet unoccupied by either power. Thailand became the official name of Siam in 1939.

the Prime Minister: Robert Arthur Talbot Gascoyne Cecil, third Marquess of Salisbury (1830–1903), who had recently formed his third (Conservative) administration, famous for his detestation of democracy, devolution, and Disraeli. He was at this time his own Foreign Secretary, a portfolio he had also borne in his second administration (1886–92) after dismissing Lord Iddesleigh in Jan. 1887: Iddesleigh fell dead on Salisbury's carpet on receiving this intelligence, presumably causing him less dismay than that occasioned by the loss of the Bruce-Partington plans. (As the circumstances of Iddesleigh's death were well known to ACD and to the public at large, this implication seems intentional.)

keep the secret: ACD's intent remains satirical: 'Mycroft's revelation that "a very large sum was smuggled through the Estimates and expended on acquiring a monopoly of the invention" is evidence that the boys were up to the same little games then as they always have been; while his expectation that, although every effort had been made to keep the secret, everyone must have heard of it, is a measure of his belief in the efficacy of governmental secrecy' (Dakin, p. 229). The allusion to the smuggling of a sum through the Estimates was justified. Before, during, and after the Supply debate in 1900 the First Lord of the Admiralty, George Joachim Goschen (1831–1907), may actually have lied to the House of Commons and certainly deliberately misled it by stating that the Admiralty was not prepared to take any steps in regard to submarines, because this was only the weapon of the weaker nation (see esp. *The Times*, 18 July 1900, Mr Harwood's speech and the First Lord's reply (at 12 midnight)). His successor, William Waldegrave Palmer, second Earl of Selborne (1859–1942), admitted in the 1901 debate that five Holland submarines had been purchased (see Reginald Longstaff, *Submarine Command* (1984)). There was no question of a monopoly, John Philip Holland (1840–1905) having sold his invention first to his own (US) government: it was the first submarine with any power by which long voyages might be endured, capable of diving by inclining its axis and plunging to the required level. The Holland submarine allowed for one bow torpedo tube, one bow pneumatic dynamite gun, and several Whitehead underwater torpedoes (in 1895 and 1900 still produced at the Royal Laboratories at Woolwich Artillery). Holland, an Irishman from Liscanor, Co. Clare, originally sought to further Fenian hostilities against Britain, but after twenty-five years' work in the USA on the submarine became convinced of the necessity to end war, whence his enthusiasm for his submarine's proliferation. 'Nations with sea ports will have to refrain from making war', he wrote ('The Submarine Boat and its Future', *North American Review*, Dec. 1900): hence Mycroft's 'naval warfare becomes impossible within the radius of a Bruce-Partington's operation'. (The Estimates are the annual requests to Parliament for money allotments on the basis of information as to anticipated needs for the work of government departments during the forthcoming year.)

43   *the next honours list*: the list of persons recommended by the government or (in a very few cases) chosen by the sovereign for honour, such as peerage, baronetcy, knighthood, or order

of distinction. ACD was knighted on 9 Aug. 1902 (at the express wish of the Sovereign), but he accepted with great misgivings, only because of the urging of the King and his own mother. Thus Holmes acts here to express his creator's alternative life.

43 *a gentleman*: Here, as with Scott Eccles in 'Wisteria Lodge', ACD notes that social status confers some degree of immunity in respect to suspicion for criminal offences—an immunity in which (on the strength of this story) the investigating authorities unwisely handicap their work.

44 *draughtsman*: Mycroft, now as spokesman for the government establishment, here virtually sets up Sidney Johnson as the alternative criminal to Cadogan West, partly by inference, partly by emotive protection of Sir James Walter. Treason from a draughtsman, a professional, seems preferable to that from a gentleman, and Johnson would have needed expert training in the making of plans, sketches, designs, and drawings. ACD, trained as a professional doctor himself, had less sympathy with the supposed moral superiority of the gentry. Sir James Walter does not commit treason, but he dies before bringing himself to disclose it in a member of his family.

45 *London Bridge*: Underground link with ground-level railway to Woolwich. Mycroft's—and thence Sherlock's—assumption that a traveller accidentally failing to alight at London Bridge would naturally reach Aldgate is erroneous.

Possibly he tried to leave the carriage: Underground doors did not close automatically at this time, nor were they of the present-day sliding variety.

47 *Aldgate is a junction*: more correctly, there is a junction of lines (but no station) shortly before Aldgate when the line from Liverpool Street forks, the eastern leg going to Aldgate East.

48 *spies . . . in England*: a request for a second opinion on his own information as recorded in 'The Second Stain' (*Return*).

mouse-coloured: dark grey with a yellowish tinge.

49 *his brother, Colonel Valentine*: Baring-Gould and others find the butler's form of allusion to his employer's brother curiously presumptuous. But the aristocratic usage wherein servants spoke of junior male members of the family by prefix and first name was, as with so much else, carefully adopted by the

professional and commercial classes of social aspiration, e.g. the publishing firm of Macmillan, headed by Daniel Macmillan in the mid-20th century, had its calm shattered by a new telephone operator one day, when she excitedly informed the chairman of a telephone call from his brother:

'It's Mr Macmillan to speak to you, sir, the Prime Minister!'
'Young woman, *I* am Mr Macmillan! *That* is Mr Harold.'

50 *Arthur*: Characters in the Holmes cycle named 'Arthur' are often the victims of injustice from those from whom they are most entitled to expect support and protection, e.g. Arthur Charpentier (*A Study in Scarlet*), Arthur Holder ('The Beryl Coronet', *Adventures*), and Arthur, Lord Saltire ('The Priory School', *Return*).

53 *I had no keys . . . safe*: this statement has elicited furious controversy, e.g. Dakin's response that its implication is 'incredible: did the senior clerk, if he arrived before Sir James, have to sit on the door-step and wait to get in? Surely the watchman must have had a set of keys, or how could he patrol the building, not to speak of letting the cleaners in and out after office hours? Indeed, a few lines earlier Johnson himself says he closed the office on Monday at five, and was "always the last man out". How could he do that without the keys?' The point is that it *is* incredible, and that Holmes did not believe Johnson, who was obviously panicking ('I beg you won't try to drag me into the matter') and anxious to divert attention from himself at all costs with actions which in fact hardened Holmes's suspicions of him. What Johnson should have stated was that this, like other Civil Service departments, worked with a general set of keys left with the watchman: it is clear there had to be such a set, but Johnson's failure to mention it was evidently noted. The Sherlockian senior civil servant Sir Paul Gore-Booth explained conventional practice (*Sherlock Holmes Journal*, Dec. 1954): 'The offices, as opposed to the safe, were closed with keys on one of those clumsy bits of wood which, in my day when I was "twenty-seven years of age, unmarried and a clerk", were handed in at some central point and were not taken home . . . it is good Civil Servant practice, or was, anyway. The Head of the Department probably would have his private keys of the doors but there was no good reason to make a lot of spares.'

55 *third-class ticket*: at this time all trains, whether over or under ground, were divided into first, second, and third classes, the latter having little upholstery, the cheapest seats, and the largest and least salubrious crowds. Cadogan West, struggling for gentlemanly status and professional advancement, was obliged to make such economies as he could; he gave the woman he loved first-class theatre seating but gave himself the worst railway comfort.

the thief: not Sir James, whose 'rooms', or rather mansion, we know to have been in Woolwich, quite apart from his alibi; and not Johnson, also a Woolwich resident quite unable to afford city 'rooms', but suspicions of Johnson rose again when it became clear West's quarry was seeking not his own rooms but those of a spymaster.

56 *13, Caulfield Gardens, Kensington*: unlike the other two spies' addresses, this is imaginary or at least pseudonymous. Dakin (p. 232) suggests 12 or 14 Hogarth Road, near Earl's Court Station, corresponding to the house descriptions and proximity of their backs to the railway line, as well as delays in train journeys caused by the main line from Waterloo crossing at Earl's Court. But Michael Harrison (p. 146) argues for Cornwall Gardens, Kensington, on the southern side of its western half, 'for here the backs of the houses overlook a vast, open cutting in which the District and the Metropolitan lines are joined'. For a photograph of Cornwall Gardens, see Charles Viney, *Sherlock Holmes in London*, 124.

all the Queen's horses: satirical allusion to grandiose governmental responses to security breaches being unable to restore the original situation, as in the contrast in Humpty Dumpty's condition before and after his fall. And once more Sherlock Holmes finds a ludicrous analogy in response to Mycroft's pretensions.

57 *Goldini's*: presumably derived from the prolific Venetian dramatist Carlo Goldoni (1707–93) one of whose best-known works was *La bottega del caffè* (*The coffee-house*, 1750).

jemmy: crowbar used by burglars, usually made in sections.

dark lantern: oil lantern with a shutter for concealing its light, sometimes appearing in the Holmes saga as a 'bull's-eye' lantern.

a respectable citizen: Julian Symons, introducing *His Last Bow* (1974), wrote: 'Watson and Holmes together made up a double image of the conventional and the eccentric, the law-keeper and the law-breaker. The instant attraction held by the short stories for their Victorian audience from their appearance in 1891 was that they offered the chance of virtuous but outrageous excitement to readers whose lives were generally stodgy . . . Holmes was not an anarchist but he was a law-breaker, and such a figure could be admired if he was himself congenial.'

curaçao: orange-rind flavoured liqueur, deriving from Curaçao in the West Indies, despite which 'Curaçoa' is also accepted, and was used in the *Strand*.

59 *My answer was to rise from the table*: Watson turning law-breaker is far more thrilling than Holmes doing so, to add a corollary to Symons's theorem.

area: a small court in front of the cellar entrance to a dwelling, sometimes with a stair giving access down from the street especially when the cellar houses a basement flat cut off from the rest of the house. An archway under the house steps from street up to front door would help conceal persons in front of a lower door entering the house from the area. (These arrangements obtain, for instance, in the house where the Doyle family lived in Edinburgh from 1877 to 1880, 23 George Square.)

61 *agony column*: the columns in newspapers and magazines consisting of special advertisements particularly for missing relatives or friends, or messages from the love-lorn, and 'thus often gives evidence of great distress' (*OED*, second edn. (1989), i. 262). The *Daily Telegraph*, a London newspaper founded in 1855, was and is politically conservative, with particular appeal to military and naval officers—a ghost of a clue missed by Holmes.

62 *For England, home and beauty*: from Samuel Jones Arnold (1774–1852), 'The Death of Nelson', which at the time of ACD's writing had been most recently reprinted for wide circulation in H. E. Marshall, *Our Island Story: A Child's History of England* (1905), 457–8, without ascription. It uses the words several times (to rhyme with variants on 'England expects that every man | This day will do his duty'). The appropriate lines would seem to be:

> But dearly was that conquest bought
> Too well the gallant hero fought
> For England, home and beauty

Holmes's derisive quotation also invokes the spirit of Nelson defying prohibitions of offensive action by putting the telescope to his blind eye, although that event was long before the Trafalgar conflict recorded in Arnold's verse. ACD's admiring but not uncritical view of Nelson may be found in his *Rodney Stone* (1896), ch. 13, where the words 'there ran through his complex nature a sweet and un-English power of affectionate emotion, showing itself in tears if he were moved' are akin to the lines above when Holmes responds to Watson's agreement to join him in burglary.

63 *the great church clock*: Baring-Gould suggests St Stephen's Church on Gloucester Road.

the bird that I was looking for: commentators are agreed that the bird Holmes had incorrectly sought was Sidney Johnson, whose suspicious manner and replies on interview deepened an impression already fostered by Mycroft, as ever overvalued by his brother.

64 *beyond my comprehension*: Holmes's bitter acknowledgement that gentlemanly status had given unjustifiable immunity from suspicion.

the more terrible crime of murder: ethically a most important gradation since chauvinism usually clouds the public mind from any such recognition. Where treason demonstrably takes human life it is murder; where it only endangers it, to however large an extent, it cannot be said to outweigh murder in turpitude.

65 *he never held up his head again*: yet the revered Sir James died without saying one word to clear the name of a subordinate who had given his life in defence of the secrets Sir James had guarded so inadequately. ACD noted that privileged families protect themselves.

66 *fifteen years in a British prison*: why was Oberstein not executed? Dakin suggests that his knowledge of other powers would have given him information with which to bargain, and it is also possible ACD was hinting that Oberstein was in a position to blackmail major British figures into using their influence to have a death sentence commuted (he concludes his 'The Lost Special' (*Round the Fire Stories*) with such a diplomatic move).

all the naval centres of Europe: 'Oberstein would have written to all the naval centres and then considered their offers before deciding which to accept. If he had any sense, he would have reported the larger bids to the others in the hope that they would increase theirs. This sort of bargaining could be carried on for weeks. In fact, with still more vision, he could have diddled the lot by having several copies made of the plans, thus not only making their recovery by the British government virtually useless, but enabling him to send them simultaneously to all the interested governments, extracting the cash and leaving them to bite their nails in baffled fury when they found their rivals similarly equipped with submarines' (Dakin, 233). In fact this—but perfectly openly and with no subterfuge—is exactly what Holland did do, with the permission of the US government under William McKinley (1843–1901). There was a general sale but no auction.

Whence Bruce-Partington? Did ACD know Holland's wife, like his own mother, was an Irish-born Foley? Bruce seems chosen as the symbol of an independence-fighter against England. 'Partington' was Abraham Lincoln's rude name for the Whig Lord Hartington (Rector of Edinburgh University elected before ACD's eyes in 1877), alluding to what he saw as Hartington's support for disunion in America. It was a demurely circuitous route of asserting English dependence on the Fenian submarine. Holland's Fenian antecedents were generally known, and the irony of Britain's submarine fleet being built up by the work of her former Fenian foe would have delighted ACD (and provided a common chord with his 'The Green Flag').

67 *the last word upon the subject*: at any rate until Dr Lucie Balmer published her *Orlando di Lassos Motetten: eine stilgeschichtliche Studie* (Berne/Leipzig, 1938), which Gerald Abraham roguishly hazarded (*Music and Letters*, xx (1939), 89–91) was in fact Holmes's work posthumously published under a pseudonym! Orlandus Lassus (1532–94) wrote some 530 motets, comprising about half his collected works as they appear in the first modern edition, by Haberl and Sandberger (which began publication in 1894, one year before the story). The opening allusion to 'the music of the Middle Ages' is therefore chronologically inexact.

the Bruce-Partington plans: ACD was actually consulted on the theft of the Irish Crown Jewels in July 1907, by his remote kinsman Sir Arthur Vicars (1864–1921), the Ulster King of Arms in whose custody the purloined regalia in Dublin Castle

had been officially placed and who suffered disgrace and
dismissal. Vicars believed the thief was his own familiar
friend Francis Richard Shackleton (1876–?1925), brother of
the Antarctic explorer. ACD was kind about the ruined
Vicars (without mentioning his ruin) in *Memories and Adventures*: saying nothing of the missing jewels in that appropriate
place, he is hardly likely to have written the case up as this
very story, as various writers have baselessly claimed, with
Vicars as Sir James Walter and Shackleton as Colonel Valentine (no resemblance being evident). The irresponsibility of
such conduct in breach of the confidence of an unhappy
victim while the case was still under investigation is alone an
excellent reason for dismissing the thesis. The only allusion
lies in Queen Victoria's gift to Holmes: emerald is the Irish
colour, an emerald tie-pin is a jewel, the jewel's origin is the
Crown, and in that sense one of the Irish Crown Jewels (still
missing as I write) came into the possession of Sherlock
Holmes long before the theft. That little joke would have
been no betrayal of Vicars and might have won a wan smile.

THE DEVIL'S FOOT

First published in the *Strand Magazine*, 40 (Dec. 1910), 639–53, with
7 illustrations by Gilbert Halliday (to the disgust of ACD, as stated
to Greenhough Smith in an undated letter). Title as here but
superscribed 'A Reminiscence of Sherlock Holmes'. First American
publication in the *Strand Magazine* (New York), 40 (Jan. 1911),
722–30; 41 (Feb. 1911), 3–9. Halliday's illustrations from the London
Strand were used, though an extra drawing was required from him
because of the two-part publication. Halliday was never again used
as a Holmes illustrator. The title and several of the story's ingredients
are found in 'Song' (*c.*1593) by John Donne (1573–1631), stanza 1:

> Goe, and catche a falling starre,
>   Get with child a mandrake roote,
> Tell me, where all past yeares are,
>   Or who cleft the Divels foot,
> Teach me to heare the Mermaides singing,
> Or to keep off envies stinging,
>   And finde
>   What winde
> Serves to advance an honest minde.

68 *occasional indiscretions of his own*: Sherlock Holmes's cocaine addiction (denied in *A Study in Scarlet* but asserted in *The Sign of the Four* and given limited use thereafter) caused concern to Jean Leckie (later ACD's second wife) who feared evil effects from an adoring public capable of adopting him as role-model, a thought amazing to ACD (who had never imagined anyone would take his creation so seriously). Hence in 'The Missing Three-Quarter' (*Return*) Watson recorded weaning Holmes 'from that drug mania which had threatened once to check his remarkable career' and that 'I was well aware that the fiend was not dead but sleeping', and the sleep 'a light one and the waking near when in periods of idleness I have seen the drawn look upon Holmes's ascetic face'. Watson's medical-moral ascendancy over Holmes is an unspoken subtext to Holmes's more famous intellectual superiority over Watson; they are doctor and patient as well as pupil and tutor, squire and knight, biographer and subject.

Harley Street: proverbial London location for fashionable medical specialists; ACD optimististically occupied rooms nearby for a few months in 1891 as an eye specialist, after an ultimately successful nine years as a Southsea general practitioner; but his failure to attract London patients increased his literary drive, finally launching him as a full-time writer via the Holmes short stories.

69 *would*: 'should' (*Strand*).

Poldhu Bay: more accurately, Poldhu Cove, almost exactly on 50° latitude, about 6 miles south of Helston ('Poldhu' = 'black pool' (Cornish)).

Mounts Bay: a great semi-circle of coast from Land's End to the Lizard, with Penzance at its apex, half-protects, half-exposes Mounts Bay.

Chaldean: the language spoken by Abraham and other inhabitants of Ur, that spoken by Nebuchadnezzar and other inhabitants of Babylon, that spoken by the Jewish peoples at the time of Christ, would all be comprehended in this, i.e. 2,000 years of Middle Eastern history. But Holmes's interests would also seem to include Carthaginian, from Dido (if she existed) to Hannibal and beyond. In fact, this is a joke, based on the 'Chaldee' alleged MS 'translated' in *Blackwood's Magazine* for Oct. 1817, satirizing the Edinburgh literary scene of its day in a biblical parody (to the fury of local Christians), being the work of James Hogg (1770–1835), John Gibson Lockhart (1794–1854), and John Wilson alias 'Christopher North' (1785–1854), brilliant and notorious literary thugs. ACD's boyhood mentor John Hill Burton (1809–81) would have acquainted him with this famous coup of Scottish cultural warfare, in the intervals of training him as a bibliophile: variations of the Chaldee-Caledonian joke were still being perpetrated in the Edinburgh of the 1870s (e.g. 'St Chaldean', *Ancient History of Caledonia*, 1874). ACD studied the extinct Cornish language on his convalescent sojourn in Feb. 1909 and enjoyed speculating about the linguistic impact of pre-Christian tin-traders, but would certainly have found Cornish links with Irish and Scots Gaelic as well as common features between the Cornish dialect of English and the Scots language.

'The Devil's Foot' as a story is a metaphor for this, with its African root matching the Phoenician-Carthaginian supposed linguistic roots out of Africa, but only finding its outlet through a Cornish family whose feud in its vicious spiral rivals the most hideous stories of Highland vengeance recounted by ACD's two greatest preceptors: Scott and Macaulay.

70 *a consignment of books upon philology*: probable candidates for inspection by ACD (and hence presumably Holmes) are: Edward Norris, *Ancient Cornish Drama* (Penzance, 1859); Revd Robert Williams, *Lexicon Cornu-Britannicum: A Dictionary of the Ancient Celtic Language of Cornwall of which the Words are Elucidated by Copious Examples from the Cornish Works Now Remaining with Translations in English. The synonyms are also Given in the Cognate Dialects of Welsh, Armorican, Irish, Gaelic, and Manx; Shewing at One View the Connexion between Them* (Llandovery, 1865); John Bannister, *Glossary of Cornish Names* (Truro, 1871); Courtney and Couch, *Glossary of Words in Use in Cornwall* (Penzance, 1880); Fred W. P. Jago, *Dialect of Cornwall* (Truro, 1882); Jago, *An English–Cornish Dictionary* (London 1887).

Tredannick Wollas: imaginary name, to cover the similarly named Predannack Wollas, a small village lying between Poldhu Cove and the Lizard; and the similarly described Cwry nearby. 'Tredanek' actually means 'electric' (and thus one of the very last words born in Cornish): ACD seems to be making a little joke about its primitive conditions (a grim joke; the murders were to depend on the want of electricity).

Roundhay: the portly Revd Roundhay, archaeologist and local historian, seems a direct origin of the Revd Reggie Portway in Angus Wilson's *Anglo-Saxon Attitudes* (1955) where pagan phenomena also come to light apparently through ancient and possibly supernatural forces but ultimately prove to have been produced by the human agency of an exceptionally malignant individual seeking vengeance on his own family. Another precursor of Wilson's novel in the Holmes cycle is the unnarrated case of 'the singular contents of the ancient British barrow' ('The Golden Pince-Nez', *Return*).

Mortimer Tregennis: the eponymous narrator's dandy uncle in *Rodney Stone* (1896) is Sir Charles ('Buck') Tregellis, also present in 'An Impression of the Regency' (1900) and 'The Fall of Lord Barrymore' (1912). 'Tre' and 'genys' seem to mean 'well-born family' in Cornish, which looks like the author's intention. Mortimer probably derives from the Great Refrain to the Scots poet William Dunbar's (?1460–1530) *Lament for the Makeris* 'Timor Mortis Conturbat Me' (The fear of death disquiets me).

an independent gentleman: a person of refinement and assured income needing no employment.

71 *view-hallo*: fox-hunting term for the call or cry given by huntsman on obtaining a view of the fox, with sinister allusion in John Woodcock Graves's song 'John Peel': 'Oh, Peel's view-hallo would awaken the dead', and 'From a find to a check, from a check to a view, | From a view to a death in the morning.' Both quotations seem apposite in the light of later developments.

Owen: 'own' or 'owne' means 'fear' or 'dread' in Cornish.

George: ACD's 'An Impression of the Regency' (*Uncollected Stories*) contains a horrifying cameo appearance of the mad King George III.

Brenda: possibly suggested by the Cornish 'Brentyn' ('noble' or 'excellent').

Wartha: 'Awartha' in Cornish means 'above' or 'on high'; Upper Tredannick.

73 *his dark eyes . . . scene*: itself a reflection or reversal, of the old superstition of a murder victim's eyes reflecting the murderer. Creation of atmosphere, not concealment of criminal, is the priority in Holmes stories.

73 *my elder brother George*: hence a possible beneficiary at the expense of a younger brother in a family business settlement of inheritance.

Redruth: railroad town about 15 miles due north of the Lizard. The collapse of the tin-mines left the workers less fortunately situated than the owners, and many were forced to emigrate to Pennsylvania, Michigan, etc.

75 *snatches*: cf. the mad, drowning Ophelia: 'she chanted snatches of old tunes / As one incapable of her own distress' (*Hamlet*, IV. vii. 177–80).

Helston: market town of the Lizard peninsula about 6 miles north of Poldhu Cove.

76 *flower-plots*: *Strand* and American texts, but elsewhere corrupted to 'flower-pots'.

St Ives: town and bay on north coast of Cornwall, about 7 miles due north of Penzance, famous as the title of a novel left uncompleted by Robert Louis Stevenson (1850–94) at his death. ACD declined to write a conclusion and it was ultimately finished by the Cornish writer Arthur Quiller-Couch (1863–1944).

79 *celts*: not here an allusion to the Iron Age immigrants of the British Isles who supplied Cornwall with its language, but the popular archaeological name for stone hatchets, adzes, or chisels derived from either *cellt* (Welsh for a flintstone) or *celtis* (Low Latin for a chisel).

Leon Sterndale: Leon is the pronunciation of Cornish 'lyon' (a lion), also the Irish-Gaelic word for it. Sterndale derives from *an Steren*, Cornish for the Pole Star whilst *Dyal* is Cornish for revenge. 'The Pole Star for Revenge' is the reworking of the old story on those lines instead of the death-wish of the original Captain of the *Pole-Star*.

Beauchamp Arriance: Venten or Fenten Arriance, near Mullion.

81 *He is deeply interested*: i.e. he has interests and investments, emotional and/or material, involved in the situation.

82 *lamp*: non-electric, paraffin-fuelled, the flame capable of increase and decrease by small hand-turned wheel, wick protected by a delicate mantle, enclosed in an open glass or talc chimney frequently bulging wide at its centre: a standard

item in rural non-electrified houses in the British Isles throughout the 19th century.

83 *foxhound drawing a cover*: hunting-dog prospecting through a covert in quest of a fox. But he has been anticipated as regards a death in the morning (see note on 'view-hallo' above).

an ordinary standard: not a 'standard' lamp in the electricity-age sense, self-standing, around 6 to 8 feet in height, but a lamp of ordinary standard make.

talc shield: in Longman's words, ' "Talc" is a name loosely applied to muscovy glass, a glass material manufactured from mica and used in lamps and lanterns. Its naturally "smokey" appearance masks carbon deposits left by the burning oil. The smoke guard on the lamp Holmes is examining is made of talc' (p. 222).

84 *ever to forget*: Robert Christison, 'On the Properties of the Ordeal Bean of Old Calabar' (*Monthly Journal of Medicine* (1855), 815–20), a characteristically dry and scientifically measured description of his own near-death from auto-experiment, was much quoted in his several obituaries after his death on 27 Jan. 1882, just following ACD's return from a voyage on the *Mayumba* to Calabar.

combustion: the action of burning.

something was burned . . . strange toxic effects: Steven Saxe, 'Tregennis and Poe' (*Baker Street Journal*, OS 1/1 (Jan. 1946), 86–7), drew attention to inspiration here from Edgar Allan Poe's 'The Imp of the Perverse' whose relevant passage runs: 'in reading some French Memoirs, I found an account of a nearly fatal illness that occurred to Madame Pilau, through the agency of a candle accidentally poisoned. The idea struck my fancy at once. I knew my victim's habit of reading in bed. I knew, too, that his apartment was narrow and ill ventilated. But I need not vex you with impertinent details. I need not describe the easy artifices by which I substituted, in his bed-room candle-stead, a wax-light of my own making, for the one which I there found. The next morning he was discovered dead in his bed, and the Coroner's verdict was, "Death by the visitation of God".'

90 *reddish gravel*: Dakin (p. 242) remarks that Sterndale 'would do his clothes a bit of no good by pocketing a handful of gravel from his garden on his way to the vicarage to carry out his

vendetta; but ... why should he take it at all? There would
be plenty of material in the vicarage garden to throw at Tregennis's window. Was he *trying* to make it easy for Holmes?'
The point is that, like so many of the Holmes saga
clues, human enslavement to convention supplied the basis of
much deduction. Sterndale, a hunter, packed his necessaries
before going on safari.

91 *I could not divorce*: divorce was not possible in England at this
time unless one party could prove sexual fidelity to the other
while proving the other guilty of adultery, and even then the
divorce might not be granted. ACD had become president of
the Divorce Law Reform Union in 1909.

Buda: situated on the west bank of the Danube, it forms
together with Pest (on the east bank) the capital of Hungary,
then part of the Austrian Empire.

92 *pharmacopoeia*: originally the register of drugs and chemicals
permissible for medical use, but more recently of all such
substances.

toxicology: the study of poisons. Christison was the foremost
toxicologist of his time.

ordeal: the use of the word here is very suggestive, given Christison's use of it in the article recording his own auto-experiment.

Ubanghi: river of Equatorial Africa, entering the Congo river
on the Equator about 17°E. Its mouth was discovered by the
Revd George Grenfell (1849–1906) of the Baptist Missionary
Society in 1884, the journeys also enabling him to meet
several cannibal and dwarf tribes hitherto apparently unac-
quainted with whites. ACD would have heard of his work
through his own study of recent Congolese history.

94 *Cornish branch*: ACD's first notable piece of writing in praise
of Cornwall predates his vacation (see Introduction) and is in
Through the Magic Door, 87–8: 'There is something wonderful,
I think, about the land of Cornwall. That long peninsula
extending out into the ocean has caught all sorts of strange
floating things, and has held them in isolation until they have
woven themselves into the texture of the Cornish race. What
is this strange strain which lurks down yonder and every now
and again throws up a great man with singular un-English
ways and features for all the world to marvel at? It is not
Celtic, nor is it the dark old Iberian. Further and deeper lie

the springs. Is it not Semitic, Phoenician, the roving men of Tyre, with noble Southern faces and Oriental imaginations, who have in far-off days forgotten their blue Mediterranean and settled on the granite shores of the Northern Sea?

'Whence came the wonderful face and great personality of Henry Irving? How strong, how beautiful, how un-Saxon it was! I only know that his mother was a Cornish woman. Whence came the intense glowing imagination of the Brontes —so unlike the Miss-Austen-like calm of their predecessors? I only know that their mother was a Cornish woman . . .'

THE RED CIRCLE

First published in the *Strand Magazine*, 41 (Mar. 1911), 259–66; (Apr. 1911), 428–34, with 3 illustrations by H. M. Brock and 1 by Joseph Simpson. Title as here but superscribed 'A Reminiscence of Sherlock Holmes'. First American publication in the *Strand Magazine* (New York), 41 (Apr. 1911), 291–8; (May 1911), 472–8; illustrated as above. The break in the story for its magazine publication (against ACD's wishes) as here, designated 'Part 1' and 'Part 2' in first British and American book texts.

The surviving MS of this story (its opening reproduced in Baring-Gould, ii. 704) indicates an original title, 'The Adventure of the Bloomsbury Lodger', discarded in favour of the present one. 'Lodger' was a title-word of dramatic and even sinister resonances, as Marie Belloc-Lowndes (1868–1947) was to prove two years later with her fictional investigation of the Jack the Ripper theme in *The Lodger* (1913), and ACD would use it in his penultimate, and last great, Holmes story, 'The Veiled Lodger' (*Case-Book*). It may be that to blazon the word from a title in 1911 was potentially distasteful to his mother, Mary, still alive and still living in a rent-free cottage on the estate of her former lodger, Bryan Charles Waller (1853–1932), in north-west Yorkshire.

'Circle' reminds us that ACD's use of secret societies in his writing was usually grounded on those he knew best, the Irish variety. The Fenian, or Irish Republican, Brotherhood was organized in 'circles' under James Stephens (1824–1901), its founder, who appears in ACD's story 'Touch and Go' (1886, reprinted in *Uncollected Stories*).

96 *girl*: maidservant, resident or non-resident, to be found even in working-class homes especially if, as here, money is coming from lodgers. ACD's father initially took lodgings with his

maternal grandmother in Edinburgh, and from 1875 to 1881 his mother took in at least one lodger and may have done so at some other times. The Census of 1861 notes a maidservant for the Doyles, that of 1871 (with no lodger and the father drinking heavily) none, that of 1881 (with lodger) one. So detailed a working-class portrait as Mrs Warren is unusual in ACD (but see Mrs Merrilow in 'The Veiled Lodger' (*Case-Book*), also a landlady): in circumstance at least it will be a portrait of his mother, the alternation of diplomacy and directness also being characteristic of her.

96 *fifty shillings*: £2.50 sterling; even with all food, house-cleaning, parlour space, and privacy, a considerable sum for those days ($ US 12.50 at this point).

97 *DAILY GAZETTE*: fictitious newspaper, to which ACD henceforth resorted (despite his previous success in parody of existing newspapers) with increasing frequency, no doubt because of his growing fame as a controversialist and with it the greater danger of libel threats (e.g. in this instance from actual 'agony' advertisers who could prove some similarity of entry should an actual newspaper be given).

thumb-print: not, as sometimes supposed, an allusion to the fingerprint system (adopted by Scotland Yard in 1901 and pointedly exhibited as a potential source of false clues with resultant injustice in 'The Norwood Builder' (*Return*)), since whatever his or her apprehensions the lodger was hardly likely to suspect the landlady of automatically sending her tenants' marks for analysis by the scientific branch of criminal investigation. It was the size and hence the sex rather than the texture of the thumb-skin for which the lodger sought concealment.

98 *you can read great things out of small*: a conflation, probably unconscious, of at least two texts:

> sic canibus catulos similis, sic matribus haedos
> noram, sic parvis componere magna solebam.

(I measured great things from small ones, such as dogs from kindred pups, and goats from their kids.)

(Virgil, *Ecloga*, i. 22–3)

Pour juger des choses grandes et hautes, il faut une âme de même, autrement nous leur attribuons le vice qui est le nôtre.

(To judge great and high things, such a soul is needed; otherwise we attribute to them our own particular vices.)

(Montaigne, *Essais*, I. xiv, ed. Rat)

These may appear somewhat sophisticated literary references for Mrs Warren, but that is only to look at the ingredients: what ACD wanted to show was that a landlady could on occasion speak with the tongue of poets and sages, believing himself the son of such a one.

cigar: 'a cigar' in the *Strand*, but not in British or American book texts.

100 *nothing in to-day's*: 'A Spaniard would write to a Spaniard in Spanish' (see 'Wisteria Lodge'), but this law, although unwisely ignored elsewhere in English literature, cannot apply here: advertisements in Italian in the midst of a mass of English notices would have excited remark from Italian readers of the paper, with the consequent danger of sympathizers with the Red Circle noting the contents and taking steps. An ethnic secret society would have large peripheral sympathies in the local immigrant group, especially if the body's antecedents were patriotic: many fellow-ethnics who would not join it would act as sentinels in certain circumstances. The other advertisements printed seem akin to the humour in the named but unrecorded Holmes cases and, as such, invitations to our imagination which could well feast on the boa-constricted skater, the Jacobean matricide, the Brixton cataleptic, and the diurnal tell-tale heart. (A boa was a fashionable female neck-wrap composed from deceased rodents or birds rather than reptiles.)

101 *He shall pack . . . baggage*: i.e. he shall depart thence with his possessions. The usage seems less from Edwardian London than from Edwardian Yorkshire.

my old man: clearly Cockney London here, the mixture of regional conventions being appropriate for rural–urban immigrants. Cockneys were widely credited with habitual allusion to marital partners as personal possessions of antiquity, and music-hall songs made much of this. Marie Lloyd (1870–1922) was at the peak of her fame in 1910, one of her best-beloved numbers having as its chorus:

> My old man
> Said 'Follow the van,
> And don't dilly-dally on the w'y!'

Off went the van
With the old man
In it;
I walked be'ind with me old cock linnet.
I dallied and dillied,
Dillied and dallied,
Lorst me w'y and don't know where to roam,
'Cos you can't trust the speshuls like the
        old-time coppers,
When you can't find your w'y 'ome.

This seems to include several of the ingredients for the ensuing passage, if not in the same order or conjunction, and no doubt supplied conscious or unconscious inspiration for it.

101 *Tottenham Court Road*: at this date a thoroughfare synonymous with commercialism, usually brash. See Saki, 'Reginald on Christmas Presents': 'there is . . . the female relative in the country who "knows a tie is always useful", and sends you some spotted horror that you could only wear in secret or in Tottenham Court Road' (*Reginald*, 1903). It divides Bloomsbury from Soho, continues the Charing Cross Road northward, becoming Hampstead Road and Camden High Street.

Hampstead Heath: great undulating parkway in north London with many lonely areas, easily reached by vehicle going north on Camden High Street.

102 *Great Orme Street . . . Howe Street*: London has no such streets, but Howe Street is a prominent Edinburgh thoroughfare (one of several cases of ACD putting Edinburgh names to work in London locations), continuing Frederick Street north after Heriot Row (where Stevenson lived). Orme is an Edinburgh name (a University student leader of ACD's time, who founded the Student Union, was David Orme Masson, known by his second name to distinguish him from his otherwise homonymous father, the famous Professor of English Literature). It has been suggested Great Ormond Street is vaguely intended: famous for its children's hospital, it is separated from Tottenham Court Road by Bedford Square, the University of London, the British Museum, and Russell Square.

104 *Art for Art's sake*: doctrine enunciated in this form by Henry Crabb Robinson (1775–1867), an associate of Coleridge and Wordsworth, pupil of Schelling, and student of Kant. Re-

ported by Benjamin Constant (1767–1834) in his *Journal intime* for 11 Feb. 1804: 'L'art pour l'art et sans but; tout but dénature l'art' (Art for art's sake and with no purpose; any purpose perverts art). The doctrine was preached by Oscar Wilde, whose genius was far too complex and avowedly self-contradictory to practise it consistently, but ACD's use of it here is a salute to Wilde and a reminder that Holmes had been conceived in the same vortex (see James Edward Holroyd, *Baker Street By-Ways* (1959), 103–13).

the greatest for the last: appropriately, when ACD died the *New York World* published a cartoon of Holmes standing on a cliff looking over the sea to sunset, captioned 'His Greatest Adventure'.

105 *Twenty . . . That should mean T*: MS originally read 'Nineteen', presumably because the Italian language has no 'K'; but this would have Holmes read it, English-style, as 'S', with consequent bewilderment. We must assume use of Italian in the English alphabet.

Dakin, supporting the idea of a common Western European alphabet of twenty-six letters, finds 'A greater mystery is why Gennaro should have chosen such a protracted [4¾ minutes] and cumbersome [477 waves of the candle] way of sending Emilia a (three times repeated, with Gorgiano at his heels at any moment!) rather pointless message about a danger of which she was already aware and couldn't do anything about anyway' (p. 226). We are back once more to the sporting metaphor Hesketh Pearson has seen at the heart of the stories. The message was not primarily for Emilia; it was, like the bust in 'The Empty House' (*Return*), bait, and again like it, it worked (see Baring-Gould, ii. 698, and works therein cited.)

it: 'he' in *Strand*.

106 *Journeys end with lovers' meetings*: correctly, 'Journeys end in lovers meeting' (Shakespeare, *Twelfth Night*, II. iii. 46). Frequently misquoted, once again by Holmes in 'The Empty House' (*Return*), that time 'in' correct but still pluralizing 'meeting', for the unappreciated benefit of the recently apprehended Colonel Sebastian Moran. Both are ironic usages, but there is a distinction between a celebration of capture of a murderer after surviving three years of his vendetta, and an encounter with a fellow-sleuth however little mutual love is lost.

106 *on my side*: not remotely near the generosity of Lestrade's *amende honorable* in 'The Six Napoleons' (*Return*) but sufficient for Gregson's minor role in the saga (*A Study in Scarlet*, 'The Greek Interpreter', 'Wisteria Lodge') for what is *his* last bow. The American cabman motif linked with him is an amusing echo of his failure in *A Study in Scarlet*.

107 *The hero of the Long Island Cove mystery*: hitherto invariably printed as 'Cave'. But there are no caves in Long Island, NY, Glen Cove is a noted landmark for the golfer and the starch-manufacturer, and ACD's handwriting, while good, has had its 'o' taken for 'a' in other cases. Pinkerton's was the most famous American detective agency, founded in 1850 by Allan Pinkerton (1819–84) (see *The Valley of Fear* in the present series).

Gorgiano: 'Gorgo' (Italian) means an abyss or a whirlpool. 'Gorgie' in Edinburgh is both a district and, among school-boy street-gangs, a Protestant war-cry which may have been in use when the youthful ACD led a Catholic street-gang, or which he may have heard among youthful Unionist suppor-ters for his Edinburgh Central candidacy—or even among opponents when his Jesuit education became an issue in the election (1900):

> Hallo, hallo, we are the Gorgie boys!
> Hallo, hallo, you'll know us by our noise!
> We are up to our knees in Fenian blood.

It has considerable common ground with Emilia Lucca's portrait of Gorgiano (John M. Simpson of the Department of Scottish History, University of Edinburgh, kindly gave me the text of the war-cry).

108 *never*: save when confronted by the hound of the Baskervilles?

pole-axed: a pole-axe is an axe with a hammer at its back, employed by butchers.

109 *Dio mio*: my God! (Italian).

110 *Vieni*: Come (Italian).

Notting Hill hooligan: 'hooligan' suddenly came into use as a word in several newspapers in the summer of 1898; a derivation from 'Hooley's gang' has been suggested, but no solid evidence has come forward, Hooley (if he ever existed) having all his con-quests, glories, triumphs, spoils shrunk to the little measure of an unattributable root. Notting Hill lies north of Holland Park,

west of Bayswater and Paddington. It may not be coinciden-
tal that it had recently been depicted as overcoming all other
London boroughs by force of arms in G. K. Chesterton's
hypertopian satire *The Napoleon of Notting Hill* (1904).

111 *of that port*: 'of that part' in all previous edns., but it makes
little sense, and would again seem a victim of an erroneous
reading of 'a' for 'o'. At best, 'part' would presumably mean
that her father was chief lawyer and former deputy for the
volcanic north-western district adjoining Naples. But 'port'
would mean her father was the chief lawyer and former
deputy of Naples, which would make him a figure of the
highest social and political status and consequence from
whom his errant progeny and her lowly swain might well flee.

the Bowery: famous New York City street, to which gentlefolk
might go for thrills or sensations only to discover themselves
at the mercy of criminals.

Brooklyn: a separate city to the south of New York City until
their amalgamation in 1898. The events of this story could be
before or after that, but are clearly after 1883 when Brooklyn
Bridge was opened, linking Brooklyn with Manhattan across
the East River.

112 *the old Carbonari*: in the MS originally 'the famous Camorra'.
The change arose because the secret society in question had
to be one which Gennaro Lucca might reasonably enter from
altruistic and philanthropic motives, and while the Carbonari
had its origins in patriotic liberal and radical republican
organization during the Napoleonic occupation, seeking re-
forms from the restored Bourbon monarchy of Naples, and
winning support from figures of some repute including the
future Napoleon III, the Camorra was a wholly self-seeking
criminal body. Entrants to the Carbonari were likely to be
poor, as the name (charcoal-burners) implied, while those
seeking admission to the Camorra (whose name means 'clique')
were social élitists or well on the road to it. ACD's brother-
in-law E. W. Hornung (1866–1921) had given his criminal
imitation of Holmes, A. J. Raffles, a couple of very unpleasant encounters with the Camorra in *The Black Mask* (1901) and
ACD may have felt the series had rather too much common
ground. But ACD was thinking primarily of the Invincibles
(the murder-gang who assassinated Chief Secretary Lord

Frederick Cavendish in Dublin's Phoenix Park on 6 May 1882) and the dynamiters who threatened London in 1883–5, both of which groups evolved from the original and much more obviously romantic patriot Fenian, or Irish Republican, Brotherhood.

112 *lodge*: the place of meeting originally which became a section or division of the brotherhood or society. Had 'The Bloomsbury Lodger' been retained as the title it would have borne a second, sinister significance. 'Held' is used to mean 'convened'.

115 *the old university*: 'I was educated in the University of Life', a popular Scotticism, is here pressed into service by ACD (though presumably without thought of the alternative usage 'I was educated in the University of the Gutter').

Covent Garden: the Royal Opera House in that popular market-place for vegetables, fruit, and flowers, was being weaned from its exclusively Italian obsession from 1892, Wagner seasons being performed in Oct. 1897 and Sept. 1902, for instance, both of which might involve wintry evenings. ACD's decision to have Holmes turn Wagnerite is unlikely to have eventuated without a thought of his former Hindhead neighbour George Bernard Shaw, prophet of Wagner among music critics and classifier of Holmes as 'a drug-addict without a single amiable trait'. Shaw openly admired the Brigadier Gerard stories, stating of his own Mendoza in *Man and Superman* (1903), 'the theft of the brigand-poetaster from Sir Arthur Conan Doyle [*The Exploits of Brigadier Gerard*: 'How the Brigadier Held the King'] is deliberate'. Was ACD now deliberately tempting GBS to more wholesale appropriation? A year after the appearance of 'The Red Circle', Shaw was at work on *Pygmalion* whose Professor Higgins derives from Holmes, and Colonel Pickering from Watson. Meanwhile ACD in late 1911 was writing *The Lost World*, whose Professor Challenger contained several personal touches of GBS.

THE DISAPPEARANCE OF LADY FRANCES CARFAX

First published in the *Strand Magazine*, 42 (Dec. 1911), 603–14, with 5 illustrations by Alec Ball. First American publication in *American Magazine* (New York), 73 (Dec. 1911), 131–42, as 'The Disappearance of Lady Carfax', with 5 illustrations (and cover) by Frederic Dorr Steele.

116 *Latimer's, in Oxford Street*: Hugh Latimer (?1485–1555), Protestant leader, was burnt as a heretic at Oxford under Mary I; the 'boot' was a later form of torture of Stuart times used by Anglicans against Protestant Dissenters, involving constriction and crushing of the feet; a Turkish bath subjects the frame to heat, sometimes excessively. A chilling association of ideas, perhaps unconscious.

you had a companion: implying simply that Watson gave a lift to a fellow-patron of the Turkish bath, who was of course male, and that his irritation at the doubling of mystification was perfectly natural. Had it been a woman, Watson would surely have sat on the right-hand side of the hansom (a horse-drawn cab for two with the driver mounted at back holding reins over the roof, first invented by Joseph Aloysius Hansom (1803–82)). The plethora of works handing out unrecorded wives to Watson and romances to Holmes seem to forget that (unlike his fellow-pupil of the Jesuits James Joyce), ACD did not try to have his short stories published by Mills & Boon.

117 *Carfax*: it is a long shot, but the revival of interest in Wilde's works by the efforts of his literary executor Robert Baldwin Ross (1869–1918), who had directed the Carfax Gallery since 1900, renewed interest in *The Importance of Being Earnest* whose heroine, the Hon. Gwendolen Fairfax, loves John Worthing whose origins in a handbag were indeed helpless and migratory. (Ross's partner More Adey suggests Moore Agat (p.68).) The Burke and Hare plot would have preceded the name-choice.

them: 'it' (*Strand*).

118 *Hôtel National at Lausanne*: it was in existence 1886–1951, with a listing in Baedeker's *Switzerland* from 1902. The lake is Lake Geneva.

The family: the present Earl of Rufton (imaginary title), a cousin to Lady Frances in the first or second degree, and/or his immediate siblings or progeny, whose readiness to disgorge funds and whose absence from any personal initiative are an additional clue to the nature of Lady Frances's isolation. They pay for her, but make no effort to extend loving welcome to her, a commonplace situation in wealthy households. Her governess seems her only loving link with her origins (ACD's governess sisters would give him firm ground here).

118 *Montpellier*: rendered incorrectly in all British texts as 'Mont-pelier'; 8 kilometres north of the Mediterranean coast, with the Rhone valley dividing it from Lausanne, Lyons midway between them, thus making Crédit Lyonnais the appropriate banking-house for the author to assign.

119 *twopence a word*: 3 pence from Switzerland (four words for 5 new pence).

Un sauvage—un véritable sauvage!: a wild man, a really wild man!

120 *Baden . . . Englischer Hof*: usually identified as Baden-Baden in the state of Baden-Württemberg, with thermal baths approved by the ancient Romans and near enough to the Rhine, its Englischer Hof famous enough, although it wisely changed its name from 1914. But surely it must be the simple 'Baden' (as written), Swiss health resort, today one and a half times the size of Baden-Baden, 14 miles north-west of Zurich, famous for its hot sulphur springs approved by even more ancient Romans, including Tacitus (Baden-Baden can claim only Hadrian, questionably). It is on the Limmat, a tributary of the Rhine tributary the Aare, which enters the Rhine above Meiringen (making it 'full of the most interesting associations', as Holmes would say, if not necessarily those Watson would want to recall from those ghastly hours when in 'The Final Problem' (*Memoirs*) he was forced to conclude Holmes was dead). It was an obvious location for ACD to choose, its proximity to Lausanne explaining the surprise at the 'circuitous route' for Lady Frances's luggage.

kingdom of the Midianites: both as an infant Roman Catholic and as a creative disciple of Macaulay, as shown in *Micah Clarke*, ACD was conscious of the field for human exploitation opened up by the assertion of the right of private scriptural judgement, essential though he held it to be. There was no kingdom or king of the Midianites, a nomadic people, but Lady Frances's pursuit of the consolations of religion was clearly too deeply related to establishing a psychological barrier against her pursuer to furnish her with working critical knowledge, and Watson was evidently in no better case. Longman notes a metaphor here with Shlessingers as Midianites and the Lady as Israel, and the texts are supportive:

And so it was, when Israel had sown, that the Midianites came up . . . And they encamped against them, and destroyed the increase of the earth, till thou come unto Gaza, and left no sustenance for Israel, neither sheep, nor ox, nor ass. For they came up with their cattle and their tents, and they came as grasshoppers for multitude . . . And Israel was greatly impoverished because of the Midianites (Judges 6: 3–6).

123 *a very pretty hash*: the text now in question appears to be Proverbs 16: 18: 'Pride goeth before destruction, and an haughty spirit before a fall', applying first to Watson, then to Holmes. Like most Jesuit pupils, ACD had an unfulfilled yearning to deliver a retreat sermon or two.

give the alarm: here, as in 'The Solitary Cyclist' (*Return*), ACD shows Holmes anxious to avoid Watson's errors only to fall into the contrary blunder.

124 *mob cap*: a cap worn indoors by women, covering all their hair as a protection against dust, etc.

you found it better . . . Africa: a polite version of 'And bold and hard adventures t'undertake, | Leaving his country for his country's sake' (Charles Fitzgeffrey, *Sir Francis Drake* (1596), 213).

not worse than others of my class: i.e. the aristocracy. The self-exculpation is not endorsed by the author, to judge by the wide range of moral dubiety afforded by the Hon. Philip's peers in the Holmes saga—John Clay, murderer etc. ('The Red-Headed League'); Lord Robert St Simon, mercenary marriage-hunter ('The Noble Bachelor'); Sir George Burnwell, seducer, thief ('The Beryl Coronet', *Adventures*); the Duke of Holdernesse, kidnapping accessory ('The Priory School'); Lord Mount-James, miser ('The Missing Three-Quarter'); Sir Eustace Brackenstall, dog-burner ('The Abbey Grange'); Lady Hilda Trelawney Hope, traitor ('The Second Stain', *Return*). The squirearchy do little better, to judge by Dr Grimesby Roylott ('The Speckled Band', *Adventures*), Reginald Musgrave ('The Musgrave Ritual'), and the Cunninghams ('The Reigate Squire', *Memoirs*), and the ex-bushrangers, mutineers, etc. ('The Boscombe Valley Mystery', *Adventures*; 'The *Gloria Scott*', *Memoirs*).

pure as snow: the Hon. Philip has no idea of what he is saying, but ACD has manœuvred him into a quotation from *Hamlet* all too apposite: 'Be thou as chaste as ice, as pure as snow, thou shalt not escape calumny. Get thee to a nunnery, go; farewell' (III. i. 150–1).

124 *Barberton*: town in Transvaal, South Africa, founded in 1886 on the discovery of gold in the neighbourhood.

Langham Hotel: an actual hotel, on Langham Place, off Upper Regent Street, famous for housing the meeting in Aug. 1889 of Oscar Wilde, ACD, and the commissioning editor for *Lippincott's*, Joseph Marshall Stoddart (1845–1921), as a result of which *The Sign of the Four* and *The Picture of Dorian Gray* were born (although Wilde initially seems to have written 'The Fisherman and his Soul' in response to it). As a result, the hotel received its place in the Holmes saga, opening with the disappearance of Captain Morstan from it in *The Sign of the Four*, and subsequently housing the King of Bohemia alias Count Von Kramm ('A Scandal in Bohemia', *Adventures*). It later became an annexe to the radio broadcasting studios and offices of the British Broadcasting Corporation opposite in Portland Place. It is now once again a hotel.

125 *Adelaide*: capital of South Australia, named after the Queen of William IV and counterpointing ACD's birthplace by calling itself 'the Athens of the South', while resembling Barberton in gaining significance by the discovery of gold near at hand. Peters's bitten ear recalls the apocryphal story that Burke's scirrous testicle derived from a murder victim's dying bite.

126 *registration*: the passport system existed on a voluntary basis for British subjects (i.e. nationals) at this time and was greatly relaxed elsewhere.

possess our souls in patience: 'in patience possess ye your souls' (Luke 21: 19).

Holmes's own small . . . organization: possibly the 'Baker Street Irregulars' or urchins appearing in *A Study in Scarlet*, *The Sign of the Four*, and 'The Crooked Man' (*Memoirs*). The originals of the Irregulars were probably ACD and his gang in Sciennes Hill Place, Edinburgh (see *Memories and Adventures*, 16–17). Yet they had not appeared in any post-Reichenbach stories, and may have seemed a less plausible device as ACD learned more of London class divisions. Other figures of the kind appear in the *Case-Book*, e.g. Holmes's 'general utility man' Mercer ('The Creeping Man'), his 'agent in the huge criminal underworld of London' Shinwell Johnson ('The Illustrious Client'), and his 'human book of reference upon all matters of social scandal' Langdale Pike ('The Three Gables').

silver-and-brilliant: a diamond of finest quality cut in two flat faces joined with facets and suspended on a silver chain. Burke excited remark by giving away, not selling, the property of some of his victims, which became (unused) evidence in indictment counts against him where no corpse remained; but he was in fact convicted for the one case for which a corpse could still be found.

Bevington's: corrupted to Bovington's in Doubleday. Perhaps ironically derived from Bravington's, the fashionable Victorian jewellers.

127 *knowledge and consent*: this course of conduct is a reminder that Holmes derives from both priest and doctor in ACD's experience. The Hon. Philip will himself be the better for playing a part in finding Lady Frances, but he must in any case win her for better reasons than his recent wealth, his violent temper, his old acquaintance, and his aristocratic status. It is a use of the chivalric quest, very much a feature of the Holmes stories: the moral arbiter no less than the medical arbiter sets the terms.

Crimean War: the Crimean War ultimately turned on the siege of the Russian fortress Sevastopol, which was consolidated in May 1855 by the British success in sweeping the Sea of Azov clear of Russian shipping, thus isolating the Crimean Peninsula which divides the Black Sea from the Sea of Azov.

ferret eyes: presumably red-rimmed, green-brown eyes. Red rims imply weeping, in ACD texts, whence it seems indicated that Peters governed his mistress, no less than his victim, in part by fear. In the mistress's case, however, that was compatible with love.

130 *Thrice is he armed . . . just*:

> *King Henry*. What stronger breastplate than a heart
> untainted!
> Thrice is he arm'd that hath his quarrel just;
> And be he naked, though lock'd up in steel,
> Whose conscience with injustice is corrupted.
> (Shakespeare, *2 King Henry VI*, III. ii. 232–5)

As a novelist of medieval history ACD would know the passage's ironies for Henry's own questionable regal title and weakness of mind; but it remains an appropriate text for Holmes. ACD may also have known another version: 'Thrice is he armed that hath his quarrel just, | But four times he who gets his blow in fust' (Henry Wheeler Shaw, *Josh Billings, his Sayings*, 1865).

131 *When a man's conscience . . . him*: Holy Peters, with second-nature hypocrisy, has so far outflanked Holmes as unconsciously to throw his Shakespearean quotation back at him.

132 *Brixton Workhouse Infirmary*: hospital for the poor and incapacitated maintained at public expense, in Brixton, a depressed district of south London below Kennington and famous as the scene of the first murder in *A Study in Scarlet*, though at an address which, like Poultney Square and Firbank Villas, is fictitious.

134 *no servant*: a reminder of the nadir of ACD's family fortunes as a boy when his mother was forced to do all the housework, but here of course a servant was impossible if the secret of Lady Frances was to be kept.

135 *The authority in Holmes's voice*: 'Then all the Midianites and the Amalekites and the children of the east were gathered together, and went over, and pitched in the valley of Jezreel. But the Spirit of the LORD came upon Gideon, and he blew a trumpet' (Judges 6: 34).

sovereign: £1 sterling (term derived from gold coin).

it seemed that we were: the 'we' is the medical writer's method of recording the medical narrator. It is, of course, Watson who is saving the life of Lady Frances Carfax but as a professional he speaks of himself as part of a team. The point is in striking contrast to his absurd and foredoomed attempts to preen himself on his detective work in Switzerland. And the episode is instructive on roles: as a doctor Watson must take the open way, not only being easily 'humiliated' as here when his illegal status is thrown in his face by a law-breaker and probable murderer, but putting forward enquiries with a formality capable of bearing any subsequent enquiry, so that Holmesian forms of investigation could never be his and it was foolish of Holmes to behave as though they could. Their ideal form of collaboration when in detective work is an open role for Watson and a covert one for Holmes as in *The Hound of the Baskervilles* where on medical questions, such as the state of Mrs Barrymore's eyes, Watson observes and deduces professionally. The present case therefore concludes with Watson saving Holmes from disgrace and dishonour.

137 *annals of crime*: the use of chloroform to ensure painless death reverses its introduction to facilitate painless birth in Edinburgh by James Young Simpson (1811–70), Professor of Midwifery.

THE DYING DETECTIVE

First published in the *Strand Magazine*, 46 (Dec. 1913), 604–14, with 4 illustrations by Walter Paget. Title as here but superscribed 'A New Sherlock Holmes Story'. First American publication in *Collier's Weekly Magazine* (New York), 52 (22 Nov. 1913), 5–7, 24–5, with 3 illustrations by Frederic Dorr Steele.

Text: from the Westminster Libraries/Arthur Conan Doyle Society facsimile of the original typescript, *The Adventure of the Dying Detective* (1991). MS dated 27 July 1913.

138 *his payments were princely*: Bryan Charles Waller (1853–1932) came to the Doyle family as a tenant in 1875, and from 1877 paid the rent for the much more expensive residence at 23 George Square, Edinburgh, whither they now moved from 2 Argyle Park Terrace. Similarly, Holmes first meets Watson in *A Study in Scarlet* because, financially, he requires to share rooms with another person; but it is clear that his income had advanced sufficiently to pay the full rent after Watson's marriage at the end of *The Sign of the Four*. A few months after Holmes becomes the sole paying tenant, the establishment has run to a page, and it is he who is most in want of such a servant (ACD's brother Innes, fourteen years his junior, fulfilled the function for him at 1 Bush Villas, Southsea from 1882): so payment of the page's wages and upkeep by Holmes is intended to be assumed, although the landlady already has a maid when Holmes and Watson first take up residence. Holmes's increase in income arising from wealthy clients enables him to put up money for a relative to purchase Watson's practice from him after his return, in 1894. Waller seems to have paid for all from his family estate, the move from Argyle Park Terrace to George Square taking place after the death of his father on 12 Mar. 1877.

second year of my married life: this sets this story much earlier in time than its fellows in this collection, all of which are 1895 or later. There is almost a quarter-century between the time of writing and the supposed date of events of the story, the first time any such historical element entered into the composition. ACD has to posit a relationship much less deep-seated and less medically based than would be the case after the return of Holmes. It is specifically in contrast to the expressions of affection in 'The Bruce-Partington Plans' and 'The Devil's Foot', or even the mutual but confident irritability of 'Lady Frances Carfax'. At the time of 'The Dying Detective' the doctor has so far made but a few (unsuccessful) attempts to discourage his friend from drug-taking. Certainly the story is a landmark for both men, and it would be possible to infer a deeper medical supervision of Holmes by Watson in the future, a stage ACD is here formally establishing in their doctor–patient relationship.

139 *Rotherhithe*: dockland, south bank of the Thames, with Rotherhithe Street following a sharp curve of the river from east to south, stretching from Bermondsey Wall East to Greenland Dock and South Dock and opposite the stretch from Wapping to the Isle of Dogs—where the river chase in *The Sign of the Four* commenced. Cholera attacked London from there in 1832, the city's first known outbreak (although Sunderland and Scotland were hit in 1831). Longman finds ACD 'has deliberately picked a place associated with virulent disease [originating in the Orient] for this reference' (p. 215).

have: 'has' (*Strand*).

enough?: no question-mark in MS.

140 *Coolie disease from Sumatra*: a disease carried by Chinese and Indonesian labourers. Sumatra, separated from Singapore and the Malay peninsula by the Malacca Strait, was then under Dutch rule and now forms part of Indonesia. Sumatra has other mentions in the Holmes saga, including Holmes's 'immense exertions' on 'the Netherlands–Sumatra Company and the colossal schemes of Baron Maupertuis, 'the most accomplished swindler in Europe' whom he 'outmanœuvred at every point' ('The Reigate Squire', *Memoirs*); and ten years hence Holmes would allude to the ship *Matilda Briggs* 'associated with the giant rat of Sumatra, a story for which the world is not yet prepared' ('The Sussex Vampire', *Case-Book*).

friend?: no question-mark in MS.

something in which: 'someone in whom' (*Strand*). The inanimate seems deliberate.

141 *You mean well, Watson*: substituted in MS for 'Obstinate old Watson!'.

Tapanuli fever . . . black Formosa corruption. Tapanuli, on the north-west coast of Sumatra, of some 15,000 square miles with a population of 1 million, is mountainous, producing maize, rubber, rice, etc. Formosa, correctly Taiwan, is an island off the south China coast which had a formidable reputation for mortality among its invaders in the late 19th century (including Cantonese, Japanese, Chinese, and French). ACD might have heard of the fate of Japanese troops from his friend Professor William Burton of the Imperial University, Tokyo, to whom he had dedicated *The Firm of Girdlestone* (1890). Hugh L'Etang has suggested the diseases are to be identified with tsutsugamushi fever or scrub typhus, involving an ulcer 'with a striking black crust' ('Some Observations on the Black Formosa Corruption and Tapanuli Fever', *Sherlock Holmes Journal*, 4/2 (Spring 1959), 58–60). The Taiwanese aboriginal inhabitants should have interested ACD, as many of them believed the disease came from the anger of departed souls.

either: substituted in MS for 'them'.

There are many problems of disease: 'interesting' deleted in MS before 'problems'.

as: 'so' in *Strand* and later texts, clearly from hasty reading.

have a medico-criminal aspect: 'had' in MS deleted for 'have'.

contracted this complaint: 'which threatens to remove the last restraint from/upon one or two gentlemen whom I could mention' in MS then deleted.

142 *not from the man you mention*: 'mention' substituted in MS for 'choose'.

The first three sensible words . . . Watson: this kind of delirious condescension is in fact characteristic of drunks in speaking to members of their families or other intimates trying to stop them drinking or bringing them home. ACD had attended many cases of alcohol dependence, beginning with his father.

under: 'in' (*Strand*); 'under' seems closer to ACD's Scots deliberation.

142 *second to that caused by his spring*: 'which' deleted in MS before 'caused'.

silent figure in the bed: next word 'and' deleted in MS; full stop inserted.

pictures of celebrated criminals . . . adorned: the *Strand* text was illustrated by Walter Paget (1863–1935), brother of the late Sidney Paget whose illustrations of the first thirty-seven short stories and *The Hound* had established a popular iconographic conception of Holmes based on Walter. Walter Paget's page-size illustration of this incident shows only one picture adorning a wall, and the subject bears a striking resemblance to ACD.

143 *Of all ruins . . . deplorable*: not a misquotation of Ophelia in *Hamlet*—'O, what a noble mind is here o'erthrown!' (III. i. 153)—but a medical corollary to it.

half-crowns: coins each for the value of 2 shillings and 6 pence, i.e. 12½ new pence

trowser-pocket: 'trouser-pocket' in all British printings; in the US, 'trouserpocket'.

balance you so much better: 'so much' inserted in MS.

He shuddered and again made a sound: 'again' inserted in MS.

Culverton Smith: here and a few lines later it appears corrected from 'Colverton' in MS. A 'planter' is the owner of a plantation (coffee, rubber, coconut, maize, nutmeg, or rice in Tampanuli, apparently Smith's Sumatra home).

13 Lower Burke Street: another shadow of Burke and Hare. The address symbolizes Culverton Smith as a 'Burker', i.e. a murderer who leaves no sign of murder; also that he is lower than Burke, morally.

144 *Sumatra*: 'Sumatra' deleted in MS, 'Formosa' substituted and deleted, 'Sumatra' substituted.

An outbreak of the disease . . . consequences: this sentence was apparently substituted on revision for 'You will find the gentleman, whose habits I have studied, seated at this present moment in a bamboo chair, his feet extended, a tumbler by his side, and a long manilla cigar between his curiously animal teeth.' ACD may have written the deleted sentence as a joke, describing himself and his situation at the time of writing, in allusion to his own unsuccessful attempts to kill

Holmes. Printed texts have 'distant' for uncorrected MS 'far absent'.

in his study: substituted in MS for 'in his flat'.

oysters: Holmes purchased oysters (and a brace of grouse) to be consumed for dinner with 'something a little choice in white wines' by Watson, Athelney Jones, and himself before the river chase in *The Sign of the Four*. Bryan Charles Waller, lodger and subsequent provider of free housing to ACD's parents, is recorded by his maidservants as voracious in his demand for oysters and (cf. 'Silver Blaze', *Memoirs*) for curries.

Culverton: now corrected from 'Colverton', 's' deleted before 'ton', possibly before writing it (MS).

between us: MS follows with sentence deleted on revision, 'Lately I have crossed his path.'

145 *down to it*: inserted on revision of MS.

Make any excuse . . . him.: inserted on revision of MS.

a happy thought: i.e. a fortunate inspiration.

unofficial tweeds: implies that Morton is a police inspector not in uniform. But ACD was careless of uniform/plain-clothes distinctions, and could well have intended Morton to be a detective.

too fiendish: 'thought I' deleted after this in MS.

exultation: 'or amusement' deleted after this in MS.

Lower Burke Street: from this point the MS ceases to be in ACD's hand but is apparently in that of his secretary, Alfred Wood. The second hand, apart from corrections, lasts until 'It was with a sinking heart . . .'; 'was a' deleted as next two words.

electric light behind him: income division was well demonstrated in the London of the 1880s and 1890s by forms of illumination in private homes. Electric light, as here, denotes opulence, as indeed might be expected from the wealth inherited by Culverton Smith on the decease of his nephew. Gas-light, as in the Holmes flat at 221b Baker Street, betokens a more moderate income, despite Holmes's 'princely' payments; we have to take it that they became more princely after this case. Candlelight, as in the home of the poverty-stricken British Museum hack Henry Baker ('The Blue Carbuncle', *Adventures*, betokens actual poverty. It is a nice point that the gas-light provides the view-hallo to Culverton Smith's pursuers running him to earth for the means whereby he could afford electricity.

145 *Yes, Mr Culverton Smith is in*: 'Culverson' in MS, consistently for the portion in the strange hand. Does 'is in', substituted for 'was in', suggest ACD toyed with indirect speech for the butler's remarks? In 'The Six Napoleons' (*Return*) he moves effectively from indirect speech to direct when the German manager of Gelder & Co. of Stepney stops giving conventional and untroubled answers to Holmes's questions and sees the photograph of the employee who had disgraced his firm.

Very good, sir: 'Dr Watson' deleted and 'sir' substituted on MS.

146 *should*: thus in MS and *Strand*, but 'could' in British and American book texts.

With a shrill cry: 'shrill' inserted on MS.

double chins: 'double chin' (*Strand*).

sullen: obliterates 'sallow' in MS (evidently erroneously recorded).

Didn't I send you word: substituted for MS original 'Didn't I tell you?'

147 *The man motioned me*: 'little' deleted in MS before 'man'.

gelatine cultivations: microbes in a laboratory are grown in cultures made of gelatine.

148 *I have another appointment*: substituted in MS for 'I cannot wait an instant'.

I will go alone: substituted in MS for 'I will follow after you'.

within half an hour at most: substituted in MS for 'almost as soon as yourself'.

It was with a sinking heart: from here MS continues in ACD's hand.

His appearance: 'it is true,' deleted from MS just after this.

and he spoke: 'in a feeble voice it is true but' inserted in MS following this.

149 *upon his haggard face*: 'haggard' seems a subsequent addition (MS).

his sudden access of strength departed: these words later inserted in MS.

droned away: 'suddenly' following these words deleted from MS.

From the hiding-place: 'my' deleted in MS in favour of 'the'.

I heard the footfalls: 'ring' before 'footfalls' deleted in MS, presumably originally imagined as 'ring of' or 'ringing'.

insistent: inserted in MS, spelled 'insistant'.

Can't you hear me: conjectural alteration from 'can' in MS ('can't' in all printings).

Coals of fire: 'If thine enemy be hungry, give him bread to eat; and if he be thirsty, give him water to drink: for thou shalt heap coals of fire upon his head, and the LORD shall reward thee' (Proverbs 25: 21–2). Culverton Smith was citing and, later, practising, Scripture for his purpose; and was following diabolic precedent in so doing (Matthew 4: 6; Luke 4: 10).

who does: closing quotation mark deleted in MS following 'does', as though ACD intended Holmes to reply, and then, before framing that reply, thought better of it and gave Smith another sentence.

150 *special study*: 'study' substituted for 'trouble' in revision of MS.

sick man: 'sick' substituted for 'dying' in MS, after 'dying man' substituted for 'sufferer'.

You're precious near ... you: 'Here you are!' before 'You're' deleted in MS and 'That's why I give you water.' inserted after 'you.' in revision of MS.

whispered: altered from 'groaned' on revision of MS.

just now: inserted in revision of MS.

East-end: 'East End' in book texts; MS and magazine texts use the older 'East-end' (the hyphen conjectural in MS, as with most of ACD's hyphens).

You came across: Substituted in revision of MS for 'You crossed the path of', a phrase previously deleted during the writing itself. It echoes Professor Moriarty's 'You crossed my path on the fourth of January' ('The Final Problem', *Memoirs*), but lacks his sinister progress through 'incommoded', 'inconvenienced', 'hampered', and 'positive danger of losing my liberty'. It also reveals that ACD was thinking of the precedent of the most famous Holmes dialogue with a villain, though he then distanced himself from it: Smith's sadism has little in common with Moriarty's austerity, or his hard-bitten informality with the professor's diplomatic malevolence.

151 *You shall hear me*: inserted on revision of MS.

Who asked you to cross my path?: the phrase can do its own work now in its context, unencumbered by the Moriarty precedent. The tension is far too high by this stage and Smith too firmly drawn for ACD to be accused of self-plagiarism.

It drew blood: Hugh L'Etang (see note on 'Tapanuli fever', pp. 214–15) has suggested the principle of a snake's fang in the lid of the box, perhaps loaded with cobra venom. But the principle of blood-drawing coupled with infection offers a range of fatal diseases, and the most obvious would seem to be the injection of a germ of some tropical disease (whether Tapanuli fever, the black Formosa corruption, or something worse) extracted and nurtured by Culverton Smith. Cobra poison would take a much shorter time than is quoted in the case of Savage and the presumed case of Holmes, unless one sees Smith, for no conceivable reason, preparing a 7 per cent solution, or some other delaying adulteration. The author of 'The Speckled Band' (*Adventures*) associated the action of snake venom with an effect varying between a few minutes and about two hours.

152 *food, nor drink*: 'nor drink' substituted for 'drink nor tobacco. It is the latter which', and then the alteration was made in the MS before the writing of the passage continued with 'until you were'.

irksome: closing quotation mark deleted at this point in MS, indicating that the decision to allow Holmes to have a cigarette was an impulse on reaching the point. In view of the frequent charges of ACD's dislike of Holmes, this humane attitude seems worthy of note, but it also underlines the relationship of tobacco to drugs in general (its potentially lethal consequences being then unknown).

the usual cautions: the statutory statement that anything said by the party about to be arrested and charged may be taken down and used in evidence at the trial of the accused. The ceremony is satirized rather movingly in 'The Dancing Men' (*Return*):

'I guess the very best case I can make for myself is the absolute naked truth.'

'It is my duty to warn you that it will be used against you', cried the inspector, with the magnificent fair play of the British criminal law.

Slaney shrugged his shoulders.

'I'll chance that', said he.

to give our signal . . . gas: 'our' substituted for 'the' in MS. Turning up the gas increased the light very dramatically and visibly from the street.

153   *not me*: altered on the revisal of the MS from 'not I'.

Culverton Smith: altered on writing or on revision from 'Colverton Smith' in MS.

Have you the cab below: as in MS. All printings add a question mark, but the Victorian imperative rather than the Georgian inquisitive seems likely. See 'Charles Augustus Milverton' (*Return*):

'And a mask?'

'I can make a couple out of black silk.'

'I can see that you have a strong, natural talent for this sort of thing. Very good, do you make the masks.'

vaseline: a petroleum jelly, normally restorative, known by this term from the mid-1870s.

belladonna: deadly nightshade, a poison used for the making of cosmetics and atropine, capable of markedly dilating the eye-pupils.

writing a monograph: an unobtrusive usurpation of Holmes's literary plans by ACD himself. A doctor is much more likely than a detective to contemplate writing a monograph upon malingering, likely to be encountered frequently in the course of a busy practice.

154   *a reversion*: money and/or property directed to revert to a certain person (in this case Culverton Smith) only in the event of the decease of another particular person (Victor Savage). In all probability Savage was in the direct male line of descent from the testator and only by his decease would the descendant through a female inherit. Obviously, either Smith or Savage must have been related via a female ancestor, as their names were dissimilar, and at this time descent through the male line was traditionally honoured before descent through the female, if all did not have equal shares. Of course Smith

might already have inherited a share of an estate and simply wished to obtain Savage's as well; in that case Smith's could have been the male line and Savage's the female.

154 *It was clear . . . the true artist*: inserted after the conclusion of the writing, probably during the general revision.

out of place: in the early summer of 1892 Joseph Bell had suggested a 'bacteriological criminal' to ACD for a future Holmes story. This was the only one of his old surgical chief's plot suggestions which ACD seems to have used (and then twenty years afterwards). Possibly he recalled the idea after Bell died in Oct. 1911.

HIS LAST BOW

First published in the *Strand Magazine*, 54 (Sept. 1917), 227–36, with 3 illustrations by A. Gilbert. First American publication in *Collier's Weekly Magazine* (New York), 60 (22 Sept. 1917), 5–7, 47–9, with 4 illustrations (and cover) by Frederic Dorr Steele.

Text: from the *Strand*, which differs more dramatically and frequently from the first British and American edns. of the collected stories entitled *His Last Bow* (as whose final chapter it was printed) than is true for any other Holmes story. The story was evidently revised, probably in proof, for the *Strand*, after the collection had been sent to the book publishers, John Murray of London (publishing ACD for the first time in his own right, the firm having bought Smith, Elder with the ACD titles in its list) and George H. Doran (afterwards Doubleday Doran) of New York. It would be natural to assume the book text as the final version, but its many discrepancies include some impossible to accept as attempted improvements on the magazine, e.g. the book has 'Carlton Terrace' and the *Strand* the correct 'Carlton House Terrace'; the book has the 'American' complete his present participles where the *Strand* clips the final 'g' in authentic informal American style, as well as giving the American usage 'too' for the book's over-British 'also', the American 'mutt' for the British 'mug', and the American 'durned' for the British 'damned'. Towards the close of the book text 'the two friends walked him very slowly down the garden walk' is a perfect example of the type of first-draft repetition with which every writer is all too familiar, but no writer would deliberately delete a better text to impose such a blunder. In fact the *Strand* text is exceedingly felicitous at this point, reading as it does 'down the garden path', a pleasingly ironic reversal of the plot of the story in which it is now evident Von Bork has been, in another sense, led *up* the garden path.

Why the mistake was not detected and put right in subsequent versions is unknown. ACD was preoccupied with his history of the *British Campaigns in France and Flanders* and resumed work on it after completing the story. Short of demanding a revised text of the book—to the considerable inconvenience of his publishers and himself after the collected *His Last Bow: Some Reminiscences of Sherlock Holmes* had appeared—his next opportunity would seem to have been with the omnibus volume *Sherlock Holmes: The Complete Short Stories* in 1928, when he was plunged into spiritualistic campaigns.

155 *An Epilogue of Sherlock Holmes*: this is the one point where the book text has been given preference over the *Strand* text, the *Strand* subtitle being 'The War Service of Sherlock Holmes'. The origin of that—and of the story—seems to have been an incident when ACD was visiting the Argonne French front in June 1916, its director General Georges-Louis Humbert (1862–1921) showing a fine instinct for conquering the press by activating its inferiority complex. A veteran of pre-war Moroccan campaigns, Humbert was tough, and not likely to be overenthusiastic about Britain or journalists. ACD described him as 'small, wiry, quick-stepping, all steel and elastic, with a short, sharp upturned moustache, which one could imagine crackling with electricity in moments of excitement like a cat's fur. What he does or says is quick, abrupt and to the point. He fires his remarks like pistol shots at this man or that. Once to my horror he fixed me with his hard little eyes, demanded "Sherlock Holmes, est ce qu'il est un soldat dans l'armée anglaise?" The whole table waited in an awful hush. "Mais, mon général", I stammered, "il est trop vieux pour service." There was general laughter, and I felt that I had scrambled out of an awkward place' (*A Visit to Three Fronts* (1916), 71–2). But the excuse evidently haunted its maker. After all, one of Holmes's progenitors in real life, Professor Sir Robert Christison, had retired at the age of 80. It was a poor war service for Holmes simply to extricate his creator from an awkward moment by himself being proved too old.

the most terrible August . . . world: i.e. Aug. 1914. Germany had declared war on Russia on 1 Aug., when both Germany and France had mobilized. On 31 July the British Foreign Secretary, Sir Edward Grey (1862–1933), had asked France and Germany if they would respect Belgian neutrality, and Belgium if it would defend it: France and Belgium affirmed, Germany declined to say. On 2 Aug. Belgium received Germany's ultimatum demanding passage of her troops through Belgium, and rejected it on 3 Aug.

155 *earth*: 'world' in book texts.

the bay: presumably Mill Bay, on the north-east Essex coast, south of Harwich (which port is near enough for Von Herling to suspect, without being certain, that its lights are those of the inhabited area visible from Von Bork's cliff, and for Holmes and Watson to make it a rendezvous). Hollesley Bay, on the south-east Suffolk coast, north of Harwich, will not do, since to reach it Holmes and Watson would have met at Colchester or Manningtree, tempting thought as it may be to locate Von Bork in the environs of Felixstowe, the site of M. R. James's chilling 'Oh, Whistle, and I'll Come to You, My Lad'.

great chalk cliff: the cliffs to the north of Walton-on-the-Naze seem the most likely point ACD had in mind—he visited Frinton-on-Sea south of Walton, in Aug. 1913, and made slight use of it in 'The Retired Colourman' (*Case-Book*) ten years later—but when the story was in initial draft he may have been vaguely thinking of the chalk cliffs of Kent and, having settled on Harwich as a focal point, forgot that the Essex cliffs are not so obviously described.

the Kaiser: Wilhelm II (von Hohenzollern) (1859–1941), third Emperor of Germany, ninth King of Prussia, grandson of Queen Victoria, succeeded his father Friedrich II (1888), was forced to abdicate (1918), and subsequently lived in the Netherlands. Widely credited with zeal, power, and guilt for the outbreak and direction of World War I, he had been much more of a figurehead since his breakdown in 1908 and, if anything, was of the 'peace party' in Berlin in the last weeks before war. (He was clearly intended by ACD to be the inflammatory correspondent whom Holmes prevented from earlier causation of European war ('The Second Stain', *Return*) but was bellicose enough then, i.e. pre-1905.)

Baron Von Herling: should be 'von Herling', 'von Bork', 'von and zu Grafenstein', etc., but ACD was very anxious to stress the aristocratic pretensions of the German leadership and capitalized on their prefixes. The name in translation means 'of the sour grape' which sounds sufficiently appropriate in the light of the story's outcome; it may have been partly inspired by Count Georg Friedrich von Hertling (1843–1919), who was then Bavarian premier and became German chancellor a month after this story was published, lasting exactly eleven months. Von Herling's identity was probably based on the Counsellor of the German Embassy from 1908 until the outbreak of war, Dr Richard von Kühlmann (1873–1948), whom at the time the story was written the Irish Nationalist leader John Dillon, MP (1851–1927) had recently called both a baron and the Kaiser's chief spy in Ireland in July 1914 (House of Commons, 7 Mar. 1917). The obvious horror and misery at the advent of war on the part of the German Ambassador to the UK, Prince Karl Max von Lichnowsky (1860–1928), naturally invited a search for some evil genius among his subordinates who might be assumed to have supported the Berlin war party, betrayed Lichnowsky, and manipulated a spy ring; von Kühlmann was named as such by the ex-premier Herbert Henry Asquith (1852–1928) in his *The Genesis of the War* (1923) and by his wife, Margot (1864–1945), in her *Autobiography* (1920–2), the Asquiths having fallen from power in Dec. 1916; Henry Wickham Steed (1871–1956) of *The Times* took the same view—'a very interesting type of the superficially jovial, cynically friendly, and wholeheartedly intriguing German diplomatist' (*Through Thirty Years* (1924), i. 385–6). In fact von Kühlmann was in Germany, not Ireland, in July 1914, though he returned to London before war broke out; he was as faithful to Lichnowsky as might be expected from a diplomat, and he, too, was of the peace party (as he demonstrated when Foreign Minister in 1918, and was dismissed accordingly). Professor Edward F. Willis came to these conclusions in his *Prince Lichnowsky Ambassador of Peace: A Study of Prewar Diplomacy 1912–1914* (1942) but added: 'Every embassy is more or less a clearing-house for spies and political information, and the German embassy was probably no exception. Usually somebody who has the ambassador's tacit approval is in charge of this activity. It may be inferred that in the German embassy' this work was performed by von Kühlmann (p. 76). Willis interviewed von Kühlmann for his study, and 'it' might also be inferred that the statement is based on some disclosure off the record. It does not make a war-hungry spymaster of him.

155 *Chief Secretary of the legation*: Although it was an embassy, this is a correct title, and was borne on 2 Aug. 1914 by a diplomat most gratifyingly called 'von Schubert'. Steed named him with von Kühlmann as 'the real German Embassy': he was permanent under-secretary of the German Foreign Office in the mid-1920s. Since relatively little was written about him, he seems quite a good possibility for espionage co-ordination and war-party intrigue, so ACD might have hit his mark on the office if not the man.

Benz car: ACD as an early motorist had all too much experience of the arrogance of road-hogs, whom he here identifies with war-hogs. Benz were premier German manufacturers from 1885 to 1926, after which they amalgamated with Mercedes.

carry: 'waft' in book texts.

Things are moving . . . time-table: this sentence not in book texts.

156 *warm*: not in book texts.

All-Highest: Wilhelm II was so termed, and British propaganda made everything of it, but nobody produced anything as funny as 'the All-Highest quarters'. ACD evidently enjoyed his revision; it was simply 'highest' in the book texts.

with a slow, heavy fashion of speech . . . political career: cf. 'Dr James Ripley was two-and-thirty years of age, reserved, learned, unmarried, with set, rather stern features, and a thinning of the dark hair upon the top of his head, which was worth quite a hundred a year to him' ('The Doctors of Hoyland', *Round the Red Lamp*).

in a deprecating way: not in book texts.

these Englanders: not in book texts; inserted to convey a conversation taking place in German.

unexpected: not in book texts.

allow for: 'observe' in book texts, which is weakened by the last word of the paragraph.

Then you come: 'Then one comes' in book texts.

insular: used satirically so that what is intended as a sneer becomes a compliment unbeknown to speaker but obvious to audience. ACD as a Scot enjoyed using the word correctly, meaning as it does 'restricted to an island'.

'playing the game' and: not in book texts.

and convention: not in book texts.

heavy-handed in these matters: apart from handing the Allies their greatest propaganda bonus at the outbreak of war by his famous description of the guarantee of Belgian neutrality as 'a scrap of paper', Theobald von Bethmann Hollweg (1856–1921), Chancellor of the German Empire (1909–17), 'destroyed the last possibility of gaining peace through England' by publicizing Grey's confidential statement to Lichnowsky on 5 Aug. that he would always be ready to mediate and that 'We don't want to crush Germany' ('Damit hat Herr von Bethmann Hollweg die letzte Moglichkeit zerstort, über England den Frieden zu erlangen', Prince Karl Max von Lichnowsky, *Meine Londoner Mission 1912–1914* (1918)). It is just possible that both ACD and Lichnowsky were being over-charitable: the Fischer-Geiss school of modern historians argues that Bethmann Hollweg was very much of the war party; and heavy-handedness may be a usefully Machiavellian method of keeping wounds open.

157 *Your four-in-hand takes the prize at Olympia*: a four-in-hand is a carriage drawn by four horses; Olympia is the 10,000-seater amphitheatre on the north side of Hammersmith Road which opened in 1886.

Flushing: correctly 'Vlissingen', seaport in south-west Netherlands on the Scheldt, at this time served by a ferry from Queensborough, Kent, whereas Harwich serves the Hook of Holland, but some traffic went from Harwich to Vlissingen.

Everything has been most carefully arranged: not in book texts.

personal suite: the innocent Lichnowsky on 5 Aug. doubtless had no idea that his departure entailed taking his spies with him (apart from anything else, he was in reality so near collapse into insanity, according to US Ambassador Walter Hines Page (1855–1918), who took custody of his embassy, that he would not have known what he was protecting); but von Kühlmann and von Schubert would have provided for quite a few stormy petrels, the same being true of the British Embassy departing from Berlin. ACD commented on the good fortune of the departing German diplomats on not being torpedoed by one of their own submarines, already in action in the North Sea by the time they left on the 5 Aug. (war between Britain and Germany having been declared on

4 Aug.). The British government gave Lichnowsky a special train to Harwich and a guard of honour, an act of gallantry befitting Asquith, Grey, and Lichnowsky. It was also an impressive and shrewd contrast in the eyes of world public opinion to German treatment of the British and French diplomats.

157 *no binding treaty between them*: on 3 Aug. Grey told the House of Commons there was no alliance, that the Cabinet had guaranteed to France that the English Channel would be maintained free of German operations, and that Britain had a friendship with France arguably entailing obligations. 'The change of attitude on 3 August, the swing to enthusiastic support for war, was not a gradual process; it was a revolution' (A. J. P. Taylor, *The Trouble-Makers* (1957), 129).

He stood listening intently for the answer: not in book texts.

158 *It would be . . . end!*: not in book texts. Von Bork, in the eyes of his creator, is intended as an honourable exception to 'the wisest brains in Germany' who 'seem to have persuaded themselves that we had sunk to such depths of cowardly indolence' that even the German violation of Belgian neutrality 'might go through' (ACD, *To Arms!* (1914), 24). The 'mediaeval conception' is here saluted by ACD such that, as in medieval times (cf. his own *Sir Nigel* and *The White Company*), the knightly hero's opponent must also understand and believe in honour. ACD might seem harshly anti-German in many of his public utterances during the war, but he had no intention of making Von Bork into an object of hate.

Irish civil war: this is not only an allusion to German aid for the Easter insurgents of 1916 through the manipulation of ACD's former friend and colleague in his Congolese crusade, Sir Roger Casement, but also to German arms-dealing with the Ulster Volunteers under Sir Edward Carson (1854–1935) and with the Irish Volunteers under Professor Eoin Mac Néill (1867–1945). Lichnowsky (who was neither able nor, so far as we can tell, willing to foment Irish civil war) told the Romanian diplomat Take Ionescu on 27 July that the Irish question would stop the UK from going to war (Ionescu, *Some Personal Impressions* (1919)).

window-breaking furies: ACD was firmly feminist regarding his own profession, the medical, but he opposed votes for women and campaigned against suffragist violence, opposed forced feeding of prisoners, and feared (shortly before the war) that lynchings were decidedly likely. It seems difficult to believe he saw a German origin of the women's movement, but it was quite in character for Von Herling to congratulate himself on one

Mr John Bull: the classic expression to denote English or British public opinion, given its most vigorous iconographic realization by 'HB' (ACD's cartoonist grandfather John Doyle (1797–1868)), always with a markedly 'common man' touch. The German formalization used here is wholly alien to the concept, and intended to reinforce the image of German power-politics as élitist and aristocratic. In fact the popular idea of John Bull was by now less egalitarian than ACD and his grandfather assumed.

let us get away . . . real-politik: not in book texts.

and watched the movements . . . companion: not in book texts.

159 *Fords*: a slip for 'fiords', perhaps, since information about narrow inlets would be invaluable to a submarine fleet anxious to surface in unfrequented shelters in enemy waters. Otherwise it seems curious, implying an invasion. ACD had been vociferous concerning the dangers submarines posed to British food supplies since well before the outbreak of war (see his 'Danger!', *Strand* (July 1914), a parable intended to warn that a very small power with eight submarines could win a war against the UK).

Harbour-Defences: not only fortifications in harbours, but the extent of human vigilance.

Aeroplanes: ACD had already published (1913) what must have been the finest flying short story to date, 'The Horror of the Heights'.

Ireland: Unlike von Kühlmann in his Dillon epiphany, Von Bork's Ireland seems Irish-American, Fenian, and separatist. ACD could hardly make much of the Ulster-Unionist—German links with Carson being First Lord of the Admiralty at the time of writing. For an example of ACD's views on Ireland when preparing 'His Last Bow', the following is an extract from *The British Campaign in France and Flanders 1916* (1918), interdicted by the war censors from publication in the *Strand* in 1917. He was telling of the repulse of a German gas attack on the 16th Irish Division on 27 Apr. 1916 between

Hulloch and Loos (the passage did not survive into his one-volume *British Campaigns in Europe 1914–1918*): 'Coming as it did at the moment when the tragic and futile rebellion in Dublin had seemed to place the imagined interests of Ireland in front of those of European civilisation, this success was most happily timed. The brunt of the fighting was borne equally by troops from the north and from the south of Ireland—a happy omen, we will hope, for the future' (p. 19).

159 *Egypt*: On 2 Aug. 1914 Helmuth von Moltke (1848–1916), Chief of the German General Staff and nephew of the eponymous strategist formerly holding that office, was actually writing to the German Foreign Minister Gottlieb von Jagow (Imanuel Geiss (ed.), *July 1914* (1965, trans. 1967), 350): 'Attempts must be made to instigate an uprising in India, if England takes a stand as our opponent. The same thing should be attempted in Egypt, also in the Dominion of South Africa.'

Portsmouth Forts: an obvious point for espionage but receiving special emphasis in honour of ACD's residence there as a Southsea doctor in the 1880s.

The Channel: the English Channel, so termed here (despite the rival claims of the North Channel and St George's Channel) because of ACD's crusade for a Channel Tunnel, without which enemy submarines could starve Britain by blockade ('Danger!', *Strand*, July 1914). Von Bork had been working out the extent of British defences against such warfare.

Rosyth: naval base on the north side of the Firth of Forth, close to Edinburgh; again a salute to ACD's former home territory.

Naval Signals: this might almost seem to be an allusion to the *British* success just before the outbreak of war in cracking the German naval code. This phenomenal good fortune of the British arose from somebody casually failing to throw out some transcribed messages which did not seem to have come from any British department. See Admiral Sir William James, *The Eyes of the Navy: A Biographical Study of Admiral Sir Reginald Hall* (1955).

Carlton House Terrace: 'Carlton Terrace', in book texts. The terrace in which the German Embassy was situated. At the time streets were casually used in reference to the power-centres situated on them, e.g. 'Downing Street', 'the Quai d'Orsay', 'the Wilhelmstrasse', 'the Bollplatz', and 'the Quirinal'. Naturally, the embassy diplomats gave themselves what they hoped sounded like comparable airs and thus 'Carlton House Terrace' meant the German Embassy (not, of course, the German Ambassador) and 'Grosvenor Square' the American Embassy, and so on.

sparking-plugs: motor-accessories discharging an electric spark firing the petrol, oil, etc. in the engine with which to enable the automobile to proceed.

160 *Pan-Germanic Junker*: ACD very thoroughly identified the heart of German chauvinism with the Junker aristocrats ('the narrow bureaucracy and swaggering Junkerdom of Prussia, the most artificial and ossified sham that ever our days have seen' (*To Arms!*, 22)), but in fact the Junkers were far too self-obsessed to be preoccupied by dreams of unity with other Germans, in or out of the Empire. The true pan-Germans were often non-aristocrats, and some of the most important were Austrian (e.g. von Schoenerer, Hitler).

the Duke of York's steps: the steps to the 124-foot column in memory of Frederick Augustus Duke of York (1763–1827), brother of George IV and William IV, erected by public subscription in 1833 for £25,000. York's main claim to fame was his sale of army perquisites through his mistress while head of the army during the Napoleonic wars. The steps adjoined the pre-war German Embassy on Carlton House Terrace, and terminate the continuation of Lower Regent Street, both commemorating his brother George.

Tokay: Tokaj is a town in Hungary about 150 miles ENE of Budapest, its vineyard covering 135 square miles. The name includes the produce of Tokaj, Tolcsva, Tarczal, Talya, and Mad. It averaged 5 million gallons a year in 1914, and was esteemed very choice by the more fashionable wine-bibbers of London's clubland. It was rich, sweet, and aromatic.

He is absolutely vital to my plans, and: not in book texts.

I have to study him: the technique of espionage here is somewhat sophisticated. Von Bork, by being so obviously German, conceals his activity for the Germans (cf. G. K. Chesterton, *The Man who was Thursday* (1908), where anarchists disguise their destructive intentions by publicly proclaiming themselves as anarchists); meanwhile 'Altamont' maintains his cover while spying on Von Bork by arousing the latter's instincts of German scholarship, bullying him consistently, being touchy about his wine, and so on.

160 *shivered and chuckled*: thus the Holmes saga, traditionally associated with hansom cabs, concludes chronologically by giving us the long-forgotten sound of vintage cars.

Harwich: about seventy miles from London, its raised eminence would have made it a highly visible landmark; dominating the estuary of the Rivers Orwell and Stour, it was the major east coast port north of London with powerful guns on Landguard Fort.

161 *Zeppelin*: Count Ferdinand von Zeppelin (1838–1917) had just died (8 Mar.) before the writing of this story was begun. He had built the first dirigible airship in 1900, whence its name: it was a sort of controllable balloon, capable of long-range flights and used by the Germans in World War I for bombing raids on London, but was much overestimated by both sides. On 19 Jan. 1915 Zeppelins bombed Yarmouth and King's Lynn (as well as several villages) with two deaths in each town.

Martha: there is not the slightest evidence that ACD meant 'Martha' to be Mrs Hudson, of Baker Street, as some Sherlockians have assumed. The two are very different figures and, in Dakin's words (p. 246), 'from what we know of Mrs Hudson's personality, it is very doubtful if she would have had the finesse necessary for successful counterespionage'. Martha is yet another example of what W. W. Robson calls 'Conan Doyle's silent women' on whose reticence so much may pivot; here the apparently innocent but actually profoundly worldly wise old lady, descended no doubt from witch and wise-woman folklore, via Meg Merrilies in Sir Walter Scott's *Guy Mannering, or, The Astrologer* (1815), a book of major influence on the birth of Sherlock Holmes.

au revoir, Von Bork: ACD, an avid reader of Macaulay's ribald account of the Francophone affectations of Frederick the Great, was probably quite correct in assuming a German Imperial diplomat would ostentatiously employ Francophone farewells to fellow-nationals on the same social level on the eve of war against France, instead of the more genuine and more plebeian *auf Wiedersehen*.

full of the impending . . . observing that: book texts have 'so full of the impending European tragedy that he hardly observed that'.

Ford: Henry Ford (1863-1947) had opened up an English factory in 1912 for the mass production of his cheap Model-T, thus ending a decade in which motor cars 'dashed along the old narrow untarred carriage-ways, frightening the passer-by on their approach and drenching him in dust as they receded . . . visible symbols of arrogant wealth. Few things . . . did more to aggravate class-feeling' (R. C. K. Ensor, *England 1870-1914* (1936), 510). ACD had been a pioneer motor-car driver, very nearly losing his life (described, with the addition of the narrator's death, in 'How It Happened', *Strand*, Sept. 1913). Here the Ford offers the dual symbol of the obvious non-British choice gratifying simultaneously the Irish and American chauvinisms of 'Altamont', but also the little, vulnerable, common man against the aristocratically pretentious Benz and the nation it served and represented. ('One of the basic folk-tales of the English-speaking peoples is Jack the Giant-Killer—the little man against the big man. Mickey Mouse, Popeye the Sailor, and Charlie Chaplin are all essentially the same figure' (George Orwell, *The English People*)— and all three achieved fame as US products.

who lingered: 'who had lingered' in book texts.

valise: travelling-bag for hand or saddle, possibly of canvas, certainly in this case possessed of some flexibility. Mark Twain supposedly once found a hotel register whose last entry read 'Baron Rothschild and his valet' under which he wrote 'Mark Twain and his valise'.

162 *glad hand*: an Americanism for 'to express gratification with me', but the subtext is that a glad-hander is an insincere politician.

cable: meaning a telegram, but 'Altamont' is presumed still to think of communication with European recipients primarily in terms of cables.

semaphore, lamp-code, Marconi: flag-signalling, lightflash-signalling, wireless telegraphy (the last known from its inventor Guglielmo Marconi (1874–1937) and so styled in parts of the British Isles for as long as two subsequent decades).

The sucker . . . book itself: not in book texts.

lay to that: you may wager confidently on that.

162   *this copy?*: 'the copy' in book texts.

    Uncle Sam: name supposedly given to the USA to humanize the generic initials 'US'; its dubious origin is ascribed to the war of 1812. It was certainly in use by the late 19th century, and clearly interpreted by ACD as a complimentary reference to American public opinion after the manner of his grandfather's John Bull: but the goatee beard was applied by English cartoonists in the American Civil War with much more hostile intent and a strong suggestion of the cheat. In the story it symbolizes Germany counting on illusory American support, whereas Uncle Sam turns out to be as British as Sherlock Holmes when the crunch comes (the USA declared war on Germany on 6 Apr. 1917). The *Strand* drawing by A. Gilbert maintains the Americanophobe British tradition with a sinister black beard, whereas the American artist, Frederic Dorr Steele, in *Collier's*, has the strong, sardonic, benevolent, old greybeard Uncle Sam immortalized (but, on Gilbert's showing, not internationalized) by American cartoonists.

    can-opener: at that date American for the English 'tin-opener'; now universal.

    mutt: 'mug' in book texts, a mid-Victorian London lower-class epithet for 'fool', the Americanism 'mutt' implies something more animal, being used particularly for mongrel dogs. 'Bud Fisher' (i.e. Harry Conway, 1885–1954) ran the first six-day-a-week comic strip in 1907 entitled 'A. Mutt', in the *San Francisco Chronicle*: it later achieved international celebrity as 'Mutt and Jeff'.

163   *any of your crooks*: 'any crook' in book texts. Von Bork is discourteous, but not intentionally, again a symbol of the thin ethnic ice on which 'Altamont' forces him to walk as part of his 'study'. By a 'Yankee crook' 'Altamont' means a pure non-Irish-descended New England criminal, and hence one whose blue blood makes him less intelligent than the green-tinctured variety. Von Bork is assuming the reference to be American chauvinist, a reminder that for all of his deprecation to Von Herling he finds 'Altamont' faintly criminal.

    too: 'also' in book texts.

    goldarned: American for 'God-damn', possibly in recognition of the separation of Church and State guaranteed by the First Amendment to the US Constitution.

you're an American citizen: the imprisonment of US citizens by the British government was a long-standing thorn in the flesh of the alleged British—American 'special relationship', but there had been few notable cases in the 20th century (nor were there until the Easter Rising of 1916, when a plea of US citizenship made by his wife may have saved the life of Éamon de Valera). Many American grievances were to mount against the British between Aug. 1914 and Dec. 1916 (after which date Germany threw away all her propaganda advantages), but imprisonment of US nationals was not one of them.

Portland: a prison on Portland Island, a peninsula in Dorset, famous as the location of Michael Davitt's *Leaves from a Prison Diary* (1884: social criticism as lectures supposedly delivered to a pet blackbird in his cell during imprisonment 1881–2).

copper: 'Altamont' is sarcastically employing the English term for an English policeman instead of the American 'cop'; both come from the Latin *capeo*, 'I take'.

British law and order: the last major British–American flare-up on imprisonment of US (Irish-born) citizens in the 1880s had turned on British suspension of *habeas corpus*, an unconstitutional proceeding in the US.

164 *woozy*: fuddled with drink and/or drugs. 'Altamont' evidently knows more of the origin of Hollis's madness than Von Bork does, an indication of superior thoroughness.

bughouse: candidate for a lunatic asylum, with implication that he was seeing 'bugs', i.e. was suffering from advanced stages of *delirium tremens* or drug addiction.

pulled him: 'got him' in book texts. The American active voice is substituted here in place of the English middle or passive.

clear: 'off' in book texts.

salt: not in book texts.

darned sight: not in book texts. It firmly Americanizes the sentence.

down Fratton way: American for 'in the Fratton district of Portsmouth'.

very: not in book texts.

where he can't talk too much: not in book texts. This is not simple name-calling. ACD is alluding to the German manipulation of agents, particularly ideologically motivated ones, and then their cynical abandonment in circumstances that gave Germany the maximum gain with the minimum effort and expenditure. Little evidence of such conduct existed for the pre-war period, but it was the pattern of Germany's aid for the Easter Rising in Ireland in 1916. The word 'politicians' is deliberately chosen here, and ACD would hope this message went into Irish minds.

165 *a stool pigeon or a cross*: a person deliberately set up as a decoy or a piece of treachery. The Penguin text of *His Last Bow* (1981) prints 'a stool pigeon on a cross' which mixes a vivid metaphor, but would have been over-theological for 'Altamont'.

big: not in book texts.

when Von Tirpitz . . . settle up, Altamont: not in book texts. Grand Admiral Alfred von Tirpitz (1849–1930) was the great architect of the new German navy whose ambition and rivalry with British naval prowess was a major cause of World War I. As naval commander from Aug. 1914 to Mar. 1916 he championed unrestricted submarine warfare so vehemently as nearly to bring the USA into the war many months before its actual entry; it was this which brought about his fall, after which he was a zealous right-wing critic in the Reichstag. His policy was not limited to blockade enforcement, as in the model sketched by ACD in 'Danger!' but included terrorizing tactics by destruction of passengers.

durned: 'damned' in book texts. The *Strand* would probably have made a change in any case, from motives of Christian propriety rather than linguistic fidelity.

nitsky: 'nothing', probably derived, somewhat ostentatiously, from Yiddish parody of the Russian '*nyet*' ('no') and the stereotype Russian ending '-sky'.

166 *strangely-irrelevant*: hyphen not in book texts; a frivolous pseudo-Germanism.

Another: the intervening caesura vanished in the Doubleday and hence Penguin *Complete Sherlock Holmes*, thus transforming a nonpareil into a *non sequitur*.

dusty: not in book texts.

We must drink . . . reunion: not in book texts. The request is for Watson to get another glass, not to refill one. We are to assume 'Altamont' and Von Bork refreshed themselves on the former's arrival, and that Holmes returned to the Tokay, having served Von Bork with the chloroform.

he said, when . . . to the sentiment: not in book texts.

noisy: not in book texts. We are to understand the chloroform was making Von Bork snore, shout, chatter, or sing: ACD describes its action in 'His First Operation' *(Round the Red Lamp)*.

Schoenbrunn Palace: the summer residence in south-west Vienna of the Austrian Emperor Franz Joseph I (1830–1916), who was installed after the 1848 revolutions in Vienna and Budapest (as King of Hungary, the Austrian Emperor was lord of Tokay). He was the father of the Archduke Rudolf, whose suicide in 1889 produced as the next heir Franz Ferdinand; his assassination in Sarajevo on 28 June 1914 set in motion the events leading to the outbreak of World War I.

who was now: not in book texts.

to admiration: it remains unclear to the end whether Martha is simply a patriotic and resourceful old servant suborned into secret service by Holmes (like Watson, recruited at the end as a chauffeur) or if she is a member of the British secret service. (If the latter was intended, it would have been extremely flattering to the authorities, who showed no such resourcefulness in their choice of agents, then or later.) The ambiguity is intentional for she is, as Von Herling says, the personification of Britannia, kind but implacable, vigilant in somnolence. As Dakin points out, Holmes's use of her first name directly implies a servant, and hence ACD's idealized Britain answering the call is elderly, female, and working-class.

167 *the stout gentleman from London*: not in book texts.

But for your excellent . . . Martha: not in book texts.

on the hill: not in book texts.

Claridge's Hotel: illustrious and discreet establishment acquired by Claridge in 1808 and located in Brook Street (where Holmes rejected 'The Resident Patient' *(Memoirs)* living and investigated him dead) between Oxford and Bond Streets and Grosvenor Square. Too staid for Von Bork, too unostentatious for Von Herling, too English for 'Altamont', and hence an appropriate bolt-hole for Holmes.

167 *He received nine . . . these also*: not in book texts.

to him: not in book texts.

the Solent: the stretch of water between the Isle of Wight and the Hampshire mainland.

168 *stunt*: an Americanism, certainly, and one usually meaning an athletic performance or feat, ultimately applied to actual life-risking activities for the movie-camera; but it had formed part of the English vocabulary, at least since Samuel Butler used it in 1878, when (and subsequently) it carried a suggestion of publicity-seeking fraud. But Holmes's mastery of American, especially in the *Strand* text, asserted the thesis of linguistic separation H. L. Mencken was to enunciate in his *American Language* (1919), and in the case of 'stunt' the fact of separation between Holmes's (American) sense of it and Butler's is clear.

magnum opus: Latin for 'great work'.

the Queen: A. I. Root, *ABC and XYZ of Bee Culture*, a standard work at that time, may have supplied the inspiration for the title. As for the subtitle, Holmes selling the book to Von Bork implies that Germany should learn from Britain to keep its monarch from directing imperial policies.

Alone I did it: Shakespeare, *Coriolanus*, V. vi. 116. Holmes, ironically pretending an allusion to his work on bee culture, exults in his triumph over the German Empire in the final words of Shakespeare's proudest hero.

Foreign Minister: Grey had been Foreign Secretary since Dec. 1905.

Premier: Asquith had been Prime Minister since Apr. 1908.

Chicago: then the second largest American city, it had been the centre of the powerful but later discredited 'Triangle' wing of the Clan-na-Gael secret society in the 1880s, and was thus a good place to infiltrate twenty years after on the basis of reputation without unduly close scrutiny; but ACD was using this and the other names for their past fame (or, in the minds of many British readers, infamy) in Irish-American nationalist-conspiratorial politics.

Buffalo: a city in New York State on the bleak shore of Lake Erie, landing-stage for produce from the Great Lakes, linked by canal to the Hudson waterway and to New York. Traditionally, a clearing-house and rendezvous point between east and west in Irish-American nationalist politics. This is a direct allusion to the activities of two Buffalo Clan-na-Gael leaders, John A. Murphy (who was sent to Ireland to distribute relief funds after the Easter Rising of 1916) and John T. Ryan (whose attempts to forge an Irish—German alliance in the United States resulted in a warrant being issued for his arrest after the USA declared war on Germany, whereupon he fled the country).

constabulary: the Royal Irish Constabulary, a paramilitary force largely boycotted by the mass of the Irish rural population, who would have acted as note-takers at supposedly seditious meetings.

Skibbereen: ('Skibbareen' in some book texts) a small town, then 3,000 in population and declining, about 50 miles south-west of Cork city, suffered horribly in the great famine of 1845–50 and is remembered in a particularly bitter folksong 'Revenge for Skibbereen'; also famous for founding a parent institution of Fenianism (the Phoenix National and Literary Society of Skibbereen) in 1857 whose moving spirit was a local youth named Jeremiah O'Donovan Rossa (1831–1915), later a Fenian leader who became a permanent exile in the United States, from where he ran ineffectual dynamite campaigns against Britain in the late 1870s. Rossa ended his days in sympathy with Irish constitutionalist nationalism and hence with its support for Britain in World War I; but on his death a great demonstration was made on the return of his funeral to Ireland when Patrick Pearse (moving spirit of the following year's Easter Rising) delivered an oration.

169 *his long . . . papers*: not in book texts.

paymaster: merely a hint that espionage found a natural ally in government corruption.

Dear me: pleasingly mild English expression of surprise, most recently employed in the Holmes cycle by Professor James Moriarty (*The Valley of Fear*, 'Epilogue' (*Strand*, May 1915)). Not in book texts.

the late lamented Professor Moriarty: Guy Boothby's *A Prince of Swindlers* ran in *Pearson's Magazine* in 1897 between the same covers as ACD's own pirate stories of Captain Sharkey; its first paragraph concluded with a graceful allusion to 'the late lamented Sherlock Holmes'.

169 *has also been known*: the use of the perfect tense suggests Moran may still be alive, despite having been apprehended for a conclusively proved and very sordid murder twenty years before this episode ('The Empty House', *Return*); in 'The Illustrious Client' (*Case Book*), set around 1902, Moran is described by Holmes as 'living'. It would be easy to construct hypotheses concerning levers which Moran, as Moriarty's ex-lieutenant, could employ to wrest a remission from compromised politicians (such as Herbert de Lernac proposes to use in 'The Lost Special'), but the student of ACD's works can simply note that in no story is an adversary of Sherlock Holmes in a recounted case described as being judicially executed. There is a casual allusion to old Baron Dowson, whom we never meet, complimenting Holmes on his acting 'the night before he was hanged' ('The Mazarin Stone', *Case-Book*), but we cannot even be certain Holmes was the cause of his death.

He was a concoction . . . personalities: not in book texts.

170 *the separation . . . Envoy*: see 'A Scandal in Bohemia' (*Adventures*). 'Separation', if a curious description of the outcome, is absolutely correct: as a result of Holmes's intervention their association was over, however much on her terms rather than his.

Count Von und Zu Grafenstein: a piece of cheerful nonsense, again reminding us that ACD had learned his German as a schoolboy in Feldkirch. In German it would be 'Graf Von und Zu Grafenstein' and in English 'Count from and to Countstone'.

Your admiral: Tirpitz.

171 *path*: 'walk' in book texts.

'The Dangling Prussian': cf. public house names such as 'The Saracen's Head' and, of course, 'The King's Head'. It sounds as though ACD had been reading G. K. Chesterton, *The Flying Inn* (1914).

joining up with your old service: 'joining us' in book texts. Watson (*A Study in Scarlet*) variously served with the Fifth Northumberland Fusiliers (as assistant surgeon) and with the Berkshires, but this simply means 'with the army medical corps' or as near as he could get to it.

172   *east wind coming, Watson*: Germany declared war on France and invaded Belgium on 3 Aug. The UK declared war on Germany the next day.

a good many of us may wither: this serves notice that Holmes and Watson may be killed in the Great War. It was written before the deaths of Kingsley Doyle and Innes Doyle, both from effects of war service. Stories in the last Holmes collection, the *Case-Book*, such as 'The Illustrious Client', definitely assert that Holmes gave his permission for publication, leaving the reader to assume that both Holmes and Watson were still alive as late as 1924. ACD did not continue the device of Watson introducing that collection (1927), but wrote its last preface over his own signature, although basing it on a farewell communication in the *Strand* for Mar. 1927 entitled 'Mr Sherlock Holmes to his Friends.'

storm has cleared: one month (Aug. 1917) before publishing 'His Last Bow' the *Strand* ran ACD's contribution to begin a symposium on 'What Will England Be Like In 1930?' in which he said: 'I believe that, taking the history of the last twenty years, we have, in spite of some ameliorating influences, lived in the most wicked epoch of the world's history, so that all changes are likely to be for the better.'

Start her up, Watson: the most famous stage use of a motor-car as a means of exeunt by that date was Shaw's *Man and Superman* (1903), Act II, enabling Jack Tanner (part Don Juan, part Don Quixote, with a touch of Holmes) and his (Watsonian) chauffeur Straker to flee from Tanner's capture in marriage by Ann Whitefield, but they are stopped by the bandit Mendoza (a highly prettified version of the much more realistic figure from ACD, *Exploits of Gerard*, 'How the Brigadier held the King') and recaptured by Ann, described as 'a regular Sherlock Holmes'.

if he can: another twist on Holmes = Altamont = ACD. Holmes is paid (or squared) for his book, 'Altamont' for his performance, ACD for his story.

APPENDIX

Three Unsigned Pieces by P. G. Wodehouse

I. DUDLEY JONES, BORE-HUNTER.

I

As is now well known, my friend Mr DUDLEY JONES perished under painful circumstances on the top of Mount Vesuvius. His passion for research induced him to lean over the edge of the crater in such a way as to upset his equipoise. When we retrieved him he was a good deal charred, and, to be brief, of very little use to anybody. One of our noblest poets speaks of a cat which was useless except to roast. In the case of DUDLEY JONES, even that poor exception would not have held good. He was done to a turn.

DUDLEY JONES was a man who devoted his best energy to the extinction of bores. With a clear-sightedness which few modern philanthropists possess, he recognised that, though Society had many enemies, none was so deadly as the bore. Burglars, indeed, JONES regarded with disapproval, and I have known him to be positively rude to a man who confessed in the course of conversation to being a forger. But his real foes were the bores, and all that one man could do to eliminate that noxious tribe, that did DUDLEY JONES do with all his might.

Of all his cases none seems to me so fraught with importance as the adventure of the Unwelcome Guest. It was, as JONES remarked at intervals of ten minutes, a black business. This guest—but I will begin at the beginning.

We were standing at the window of our sitting-room in Grocer Square on the morning of June 8, 189—, when a new brougham swept clean up to our door. We heard the bell ring, and footsteps ascending the stairs.

There was a knock.

'Come in,' said JONES; and our visitor entered.

'My name is Miss PETTIGREW,' she observed, by way of breaking the ice.

'Please take a seat,' said JONES in his smooth professional accents. 'This is my friend WUDDUS. I generally allow him to remain during my consultations. You see, he makes himself useful in a lot of little ways, taking notes and so on. And then, if we turned him out, he would only listen at the keyhole. You follow me, I trust? WUDDUS, go and lie down on the mat. Now, Miss PETTIGREW, if you please.'

'Mine,' began Miss PETTIGREW, 'is a very painful case.'

'They all are,' said JONES.

'I was recommended to come to you by a Mrs EDWARD NOODLE. She said that you had helped her husband in a great crisis.'

'WUDDUS,' said JONES, who to all appearances was half asleep, 'fetch my scrapbook.'

The press-cutting relating to Mr EDWARD NOODLE was sandwiched between a statement that Mr BALFOUR never eats doughnuts, and a short essay on the treatment of thrush in infants.

'Ah,' said JONES, 'I remember the case now. It was out of my usual line, being simply a case of theft. Mr NOODLE was wrongfully accused of purloining a needle.'

'I remember,' I said eagerly. 'The case for the prosecution was that NEDDY NOODLE nipped his neighbour's needle.'

'WUDDUS,' said JONES coldly, 'be quiet. Yes, Miss PETTIGREW?'

'I will state my case as briefly as possible, Mr JONES. Until two months ago my father and I lived alone, and were as happy as could possibly be. Then my uncle, Mr STANLEY PETTIGREW, came to stay. Since that day we have not known what happiness is. He is driving us to distraction. He *will* talk so.'

'Stories?'

'Yes. Chiefly tales of travel. Oh, Mr JONES, it is terrible.'

JONES'S face grew cold and set.

'Then the man is a bore?' he said.

'A dreadful bore.'

'I will look into this matter, Miss PETTIGREW. One last question. In the case of your father's demise—this is purely hypothetical—a considerable quantity of his property would, I suppose, go to Mr STANLEY PETTIGREW?'

'More than half.'

'Thank you. That, I think, is all this morning. Good-day, Miss PETTIGREW.'

And our visitor, with a bright smile—at me, I always maintain, though JONES declares it was at him—left the room.

'Well, JONES,' I said encouragingly, 'what do you make of it?'

'I never form theories, as you are perfectly well aware,' he replied curtly. 'Pass me my bagpipes.'

I passed him his bagpipes and vanished.

It was late when I returned.

I found JONES lying on the floor with his head in a coal-scuttle. 'Well, WUDDUS,' he said, 'so you've come back?'

'My dear JONES, how——?'

'Tush, I saw you come in.'

'Of *course*,' I said. 'How simple it seems when you explain it! But what about this business of Miss PETTIGREW'S?'

'Just so. A black business, WUDDUS. One of the blackest I have ever handled. The man STANLEY PETTIGREW is making a very deliberate and systematic attempt to bore his unfortunate relative to death!'

I stared at him in silent horror.

Two days afterwards JONES told me that he had made all the arrangements. We were to go down to Pettigrew Court by the midnight mail. I asked, Why the midnight mail? Why not wait and go comfortably next day? JONES, with some scorn, replied that if he could not begin a case by springing into the midnight mail, he preferred not to undertake that case. I was silenced.

'I am to go down as a friend of the family,' said he, 'and you are going as a footman.'

'Thanks,' I said.

'Don't mention it,' said JONES.

'You see, you have got to come in some capacity, for I must have a reporter on the spot, and as a bore is always at his worst at meal-times you will be more useful in the way of taking notes if you come as a footman. You follow me, WUDDUS?'

'But even now I don't quite see. How do you propose to treat the case?'

'I shall simply outbore this PETTIGREW. I shall cap all his stories with duller ones. Bring your note-book.'

'Stay, JONES,' I said. 'It seems to me—correct me if I am wrong—that in the exhilaration of the moment you have allowed a small point to escape you.'

'I beg your pardon, WUDDUS?' His face was pale with fury.

'A very small point,' I said hurriedly. 'Simply this, in fact. If you begin outboring STANLEY, surely an incidental effect of your action will be to accelerate the destruction of your suffering host.'

'True,' said JONES thoughtfully. 'True. I had not thought of that. It is at such moments, WUDDUS, that a suspicion steals across my mind that you are not such a fool as you undoubtedly look.' I bowed.

'I must make arrangements with Mr PETTIGREW. Until I have finished with brother STANLEY he must keep to his room. Let him make some excuse. Perhaps you can suggest one?'

I suggested Asiatic cholera. JONES made a note of it.

On the following night, precisely at twelve o'clock, we sprang into the midnight mail.

II

I think STANLEY PETTIGREW had his suspicions from the first that all was not thoroughly above board with regard to JONES. Personally, I think it was owing to the latter's disguise. It was one of JONES'S foibles never to undertake a case without assuming a complete disguise. There was rarely any necessity for a disguise, but he always assumed one. In reply to a question of mine on the subject he had once replied that there was a sportsmanlike way of doing these things, and an unsportsmanlike way. And we had to let it go at that.

On the present occasion he appeared in a bright check suit, a 'property' bald head, fringed with short scarlet curls (to match his tie and shirt), and a large pasteboard nose, turned up at the end and painted crimson. Add to this that he elected to speak in the high falsetto of a child of four, and it is scarcely to be wondered at that a man of STANLEY'S almost diabolical shrewdness should suspect that there was something peculiar about him. As regarded my appearance JONES never troubled very much. Except that he insisted on my wearing long yellow side-whiskers, he left my make-up very much to my own individual taste.

I shall never forget dinner on the first night after our arrival. I was standing at the sideboard, trying to draw a cork (which subsequently came out of its own accord, and broke three glasses and part of the butler), when I heard JONES ask STANLEY PETTIGREW to think of a number.

His adversary turned pale, and a gleam of suspicion appeared in his eye.

'Double it,' went on JONES relentlessly. 'Have you doubled it?'

'Yes,' growled the baffled wretch.

'Add two. Take away the number you first thought of. Double it. Add three. Divide half the first number (minus eighteen) by four. Subtract seven. Multiply by three hundred and sixteen, and the result is the number you first thought of minus four hundred and five.'

'Really?' said STANLEY PETTIGREW with assumed indifference.

'My dear JONES, how——?' I began admiringly.

JONES flashed a warning glance at me. Miss PETTIGREW saved the situation with magnificent tact.

'JOHN,' she said, 'you forget yourself. Leave the room.'

I was therefore deprived of the pleasure of witnessing the subsequent struggles, which, to judge from the account JONES gave me in my room afterwards, must have been magnificent.

'After the fish,' said JONES, 'he began—as I had suspected that he would—to tell dog-stories. For once, however, he had found his match. My habit of going out at odd moments during the day to see men about dogs has rendered me peculiarly fitted to cope with that type of attack. I had it all my own way. Miss PETTIGREW, poor girl, fainted after about twenty minutes of it, and had to be carried out. I foresee that this will be a rapid affair, WUDDUS.'

But it was not. On the contrary, after the first shock of meeting a powerful rival so unexpectedly, STANLEY PETTIGREW began to hold his own, and soon to have the better of it.

'I tell you what it is, WUDDUS,' said JONES to me one night, after a fierce encounter had ended decidedly in his rival's favour, 'a little more of this and I shall have to own myself defeated. He nearly put me to sleep in the third round to-night, and I was in Queer Street all the time. I never met such a bore in my life.'

But it is the unexpected that happens. Three days later, STANLEY PETTIGREW came down to breakfast, looking haggard and careworn. JONES saw his opportunity.

'Talking of amusing anecdotes of children,' he said (the conversation up to this point had dealt exclusively with the weather), 'reminds me of a peculiarly smart thing a little nephew of mine said the other day. A bright little chap of two. It was like this——'

He concluded the anecdote, and looked across at his rival with a challenge in his eye. STANLEY PETTIGREW was silent, and apparently in pain.

JONES followed up his advantage. He told stories of adventure on Swiss mountains. A bad Switzerland bore is the deadliest type known to scientists.

JONES was a peerless Switzerland bore. His opponent's head sank onto his chest, and he grew very pale.

'And positively,' concluded JONES, 'old FRANZ WILHELM, the guide, you know, a true son of the mountains, assured us that if we had decided to go for a climb that day instead of staying in the smoking-room, and the rope had broken at the exact moment when we were crossing the Thingummy glacier, we should in all probability have been killed on the spot. Positively on the spot, my dear Sir. He said that we should all have been killed on the spot.'

He paused. No reply came from PETTIGREW. The silence became uncanny. I hurried to his side, and placed a hand upon his heart. I felt in vain. Like a superannuated policeman, the heart was no longer on its beat. STANLEY PETTIGREW (it follows, of course) was dead.

JONES looked thoughtfully at the body, and helped himself to another egg.

'He was a bad man,' he said quietly, 'and he won't be missed. RSVP.'

A brief post-mortem examination revealed the fact that he had fallen into the pit which he had digged for another. He had been bored to death.

'Why, JONES,' said I, as we sprang into the midnight mail that was to take us back to town; 'did deceased collapse in that extraordinary manner?'

'I will tell you. Listen. After our duel had been in progress some days, it was gradually borne in upon me that this STANLEY PETTIGREW must have some secret reservoir of matter to draw upon in case of need. I searched his room.'

'JONES!'

'And under the bed I found a large case literally crammed with tip-books. I abstracted the books and filled the box with bricks. Deprived of his resources, he collapsed. That's all.'

'But——' I began.

'If you ask any more questions, WUDDUS,' said JONES, 'I shall begin to suspect that you are developing into a bore yourself. Pass the morphia and don't say another word till we get to London.'

(*Punch*, 29 Apr., 6 May 1903)

II. BACK TO HIS NATIVE STRAND.

['Sherlock Holmes' is to reappear in the *Strand Magazine*.]
AIR—*'Archie' in the 'Toreador'*.

OH, SHERLOCK HOLMES lay hidden more than half a dozen
years.
He left his loving London in a whirl of doubts and fears.
For we thought a wicked party
Of the name of MORIARTY

Had despatched him (in a manner fit to freeze one).
They grappled on a cliff-top, on a ledge six inches wide;
We deemed his chances flimsy when he vanished o'er the side.
  But the very latest news is
  That he merely got some bruises.
If there is a man who's hard to kill, why he's one.
 Oh SHERLOCK, SHERLOCK, he's in town again,
  That prince of perspicacity, that monument of brain.
  It seems he wasn't hurt at all
  By tumbling down the waterfall.
 That sort of thing is *fun* to SHERLOCK.

When SHERLOCK left his native Strand, such groans were
    seldom heard;
With sobs the Public's frame was rent: with tears its eye was
    blurred.
  But the optimists reflected
  That he might be resurrected:
It formed our only theme of conversation.
We asked each other, Would he be? and if so, How and
    where?
We went about our duties with a less dejected air.
  And they say that a suggestion
  Of a Parliamentary question
Was received with marked approval by the nation.
 And SHERLOCK, SHERLOCK, he's in town again,
  Sir CONAN has discovered him, and offers to explain.
  The explanation may be thin,
  But bless you! we don't care a pin,
 If he'll but give us back our SHERLOCK.

The burglar groans and lays aside his jemmy, keys, and drill;
The enterprising murderer proceeds to make his will;
  The fraud-promoting jobber
  Feels convinced that those who rob err;
The felon finds no balm in his employment.
The forger and the swindler start up shrieking in their sleep;
No longer on his mother does the coster gaily leap;
  The Mile-End sportsman ceases
  To kick passers-by to pieces,
Or does it with diminishing enjoyment.
 For SHERLOCK, SHERLOCK, he's in town again,
  That prince of perspicacity, that monument of brain.

The world of crime has got the blues,
    For SHERLOCK'S out and after clues,
And everything's a clue to SHERLOCK.

(Punch, 27 May 1903)

III. THE PRODIGAL

[It is rumoured that SHERLOCK HOLMES, when he reappears, will figure in a series of stories of American origin.]

I met him in the Strand. It was really the most extraordinary likeness. Had I not known that he lay at the bottom of a dem'd moist unpleasant waterfall, I should have said that it was SHERLOCK HOLMES himself who stood before me. I had almost made up my mind to speak to him, when he spoke to me.

'Pardon *me*, stranger,' he said, 'can you tell where I get a car for Victoria?'

I told him.

'Do you know,' I said, 'you are astonishingly like an old friend of mine. A Mr SHERLOCK HOLMES.'

'My name,' he said coolly.

I staggered back, nearly upsetting a policeman. Then I seized him by the arm, dragged him into an ABC shop, and sat him down at a table.

'You are SHERLOCK HOLMES!' I cried.

'Correct. SHERLOCK P. HOLMES of Neh Yark City, USA. That's me every time, I guess.'

'HOLMES!' I clutched him fervently to my bosom. 'Don't you remember me? You must remember me.'

'Name of——?' he queried.

'WATSON. Dr WATSON.'

'Wal, darn my skin if I didn't surmise I'd seen you before somewhere. WATSON! Crimes, so it is. Oh, this is slick. Yes, *sir*. This is my shout. Liquor up at my ex-pense, if *you* please. What's your poison?'

I said I would have a small milk.

'Why, the last I saw of you, HOLMES——' I began.

'Guess you didn't see the last of me, sirree.'

'But you did fall down the waterfall?'

'Why, yes.'

'Then how did you escape?'

'Why, I fell over with MORIARTY. The cuss was weightier than me some, so he fell underneath. If two humans fall over a

251

precipice, I calkilate it's the one with the most avoir-du-pois that falls underneath. Conse-*quent*ly I was only con-siderable shaken, while MORIARTY handed in his checks.'

'Then you weren't killed?'

'My dear WATSON, how——? No. Guess I *sur*-vived. But, say, how are all the old folks at home? How's Sir HENRY BASKER-VILLE?'

'Very well. He has introduced base-ball into the West Country.'

'And the hound? Ah, but I remember, we shot him.'

'No. He wasn't really dead. He recovered, turned over a new leaf, and is now doing capitally out Battersea way.'

Just then a look of anxiety passed over my friend's face. I asked the reason.

'It's like this,' he said; 'I've been in the U-nited States so long now, tracking down the toughs there, that I reckon I've *ac*-quired the Amurrican accent some. Say, do you think the public will object?'

'HOLMES,' I said, 'it wouldn't matter if you talked Czech or Chinese. You've come back. That's all we care about.'

'It's a perfect cinch,' said HOLMES, with a happy smile.

(*Punch*, 23 Sept. 1903)